THE
GEOGRAPHIES
OF FASHION

D1633487

Windsor and Maidenhead

95800000072391

DRESS, BODY, CULTURE

Series Editor: *Joanne B. Eicher, Regents' Professor Emerita, University of Minnesota*

Advisory Board:

Djurdja Bartlett, *London College of Fashion, University of the Arts*
Pamela Church-Gibson, *London College of Fashion, University of the Arts*
James Hall, *University of Illinois at Chicago*
Vicki Karaminas, *Massey University, Wellington*
Gwen O'Neal, *University of North Carolina at Greensboro*
Ted Polhemus, *Curator, "Street Style" Exhibition, Victoria and Albert Museum*
Valerie Steele, *The Museum at the Fashion Institute of Technology*
Lou Taylor, *University of Brighton*
Karen Tranberg Hansen, *Northwestern University*
Ruth Barnes, *Ashmolean Museum, University of Oxford*

Books in this provocative series seek to articulate the connections between culture and dress which is defined here in its broadest possible sense as any modification or supplement to the body. Interdisciplinary in approach, the series highlights the dialogue between identity and dress, cosmetics, coiffure and body alternations as manifested in practices as varied as plastic surgery, tattooing, and ritual scarification. The series aims, in particular, to analyze the meaning of dress in relation to popular culture and gender issues and will include works grounded in anthropology, sociology, history, art history, literature, and folklore.

ISSN: 1360-466X

Previously published in the Series

Helen Bradley Foster, *"New Raiments of Self": African American Clothing in the Antebellum South*
Claudine Griggs, *S/he: Changing Sex and Changing Clothes*
Michaele Thurgood Haynes, *Dressing Up Debutantes: Pageantry and Glitz in Texas*
Anne Brydon and Sandra Niessen, *Consuming Fashion: Adorning the Transnational Body*
Dani Cavallaro and Alexandra Warwick, *Fashioning the Frame: Boundaries, Dress and the Body*
Judith Perani and Norma H. Wolff, *Cloth, Dress and Art Patronage in Africa*
Linda B. Arthur, *Religion, Dress and the Body*
Paul Jobling, *Fashion Spreads: Word and Image in Fashion Photography*
Fadwa El Guindi, *Veil: Modesty, Privacy and Resistance*

THE GEOGRAPHIES OF FASHION

Consumption, Space, and Value

LOUISE CREWE

Bloomsbury Academic
An imprint of Bloomsbury Publishing Plc

B L O O M S B U R Y
LONDON · OXFORD · NEW YORK · NEW DELHI · SYDNEY

Bloomsbury Academic

An imprint of Bloomsbury Publishing Plc

50 Bedford Square
London
WC1B 3DP
UK

1385 Broadway
New York
NY 10018
USA

www.bloomsbury.com

BLOOMSBURY and the Diana logo are trademarks of Bloomsbury Publishing Plc

First published 2017

British Library Cataloguing-in-Publication Data
A catalogue record for this book is available from the British Library.

ISBN:	HB:	978-1-4725-8956-9
	PB:	978-1-4725-8955-2
	ePDF:	978-1-4725-8957-6
	ePub:	978-1-4725-8958-3

Library of Congress Cataloging-in-Publication Data
Names: Crewe, Louise, author.
Title: The geographies of fashion : consumption, space and value / Louise Crewe.
Description: London, UK ; New York, NY : Bloomsbury Academic, [2017] |
Series: Dress, body, culture
Identifiers: LCCN 2016040876 (print) | LCCN 2017000522 (ebook) |
ISBN 9781472589552 (pbk. : alk. paper) | ISBN 9781472589569 (hardback : alk. paper) |
ISBN 9781472589576 (ePDF) | ISBN 9781472589583 (ePub)
Subjects: LCSH: Fashion–Social aspects. | Clothing and dress–Social aspects. |
Consumption (Economics)–Social aspects. | Clothing trade–Social aspects.
Classification: LCC GT525 .C754 2017 (print) | LCC GT525 (ebook) | DDC 391–dc23
LC record available at https://lccn.loc.gov/2016040876

Series: Dress, Body, Culture, 1360466X

Cover design: Adriana Brioso
Cover image © BOUDICCA: The Liquid Game. Work produced during their
Stanley Picker Fellowship, 2014.

Typeset by Integra Software Services Pvt. Ltd.
Printed and bound in Great Britain

CONTENTS

LIST OF FIGURES

ACKNOWLEDGMENTS

This book has been in the making for many years, in part as a response to the frequently asked question "What has fashion got to do with geography?" I have been exploring how best to answer this question through a long-standing lecture course at the University of Nottingham. Thank you to all of the students who unwittingly helped me to write these words. Thank you too to the team at Bloomsbury who have been so very supportive throughout the writing process. I owe a great deal of gratitude to the many wonderful colleagues who have supported me over the years, shared inspiration and much laughter. Thank you Andrew Leyshon, Steve Legg, Shaun French, Georgina Endfield, Carol Morris, Sarah Hall, Charles Watkins, Isla Forsyth, Andy Cook, Amber Martin, Kieran Phelan, Mike Heffernan, Dave Matless, Alex Vasudevan, Francesca Fois, Kean Lim and Steve Daniels. You make the School of Geography a fabulous place to work. To friends further afar—Francesca Murialdo, Nigel Thrift, Roger Lee, Ian Cook, Alex Hughes, Phil Hubbard, Michelle Lowe, Linda McDowell, Peter Jackson, Jon Beaverstock, and Jo Entwistle—you have all informed my work in so many ways. My friends have listened to my ideas, my blank-screen days, and have been a source of great support and much hilarity. I'm very lucky to have you in my life Elli, Katie, Wendy, Lou Lumby, Jussie, Mummy Milton, Hils, Jules, Lizzie, and our Janet. But mainly this book is written for my sister (Helen, who still thinks I have a face for television) and the Davies family, Dad (my hero), and my three amazing twiglets Isabella, Sacha, and Willow who are, quite literally, the light of my life. This book *Geographies of Fashion* is dedicated to my wonderful mum Norma who was my best friend, my inspiration, and my soul mate. A funnier, wiser, and more compassionate person you will never meet. I wish you were still here to read it mum.

1
FIGURING OUT THE GEOGRAPHIES OF FASHION

The encounters with fashion happen within a space at a given place and do not simply function as backdrops but are pivotal to the meaning and vitality that the experiences of fashion trace. More often than not, these environments mitigate, control, inform and enhance how fashion is experienced, performed, consumed, seen exhibited, purchased, appreciated, desired and, of course, displayed. (Potvin 2009: 1)

In the extract above, Potvin explores above how fashion is practiced, and performed and consumed in space. This way of "seeing" fashion is central in our attempts to understand why fashion matters geographically and why we as Geographers are interested in it. Think for a moment about your most valuable item of clothing and reflect on why it means so much to you. Is its value derived from where in the world it was produced (compare the symbolic geographical significance of "Made in China" to "Made in Italy," for example)? Or perhaps you cherish the brand or its marketing message (Primark versus Prada, Marks and Spencer versus Margiela). Perhaps the garment was a gift from someone special, or was purchased as a souvenir or memento of a trip, or is unique? It may be important to you because of its history and authenticity, as layers of meaning and memory become trapped within the warp and weft of the fibers. I would suggest that fashion value resides in all of these places and more. In this book I aim to bring into view these mutually constitutive relations between production, sale, consumption, possession, and space. Together these connections reveal how the geographies of fashion cannot be reduced simply to fibers or garments, or production sites, or to shops, or consumers, but must be understood in terms of relationality—as a recursive loop that is characterized by complexity and connection, fragility, and instability. In its framing of the geographies of fashion, the book draws on five key conceptual approaches.

The first conceptual device is that of *cultural economy*. This approach examines how changes in the nature of socio-economic life are driven by complex inter-relationships between people, objects, discourses, and practices. In other words, a cultural economy approach to the geographies fashion emphasizes how socio-economic life is made, reproduced, legitimated, and circulated in time and space. Fashion has been a central focus in work on the cultural economies and creative industries of cities (Currid 2012; Scott 2000). The most systematic work in this tradition emerges from the cultural economy of cities literature (Lash and Urry 1994; Scott 2000). This approach emphasizes the global significance of urban activities that are infused with aesthetic or semiotic attributes. The cultural economy approach places particular significance on symbolic meaning and value as this is constituted in contemporary economies. It foregrounds the connections between sites of consumption and spaces of production and enables simultaneous consideration to be given to the material form of the city (architectural and consumption sites) and to its symbolic significance. This framing device opens up space for the consideration of fashion not simply as an object, commodity, concept, or idea but as an active and ongoing set of practices that are co-negotiated between people and communities in space. Actions are intertwined with people's everyday practices and the structure of cultural communities in complex ways. Passivity, predictability, and rationality are poor descriptors of contemporary consumption practices. A cultural economy approach underscores the impossibility of severing commercial or financial explanations of fashion from those that emphasize the aesthetic and creative determinants of worth and value. In the fashion industry, financial pricing devices must be understood in conjunction with social and cultural mechanisms as intricate parts of circuits of commerce (Zelizer 2004). Fashion works through constant negotiations between production and consumption and involves both the sale of commodities and the exercise of the creative imagination. "It is at once highly symbolic and yet an intimate part of embodied, everyday experience" (Breward 2003: 21). One particularly powerful strategy has been the pursuit of an aggressive logic of differentiation based on the aesthetic qualities of commodities. In order to construct themselves as rare and desirable, while simultaneously catering for the demands of more inclusive and larger markets, design-led fashion firms are conjoining the creative and commercial elements of their business and are emphasizing the symbolic and immaterial qualities of their brand. Brands thus become repositories of meaning, a means of conveying distinction and value (Arvidsson 2006; Bourdieu 1984; Lury 2004; Simmel 1904). A cultural economy approach to fashion foregrounds the social and cultural relations that go to make up what we conventionally term the economic (Amin and Thrift 2003: xviii). The creative envisioning of fashion space as economic, social, and cultural practice, that is, as both a material and a representational form, enables us to more fully understand the articulations between fashion, knowledge, and practice as they combine to shape contemporary space. As Elizabeth Wilson argues, "To attempt to view fashion through different pairs of spectacles simultaneously—of aesthetics, social theory, politics—may result in an obliquity of view, or even astigmatism or blurred view, but it seems we must attempt it" (Wilson 1985: 11). A cultural economy approach to the making and placing of fashion markets in turn allows the development of more plural and critical interventions in the making of cities. Fashion both reflects and communicates many of the political, economic, environmental, and social concerns of the moment, and by taking a cultural economy approach we can better understand how multiple agents, institutions, and practices intersect to create fashion space.

The second framing device is that of the *economic sociology of markets*. The book attends to three perceived gaps in the literature on the sociology of markets: their limited attention to value; the neglect of consumption; and, most significantly, their limited attention to space, place, and scale. Drawing on studies of value from an economic sociology of markets perspective (Aspers 2010; Beckert and Aspers 2011; Dewey 1939; Karpik 2010; Stark 2011; Velthuis 2011; Zelizer 2011), the book explores the strategies that are adopted by fashion houses in order to grow their markets while retaining brand value under increasingly complex global conditions.[1] The drive for desingularization as a means to distinguish and valorize the unique (Karpik 2010), together with the financial interests that accompany the mass production of fashioned commodities, are significant forces that threaten brand valorization, uniqueness, and aura, a tendency that echoes Benjamin's early works on the demise of authenticity in an age of reproduction (Benjamin 1936). The book explores the devices and techniques that brands have deployed in order to maintain and grow markets. Fashion, and particularly luxury commodities, cannot be valorized or financialized by conventional methods because they are "multidimensional, incommensurable and of uncertain or indefinable quality" (Karpik 2010: 24). As a result of their uncertain and highly subjective valuation, fashion markets are equipped with "judgment devices," such as labels and brands, that provide consumers with sets of knowledge with which to make consumption judgments (Arvidsson 2006; Karpik 2010). The book captures the ways in which fashion markets carefully choreograph their geographical practices and representational strategies in order to both reveal and conceal social and geographical information and relations.

Third, the book places the *object*, its *materiality*, and its *possession* at the heart of its interests. This approach argues that the value of fashion may accrue, in part, from beyond-market explanations that relate to memories, social relations, love, or history. The affective charge of "love-objects" is out of all proportion to their market worth. The book argues that we attach variable degrees of meaning and value to garments as a result of our personal connections to them, their social history and geography, and the traces of wear and use embedded in them. Garments are constantly in the process of becoming: they have lives, biographies, stories to tell. They are agentive and have capacities to fail and outwit us. The contradictions between the conditions of production, and the materiality and social relations between the garment and the consumer lie at the heart of the problem of value determination. This problematic is played out through the geographical tactics of association and dissociation employed by fashion organizations that have built their competitive strategies on commodity fetishism, emphasizing certain sites and spaces of fashion and hiding others from view.

Fourthly, fashion is conceptualized here as a *performative practice* and central to our creation of identity and sense of self. Fashion spaces and places are part of a broader spatial landscape that articulates our experiences of being-in-the-world and strengthens our sense of self and space (Pallasmaa 2005: 11). Recent work in urban theory has argued that the city must be understood as a haptic, sensory space (Entwistle 2000; Thrift 2004). This parallels work in fashion theory that prioritizes the relationships between clothing and the body (Entwistle 2000). Clothes act as "identity-markers" and are one means by which contemporary consumers can affirm their sense of individuality. Our clothes are among the most personal and the most global objects we possess—they are inherently scalar objects. They are both genuinely specific and uniquely individual as a result of their wearing and in spite of contemporary tendencies toward globalization and homogenization. Our clothes produce emotions, sensory experiences, and engender memories. If one of the problems that people face is that modern freedom has left them stranded as individuals, detached from key social and cultural support structures, then clothes are a key means of actively engaging and connecting with the world. As Umberto Eco famously said, "I speak through my clothes" (Eco 1973). It is argued that consumer creativity and knowledge requires a more critical and sustained interrogation as part of a broader framing of contemporary consumption geographies. Fashion is about both the acts of looking and buying, and about consumption and wearing: fashion is an embodied practice involving people daily negotiating fashion's effects in their daily wearing practices. The increased commodification of all spheres of social life under a postmodern aesthetic of hyper-reality and illusion leads to the "attenuation of actuality," to a process of dematerialization where value is increasingly dependent not on the material properties of the commodity, nor on need or economic value, but on its position in relation to codes of meaning (Jansson 2002). If we are interested in how people relate to one another we need to understand clothes. Our clothing choices are a means of seeking identification. They are an external representation of inner intentionality, "personhood in aesthetic form" (Gell 1998), and rather than disguising who we are, clothes force us to confront who we are. As Miller argues "We cannot know who we are, or become who we are, except by looking in the material mirror" (Miller 2005: 8). Fashion is the porous boundary, the frontier between the self and world. The book argues for a geographical conceptualization of fashion that places object–subject relations, agency, value, knowledge, and the making of meaning at its center. A central argument mobilized throughout the chapter is that the decline of long-standing and relatively stable ideological identities (class, age, gender) is resulting in a much freer fashion system where reflexive individualized consumption is increasingly required in the production and representation of the self. This increased choice and a lack of fixed codes offer freedom for the consumer but comes at the price of increased individual risk and responsibility. The book explores the very real contradictions facing contemporary fashion practice: in a free-floating world of design and desire, seduction and symbol, consumers may become increasingly anxious, confused, and bewildered. Identities are increasingly transient and fragile and we are seeing anxiety and creativity in consumption, both at the same time. Fashion is thus both multilayered and double-sided, characterized by new forms of constraint but also possibilities for more active and creative engagement on the part of consumers. Clothes shopping can be an ethical, economic, and embodied nightmare. Far from wearing clothes to hide or disguise who we are, it may be that we confront and create our sense of self through the clothes we buy and wear. Our clothes conduct and connect our sense of what lies inside and outside ourselves. Our clothes can betray us, they can expose our bodily failure and social ineptitude. In spite of our best endeavors to be who we would like to be, our clothes have the capacity to let us down. The book draws on debates about identity, risk, certitude, and postmodernity to reflect on the fashion system as a means of distinction and identity formation. The fashioned body is argued to be a key geographical space through its affective and sensory capacities: it is only through our bodies that we can feel the materiality of our clothes, and their touch and fit, and it is only through our bodies that we can see, feel, understand, and comprehend the world and our place within it.

Finally, the book develops a *scalar, relational approach* to understanding why fashion matters geographically. Our understanding of fashion needs to recognize that fashion spaces are constituted through hybrid relations and connections to other places (Gilbert 2006). It is important to acknowledge the key role that fashion has played in "actively spatializing the world—dividing, labelling and sorting it into a hierarchy of places of greater or lesser 'importance'" (Agnew 1998: 2). Fashion cities are part of a broader world system and reveal deep connections and interdependencies with other places on the map. A key task in this book is to understand and explore the nature of these connections and the power relations that underpin them. Appadurai's work offers some important insights into how globalization occurs in multiple and differentiated ways, working on and through a series of overlaid "scapes," or morphologies of flow and movement (1990). This is an important counter to the world cities or global cities literature that has reified the economic function of cities and resulted in partial representations of the world that mask the important interleaving of social, cultural, political, *and* economic processes in creating urban space (King 1995). The long and continuing cultural significance of certain key fashion cities is acknowledged throughout the book, which argues that "fashion's ordering does not operate in a vacuum but instead is shaped by broader economic, cultural and even geopolitical factors" (Gilbert 2006: 18).

By emphasizing the relational nature of geographical scale the book connects the complex geographies of fashion in ways that go beyond the binary imaginings of spaces "over there" (sweatshops in China, for example) or "over here" (designer stores in London, for example) (Breward and Gilbert 2006). As Jonathan Murdoch explains, "spatial scales are not stacked on top of one another in discrete layers; rather, scale is generated by distance—that is, it stems from the consolidation of power relations between dispersed sites" (2006: 27). Garments connect global geographies in fascinating ways and reveal highly significant spatial relations, both home and away. In his chapter titled "inserting fashion into space" John Potvin argued that

> discussions of space continue to be emptied of fashion: it's as if space were unchanging and sacred, beyond the vagaries of trends and fashion cycles, beyond the purported feminine wiles of beauty and image. Likewise, spaces and places have often been overlooked in the writing of the visual and material cultures of fashion. (Potvin 2009: 1)

There are thus some critical Geographies of Fashion to be written, ones that locate fashion within various design, production, retailing, and representational nexuses, all with very particular and relational geographies. In adopting this relational conceptualization of place the centrality of mobility becomes instantly apparent. Clothes have biographies, they live lives that include movement through space and time during which value and meaning is transformed. The book thus argues that a number of issues are combining and coalescing to create a powerful new Geographical Theory of Fashion that envisions fashion as both product and practice, object and agent. Fashion is valorized in complex ways through design and desire, production and reproduction, representation and transformation and, perhaps most significantly, through relations between creator, wearer, and garment in space and through time.

The book works through a range of geographical scales and spaces in its search for questions about fashion value. It begins with an exploration of how fashion defines and brands the contemporary city and casts its eye over the myriad ways that fashion shapes contemporary urban space, from flagship stores to exploratory art installations to fashion houses that explore questions of use, reuse, reclamation, and dereliction. By critically reflecting on the connections between fashion and the city this chapter offers the potential to recast our understanding of buildings, bodies, and inhabitation and makes possible new articulations between fashion, passion, emotion, and experience through redefining the relation between the body and space. This critical approach to the fashioned city has the potential to transform the way in which we envision fashion and its urbanisms. Through a number of case studies, including Lucy Orta, Maison Margiela, Boudicca, and Comme des Garcons, the chapter argues that the fashioned city can be about far more than crass commercialization and brandscaping. A number of fashion projects are revealing new possibilities for progressive and socially inclusive urban design, polity, and policy. In short, fashioning the city can be a powerful mechanism in thinking through how we might design a world that is a better place in which to live. Chapter 3 explores how the geographies of fashion connect people, places, practices, and objects in ways that are scarcely imaginable. The chapter argues that the recent history of the garment industry encompasses not simply a relocation of the geographies of employment from the developed north to the global south, but a simultaneous reordering of the moral obligations owed to workers in garment-producing factories around the world. The violation of wage, child, environmental, health, or safety law is the product of a concentrated and powerful clothing retail sector which scans the globe in search of vulnerable, desperate workforces that can be super-exploited in the neoliberalized world order that seeks to extend the social and economic distance between employer and (hidden) employee. The chapter focuses on the ways in which the fashion industry actively puts geography to work in its search for super-profits, using strategies of geographical association and dissociation. Drawing on a range of commodities (jeans, t-shirts, handbags) and organizations (Primark, Zara, Hermes, and Louis Vuitton) the chapter critically reflects on commodity fetishism, value, and the ways in which global flows and processes enable the creation, exchange, and consumption of fashion. While commodity fetishism—the ways in which consumers are persuaded not to reflect on the hands of the makers of their clothes—has been an important focus of geographical enquiry over many years, this chapter argues that a new form of geographical *dissociation* is in the making, one that asks the consumer to reflect not simply on "who made my clothes?," or "where were they made?," but to question what our clothes are made from and to understand how contemporary capitalism has so adeptly disguised from view not just the geographical and social but also the biological origins of our clothes. Taken together, these questions of geographical association and dissociation underscore the complexities of the geographical biographies of commodities. The chapter reveals how the most highly priced fashion commodities may be socially and culturally the least desirable, if their production depends on exploitative, unscrupulous, or toxic practices. It demonstrates that "fast fashion" is an amorphous and conceptually vague descriptor for a range and variety of retail models in the low–mid range price points of the market. Equally, the social, economic, and environmental impacts of luxury fashion may not be far removed from those associated with fast fashion. Luxury fashion, so often positioned as fast fashion's alter-ego, also has a dark geographic underbelly. Looking at the specific case of luxury leather handbags, the chapter explores the secret world of leather supply and the bio-commodification that underpins this. The dislocation between how consumers and the market value luxury handbags and how their supply chains operate "on the ground" raises some important social, economic, and environmental questions. The majority of luxury fashion houses are exploiting increasingly exotic and rare species, and bio-commodification is emerging as a key means through which to capture value in global markets. The chapter concludes with a discussion of "the deceptive economy" of luxury fakes and argues that they are a perfect exemplar of the paradox of value and reveal many of the contradictions that lie at the heart of the articulation of value. An exploration of counterfeit luxury reveals a great deal about the liminal, hidden, misleading, and fictitious worlds of value. It demonstrates how vulnerable brands are to exposure and how fragile their creation is. Fake branded goods are argued to be an acute form of a doubly commodity-fetishized product. The chapter reveals a profoundly polarized fashion market that has, at its heart, a series of geographical inequalities and dislocations that, together, ensure that scale is relational, power and control is increasingly concentrated in the hands of a few global fashion corporations, and the value chains that underpin the "fast," the "luxury," and the "fake" ends of the market are spatially skewed and economically, socially, ecologically, and environmentally toxic.

Chapter 4 focuses on slow fashion and its geographies. The chapter shifts the locus of fashion value away from notions of "value for money" and towards an understanding of the ecology and material culture of our garments which so often accrue value because of our own personal investments in them, our connections to them, their histories, geographies, and our memories of their wearing. Fashion need not be fast, cheap, and disposable and a more sustainable fashion future is possible if we buy fewer, but higher quality pieces that will endure. This model of fashion is based around slow pace, craft, quality, reputational capital, knowledge, and longevity. Significantly in terms of geographical debate, the arguments forwarded here work with a very different set of spatialities and temporalities to those characterizing the fast fashion production model. In the slow fashion system, production systems are locally embedded rather than globally footloose and mobile; materials are traditionally crafted and garments have intentionally long consumption lifetimes rather than being "disposable" quick fashion fixes. The slow fashion model argues that modes of production can act as levers of the imagination: just as the distant ugly conditions that underpin the fast and the luxury leather sector weigh heavily on consumer's minds, so too can more equitable and durable visions of production inspire us, connect us to garment creators, makers, and designers. The chapter discusses the inestimable value of cultural specificity, history, craft, and skill that globalization and fast fashion will not and cannot erode. Two examples are drawn on to explore the spaces and times that slow fashion inhabits: the tailoring cluster of Savile Row, London, and the production of Harris Tweed on the Hebridean Islands of Scotland. Together they reveal how the place of production can be a space of engagement where geography, history, and reputation are woven together. The chapter raises a set of broader conceptual questions about how the competitive qualities of tradition, craft, and locality can endure and adapt to a rapidly changing international environment.

Chapter 5 analyzes the role of luxury fashion retailing, display, and consumption as a remarkably enduring and resilient feature of contemporary capitalism and a key component in the creation of brand and commodity value. The chapter explores the strategies that are adopted by luxury fashion houses in order to maintain aura and grow their markets under increasingly complex global conditions. Central to the evolution of the luxury market is the ways in which retailers actively put geography to work in their creation of value. Key to this business strategy is the role of the flagship store which stands as a highly prominent spatial manifestation of the brand. Drawing on case study retailers including Selfridges, Louis Vuitton, Chanel, and Burberry, the chapter explores the geographies of the flagship store as a key strategy in the semiotic and material expression of the brand. It reveals the significance of the collaborations between artists and fashion creatives in defining the brand's value through shop space. The collaborations constitute an important axis of aesthetic invention. The chapter makes two key conceptual points. Firstly, while art, fashion, and luxury have always been intertwined, recent decades have revealed that contemporary notions of luxury, quality, and added value are quickly combining with the immaterial qualities of retail design, display, atmosphere, and experience. This is engendering a shift away from the significance of the materiality and origin of luxury objects per se to toward their aesthetic pull. Secondly, the chapter reveals that the orchestration of fashion through artistic collaboration in store provides a critical space for reflections on the workings of commercial and creative practice and offers insights as to how, together, these may offer new ways through which to theorize value, aura, and the ordering of markets. The chapter thus offers a more critical reflection on the worlds of art and fashion and draws attention to the many ways in which the two professions are coalescing around a set of practices that enshrine value in the spaces of retailing and consumption as much as in the place of origin of goods.

Chapter 6 explores the role of possession in determining the value of our clothes, arguing that the boundaries between cost and value, between acquisition and ownership, between memory and materiality, and between object and possession are both blurred and mobile. Drawing on Michael Landy's *Break Down* project, the artist Gavin Turk and cherished garments that act as memory-objects, this chapter explores the role of possession, love, and wearing in the creation of fashion value. The chapter thus shifts the geographical focus from the global, urban, street, and store toward the body and social relations in the making of meaning. Fashion is embodied, garment value is a key component in the making of subjectivity, and the biographical histories and geographies of fashion really do matter. Finally, in Chapter 7 the geographical focus shifts from the material to the virtual. Specifically the chapter explores how conventional fashion spaces (cities, stores, magazines, designer firms, shows) must variously compete, coexist, or coalesce with digitally mediated spaces and how the relational networks between the two are unfolding. Drawing on examples including SHOWstudio, Boudicca, Net-a-Porter, ASOS, and blogging, the chapter makes three key points. First, it is argued that emergent digital technologies are *remediating* and *refashioning* existing cultural forms of signification such as fashion magazines and photography. Second, the chapter explores the potential *disintermediatory* effects that the internet is having on fashion markets and consumption, questioning to what extent digital technologies are enabling the devolution of fashion authority from traditional power brokers such as magazine editors and designers toward a more diversified assemblage of participants, including fashion bloggers and consumers. Finally, the chapter explores the transformative effects that digital technology is having on fashion consumption. The chapter explores the ways in which emergent technologies are probing and perforating the boundaries between firms and consumers, production and consumption, object and image, the material and the virtual. As with the chapters that precede it, this section of the book again underscores the relationality of fashion space, its complexity, and its power. The chapter concludes by interrogating questions of agency and power in the fashion system. The depressing interpretation of developments such as artist–fashion collaboration; the emphasis on spaces of retail and consumption; and disintermediation through crowdsourcing, livestreaming, and active enrolment of consumers into the creation of brand messages is little more than capitalism's latest tactic to co-opt the consumer in the relentless pursuit of surplus value creation. It may be that the complexities of the contemporary fashion system amount to little more than the ratcheting up of long-held forms of exploitation, but now at the places of consumption rather than production. While this is a possibility I would like to think that the developments discussed in the book really do offer transformative possibilities for fashion and its participatory politics, possibilities founded upon new modes of knowledge generation and circulation and new recursive links between production and consumption which, together, might form the basis for a new, more transparent, dynamic and participatory industry. The geographies at work at all scales signal both disruption and disturbance to the conventional power relations that structure fashion. But they also reveal new sorts of temporality within fashion characterized by immediacy, virality, and more interactive forms of engagement. Together these developments point to exciting times ahead in the practice and theory of fashion and its geographies. Finally this book has demonstrated how we are living through exciting moments of new understanding and possibility. The findings offer insights that break with conventional wisdom and imply that we need to find new languages and syntaxes to talk about fashion technologies in ways that don't follow the standard script. In theoretical terms we have great opportunities to rework our understandings of embodiment and subjectivity through the collapse of distinctions between the body, commodity, and technology. Above all there can be no end to fashion's geographies for they are continually being re-enacted, replayed, relayed anew. We increasingly inhabit multiple spaces whose interplays and relationalities are throwing up fascinating questions about business models, the market, and consumption. This strikes me as a great way to debate the shape and form that technology, fashion, and space will interweave and evolve in the future.

Note

1   The empirical focus of the chapter is on the eight largest luxury fashion organizations—Louis Vuitton (LVMH), Hermes, Gucci, Prada, Chanel, Burberry, Fendi, and Coach—and on global "flagship" spaces of display such as Selfridges and Harvey Nichols.

2

FASHIONING THE GLOBAL CITY: ARCHITECTURE AND THE BUILDING OF FASHION SPACE

This chapter casts its geographical eye over the myriad ways that fashion shapes contemporary urban space. Following Mores, who contends that "A building's exterior, much like a garment's surface, acts as a mirror of structure left open to a variety of interpretations and representations" (Mores 2006: 141), the chapter argues that fashion literally brands and defines contemporary cityscapes, from dramatic skylines, spectacular architectural structures, LED back-lit nightscapes, dazzling window displays, revolutionary interiors, and deeply sensory store spaces. The chapter reflects on the synergies and convergence between fashion and architecture and on the emotional and sensory resonances that fashion spaces generate: fabric, materiality, tissue, construction, sculpture, silhouette, model. The convergent vocabularies and practices of both fashion and architectural design are argued to offer important insights into the relational geographies of the contemporary city. The temporalities, techniques, rhythms, and spaces of fashion and architecture might be intuitively imagined as starkly different—the first fast, pliable, delicate, and embodied; the second slow, solid, rigid, and permanent. However, the chapter argues that both practices are centrally engaged in the creation of urban environments that question our notions of time, space, form, fit, interactivity, and mobility. Focusing on a number of fashion projects, including Chanel, Maison Martin Margiela, Rei Kawakubo, Issey Miyake, Comme des Garcons, and Lucy Orta, the chapter explores the ways in which the architecture of fashion is centrally concerned with questions of color, emotional response, sensory experience, temporality and visuality. New fashion spaces offer transformative possibilities for the ways in which we inhabit and understand the built urban form. They reveal the limits and possibilities of materiality and open up a physical and metaphorical space through which to revise the politics of consumption. The creative envisioning of fashion space as economic, political, and cultural practice—that is, as material *and* representational capital—ultimately reveals the impossibility of severing buildings from being, fashion from urban form, inhabitation from fabrication. Clothing and architecture overlap to fashion the contemporary city. Yet both are about far more than retinal stimulation, fabrication, and fantasy, the spectacular or the superficial. Rather, they articulate our experiences of being in the world and strengthen our sense of space and self. It is argued that the dissolution of disciplinary boundaries can bring new formations and reveal significant intersectionalities. Theorizing across disciplines need not imply dilution of significance but rather may reveal unexpected mutual effect. Escaping from subject-specific boxes can be transformative, powerful, and profound.

The particular disciplines that I conjoin in this chapter, fashion and architecture, are two subjects and objects that might at first glance appear to have little in common with one another. The clash between the durability of a work of architecture and the mutability of fashion is particularly obvious. But more substantively, the temporalities, materialities, techniques, rhythms, scales, and spaces of fashion and architecture are so often portrayed as starkly different, discordant even. Fashion and architecture move at profoundly different speeds. Their spatial vocabularies, technical practices, and operational scales appear incongruent. Their material and metaphorical presence in the world reminds us of their very different physical conditions and capacities: bricks and mortar, fabric and thread; buildings in cities, bodies in clothes. Fashion is suggestive of transience, pliability, ephemerality, and superficiality (Hollander 1975). It uses soft, sometimes fragile materials. It is characterized by rapid temporality, neophilia, and operates on the smallest, closest in scales of the body. Architecture, in contrast, calls forth notions of longevity, permanence, and solidity. Using rigid materials, architecture is considered monumental, durable, substantive; "the size of its examples (give) more command over the eye" (Hollander 1975: xiv). These representations of fashion and architecture as dualistic in turn owe a great deal to debates about gender and professionalization, whereby design and architecture have tended to equate production with the professional "masculine" sphere, reinforcing notions of subordinate feminine areas of interest into which fashion is generally relegated (Breward 2003). Further, the relationship between fashion and architecture is entwined with broader theoretical and political debates about branding, design, commodification, and consumption. For some, the new alliances being forged by the two disciplines smack of "something sinister" (Pawley, in Castle 2000; Saunders 2005, 2007), a vehicle to seamlessly meld design, branding, signature, and corporate commercialization into a mediatized, promotional selling machine driven by celebrity designers and archistars.

Other interpretations are possible however. In the following discussion I argue that a number of conceptual principles within both fashion and architectural practice are currently converging in ways that suggest mutuality and congruence.

This revisioning is significant in that it offers a conceptual means to break out of the unhelpful oppositional logic that defines fashion as fleeting, trivial, and superficial while architecture represents "supreme and eternal truths" (Mores 2006: 22). Taken together, I argue that fashion and architecture offer some critical insights into the ways in which we inhabit and understand the built form. I substantiate this claim through engagement with critical debates from within both architecture and fashion, and argue that some of the most interesting, progressive, and socially exciting developments often emerge when disciplinary boundaries are crossed or blurred. Exploring the mutual provocations and entanglements between contemporary architecture and fashion offers important insights into the relational geographies of the contemporary city. The disciplines share multiple points of connection around the analytics of construction and the theoretical practices of deconstruction (Gill 1998). More specifically the two are united through a focus on the body and its wrapping, revealing, and sheltering in space. Both buildings and clothes are a mediating layer between the body, the environment, and others. They protect us. Both are also centrally engaged in the creation and representation of urban environments and together question notions of temporality, space, form, fit, interactivity, and mobility. By bringing fashion and architecture into simultaneous view the chapter explores the ways in which the architecture of fashion is concerned with questions of transience, shelter, display, erasure and invisibility, key dimensions of city living. Critically, I argue that fashion spaces can and do offer transformative possibilities for the ways in which we inhabit and understand the built urban form. New fashion architectures make it possible to resist, escape, or offer alternatives to the dominant consumer culture. Further, I suggest that the new alliances between the disciplines offer the potential to recast our understanding of buildings, bodies, and inhabitation and make possible new articulations between fashion, passion, emotion, and experience through redefining the relation between the body and space. Boldly, perhaps, I suggest that this exercise in disciplinary boundary crossing has the potential to transform the way in which we envision accommodation, habitation, interaction, space, and the city, creating and sustaining our wider social landscape and revealing new desires and possibilities for progressive and socially inclusive urban design, polity, and policy. In short, to unite in a mutual desire to design a world that is a better place in which to live.

The chapter is in five parts. First, it begins with an outline of the alleged and often caricatured distinctions and antagonisms that have characterized the disciplines of fashion and architecture. The section then draws out a number of ways in which fashion and architecture have and continue to forge new connections and mutualities. Second, the chapter reflects on the ways in which the connections between fashion retail and architectural design are offering new ways to aestheticize, project, and (re)present the city, drawing particularly on materiality, color, and sensory geographies. It is argued that the nature of the association between fashion and architecture is shifting and that architecture is embracing the soft, sensory, emotional, and tactile characteristics more typically associated with dress. Disciplinary convergence has not simply resulted in ever more effective means of branding the city: both fashion and architecture are questioning conventional cultural practice and offering more critical interventions in the making of cities. Third, I explore a number of ways in which fashion designers are drawing on architectural techniques rather than those based on the normative principles of garment construction to create structural garments — body sculptures. Fourth, the chapter explores the ways in which the design and display of store windows can raise important questions about time, space, and visuality. Finally the discussion addresses the extent to which fashion space may open up new possibilities for political and social critique — to offer radical commentary on contemporary urbanism. In short this chapter aims to reveal the possibilities for a more progressive politics of consumption and a means for consumers to be resistant to, and critical of, the blandishments of hyper-consumption and crass commercialization. The chapter concludes by suggesting that the framing of fashion space as urban practice opens up a rich physical and metaphorical terrain through which to recast the politics of consumption.

Discordant disciplines and mutuality

There can be little doubt that much public discourse between the more vociferous members of the architectural and fashion design communities has been characterized by mutual hostility, if not outright disdain. In certain architecturally based accounts, fashion has been positioned as the inferior craft compared to its weightier intellectual relation, architecture (Wigley 2001). Throughout much of the past century architectural practitioners and scholars attempted to distance themselves from the fickle and short-term business of fashion whose "ribbon and ruffles" were denigrated as "all froth" (Jencks in Quinn 2003: 9). Fashion, its critics would suggest, is "what used to be called a minor art, something like snuffbox making, or glass-blowing" (Sudjic 2001). Among serious intellectual preoccupations, argues Lipovetsky, fashion has marginal status; it is seen as artifice, a capricious trifling, fantasy, shifting ephemera on the surface of life (1994). To be deemed fashionable or on-trend was, in architectural circles, an insult, shorthand for all that is superficial, transient, and frivolous in design terms. The denigration of fashion for its greed and pomp sees only oppressive gendered power relations. Critics emphasize not only the speed at which fashion moves but also the industry's notoriously short-attention span (Castle 2000). Fashion is, for certain architects, little more than a pantomime of merging and marketing, financing and franchising, "a lethal poison. Deadliest in even the smallest of doses" (Quinn 2003: 3). Architects, trained to think of themselves as commissioned artists associate retailers "with snake oil salesmen and pretend to be uninvolved in the 'evils' of consumerism" (Ervin Kelley 2005: 48). But as with a number of subject-specific position statements these reflections on architectural practice and convention are as much rhetorical devices to endorse distinctive scholarly credentials as they are accurate reflections of a given disciplinary "reality." In turn there has long been evidence of a sneering and conceited disdain from within the fashion industry who see the architectural profession in little more than a supporting role, adept at surveying, knowledgeable about the structural properties of steel and concrete, but ultimately more akin to engineers and builders than to creative fashion designers.[1] Their talent is denigrated as technicians not visionaries, their skills those of construction not inspiration. In addition, the realization that fashion now holds a significant allure for young architects has prompted something of a turf war between the professions. As big-name architects compete to rebrand fashion stores with ever more spectacular structures, fashion designers lament their lack of creativity and originality. Emerging as the new heroic city builders, archistars are vilified as depoliticized, desocialized celebrity elites who serially reproduce retail formats in a nasty commercialized mediatecture landscape (McNeill 2009; Sorkin 2005: 116). And in the process they become stylized urban laureates who peddle their own brand. The architect Rem Koolhaas is perhaps most notable in this respect and is alternately viewed with both reverence and disdain. In his writings on the city, Koolhaas has forcefully argued against the endless globalization of retailing and the creation of "junkspace," a kind of monotonous urban vomit. Shopping space and practice are, he suggests, the terminal human condition. Following urban theorists such as Davis (1990), Harvey (1989), and Soja (1989), Koolhaas argues that indefinite expansion represents a crisis and that the current trend of branding is toward the creation of a narrow, immutable, and invariable identity that ultimately spells the end of the brand as a creative enterprise (Koolhaas 2001).

> The danger of a large number of stores is repetition: each additional store reduces aura and contributes to a sense of familiarity. The danger of larger scale is the Flagship syndrome: a megalomaniac accumulation of the obvious that eliminates the last elements of surprise and mystery that cling to the brand, imprisoning it in a definitive identity. (Koolhaas 2001: 4)

So far so good. But the cracks in the foundation of this argument begin to emerge when Koolhaas moves from the role of urban commentator to architectural practitioner. In a valiant about-turn, Koolhaas suggests that in spite of the above, global expansion *can* be employed as a means of stretching, bending, perhaps permanently redefining the brand. When the flagship is recast as an epicenter store (in this case Koolhaas' store designs for global fashion giant Prada) it can become a device that renews rather than dilutes the brand by counteracting and destabilizing any received notion of what Prada is, does, or will become. The epicenter store acts as a conceptual window and conveys the impression that it is at least in part a public space, an attempt to return "the public back to the public" (Koolhaas 2001, unpaginated). In what strikes some as a profound contradiction, Koolhaas suggests that "In a landscape of disarray, disassembly, dissociation and disclamation, the attraction of Bigness is its potential to resurrect the Whole, resurrect the Real, reinvent the collective" (in Foster 2002: 51). Koolhaas the theoretician, Koolhaas the archistar, and Koolhaas the brand appear to be speaking to one another in tongues. How is one to make sense of the suggestion from the retail architect for Prada that "not shopping" is the only luxury left in the late modern world? Critics call this emergence a "Remchasm between practice and theory…A kind of architectural and theoretical parallel universe called Remworld…the projects that are presented are not the models of a semifictional urbanoid future but are here, now, in your face and under your arse" (Vanstiphout 2005: 80). The gulf between Koolhaas' Harvard academician-speak and his real-world built structures could scarcely be wider, the rhetoric and the reality startlingly contradictory.

Yet in spite of the evident antagonism between a number of celebrity architects and fashionistas as they jockey for position as the genuine creative talent recasting urban cultural and commercial space, the congruence between the two disciplines has a long and rich historiography. More recent interdisciplinary collaborations are collapsing the distinctions between design, fashion, architecture, art, and commerce. And so while the two disciplines are often represented as occupying mutually exclusive intellectual ground, it is perhaps more instructive to see them as "hovering on the margins of a mutual existence" (Quinn 2003: 15), evolving relationally through their shared interest in design, display, color, materiality, and space. Both envision space as simultaneously perceptual, political, and physical. Both have the capacity to communicate in non-dialogic ways. Both disciplines use the expressive capacity of materials to create signature pieces. And both have the capacity to connect the body to the built form in profound and pervasive ways. The boundaries between the disciplines appear to be folding seamlessly into one another and in the process opening up exciting possibilities for a progressive politics of consumption and for new ways of sensing space.

White cube, black dress: Building sites and wearing buildings

Whatever the alleged historical impasse between the two disciplines there has certainly been a sense of renewed rapprochement in the past 20 or so years. Densely populated urban spaces reveal the performative nature of fashion and underscore the range of encounters that individuals enact in city spaces that bombard them daily with a mix of information, communication, consumerism, and commercialism (Breward and Gilbert 2006). Progressive architecture and fast-moving fashion combine to socially and spatially shape the metropolis (Celant 2003; Scleifer 2007). A number of leading architects have competed on the world city stage for fashion projects with passion, enthusiasm, competitiveness, and success. As cities become adorned with fashion signs, symbols, and logos, retail architecture is rebranding urban space (Quinn 2002: 29); the spectral nature of fashion is exposed through the exterior built form and interior retail spaces. Both provide the framework through which the mobility of fashion can be practiced. Sudjic (1990: 13) argues that "the look of shops and the cut of clothes are … part of the same thing." Architecture and fashion have converged to aestheticize urban space via dazzling displays, staged performances, fantastic spectacles, and dramatized city skylines. This "strangely reciprocated love" between fashion and architecture (Mores 2006: 15) demonstrates how together the disciplines are capable of creating spectacle in the city. Of course this sensory appraisal of architecture is not to deny the very important role that collaboration between architects and the business of fashion plays in shaping the urban fabric. Striking architectural designs are one means through which fashion houses can define their identity (Koolhaas et al. 2001). This dramatic use of mediatecture through cladding buildings with visual, branded screens, as is particularly the case with Burberry New York and Chanel's global flagship stores, changes not only the aesthetic of the city but also the way in which buildings occupy space. The building itself, through new technological architectures and sensory stimuli, becomes a representational feature of both architecture and brand. Both architecture and fashion thus fuse to create metaphorical and material geographies. As Dercon argues, "Fashion is the representational model of this new century. Fashion has permanently overtaken film as the new, ultimate 'Gesamtkuntswerk.' Nobody and nothing can escape fashion. It is literally right on our backs" (Dercon 2009:137). Casting one's eye over the dramatic fashionscapes of world cities reveals the profound ways through which fashion retail, artistic intervention, and architectural design are combining to aestheticize, project, and (re)present luxury fashion in city spaces, drawing particularly on materiality, color, and sensory geographies in their development of a global retail strategy. Like the use of black as Chanel's signature motif, white is also a color that reveals much about the shared practices of fashion and architecture (O'Doherty 1999). The achromaticity that characterized a number of fashion houses in the 1980s revealed a shared aesthetic sensibility between fashion designers and architects about the power of color in creation. "White walls are never neutral"; they take on active roles by casting and reflecting shadows, defining, and animating space. The pristine white geometrical flagship stores of Jil Sander (see Figure 2.1) and Calvin Klein are material statements about the power of color (or its effacement). Rather than

Figure 2.1 Gabellini Associates Jil Sander showroom in Milan.

seeing such minimalist designs as nullifying and unimaginative, they can instead be read as a material and metaphorical alliance between creators of fashion and creators of the spaces in which they are displayed.

The spare, pared-down design of space and garment allows each piece to stand in stark relief against the neutral background, whose clean shades are accentuated by dramatic lighting (Ojeda and Mccown 2004: 19). "White is the great backdrop, the nullity against which all else stands out" (Ojeda and Mccown 2004: 15). Maison Martin Margiela (MMM) is a particularly insightful example of the use of the color white: "White means the strength of fragility and the fragility of the passage of time. An expression of unity, purity and honesty. It is never just white" (Maison Martin Margiela 2009: 105). For MMM the color white has been at the cornerstone of the organization and its ethos. Maison Margiela stores defy retail conventions of display, branding, labeling, and packaging. The white interiors are filled with white objects, numbers, and words that bear little relation to the clothing that is for sale. His "label" is, and has always been, a bright white rectangle roughly sewn into the garment, identifiable as Margiela only by the four white tacks that are visible on the garment, quietly aimed at the fashion savvy consumer who prefers craft over surface display and would prefer not to wear a label on their sleeve (Frankel 2003). The *blouses blanches* that shop staff wear are reminiscent both of laboratory technicians and the white cotton work coats worn in haute couture ateliers. White, in all of its hues, is used to powerful effect by Margiela and is "in no way neutral or anonymous" (Dercon 2009: 137). In both fashion and architecture, white has come to represent purity and integrity. It has ethereal qualities, simultaneously ghostly and holy. The white wedding dress is a perfect example of the moral and spiritual effective capacities of the color white. The use of color, as these examples reveal, is emotional, sensory, engaging, affective. "White is not a mere absence of colour. It is a shining and affirmative thing, as fierce as red, as definite as black" (Gilbert Keith Chesterton). Both black and white are timeless, essential structural elements; a totality—a convergence of colors. The color of garments and buildings produce emotional effects and responses. We feel and see color through our skin (Merleau Ponty 1968). My point in this discussion is to argue that fashion and architecture have more substantive and profound impacts on urban space than simply those of spectacle and display. Buildings and clothes fashion the city not merely through the surface features of glamour and glitz but via their shared understanding of the affective power of space, form, materiality, and color (Antonelli 2007). The disciplines reveal a mutual understanding of the agentive capacities of buildings and bodies, and of their relationality. Buildings and clothes touch our senses; they are the mediating layer between our bodies and the world; we feel, smell, and see them as they form a membrane between the self and world, enveloping us, touching us.

Body sculpture: Clothes as construction

Two critical public events were particularly notable for setting the connections between architecture and fashion in motion. The first was the *Deconstructionist Architecture Exhibition* in 1988 at the Museum of Modern Art (MOMA). It has been suggested (McLeod 1994) that this event raised the profile of deconstructionism and enabled its cultural dissemination beyond architecture to a range of other professions including graphic design and, crucially, fashion. McLeod, herself an architect, has been a key proponent in furthering the dialogue between the two disciplines and has argued that "architecture and fashion share a lexicon of concepts like structure, form, fabric, construction, fabrication and she can see clear points in the history of Modernism where a shared language has made a conversation between these practices possible" (Gill 1998). The second significant event that pushed further the connections between the disciplines was an exhibition for the MIT Visual Arts Centre in 1982 called *Intimate Architecture: Contemporary Clothing Design*. The exhibition examined the work of eight fashion designers from an architectural perspective and underscored the ways in which both disciplines are centrally concerned with creating symbols of originality, individuality, audacity, and risk. The really significant outcome of these events was the revelation that the direction of the shared discourse appeared to be shifting: while fashion designers had been drawing on architectural principles for many decades, it is only in the past couple of decades that architects have begun to pay closer attention to fashion design (Hodge et al. 2006: 11).

The historiography of fashion designers adopting architectural tropes and practices is a long and rich one (Lipovetsky 1994), not least the architectural fashion designers of the 1950s such as Balenciaga who pared away "extraneous detail to achieve the impact of a pure line and a breathtakingly simple sculptural shape" (Polan and Tredre 2009: 78). Pierre Cardin also fashioned many of his garments in an architectural style and revealed sculptural qualities, clean lines, and a sense of monumentality in, for example, his cocoon coat, trapezoidal cut, and use of high-tech materials such as vinyl and Perspex (Polan and Tredre 2009: 99). More recently Issey Miyake has produced fashions that veer between figurative sculpture and habitations. His collaboration with artists and architects over many-years design has resulted in commentators discussing questions of the space between the body and the cloth almost as much as the garment itself (Frankel 2001), and the subjectivities enshrined in our clothing choices are both complex and well debated: "Clothes are shorthand for being human; they are an intimate, skin-close craft form" (Wilcox 2001: 1). Miyake's A-POC project, an acronym for "A Piece of Cloth," for example, tried to revolutionize the way garments are constructed by delving into three-dimensional worlds that transcend conventional or normative fashion practice (Miyake and Fujiwara 2001). Miyake's designs drew more on the style of the kimono than on the more formal tailoring practices of European fashion production with their seaming and stitching that eliminates the space between body and cloth. Miyake's designs are explicitly focused on the empty space between the skin and the fabric.

By using one long piece of fabric to create multiple garments Mikaye could be argued to be making an implicit commentary on standardized manufacturing, mass production, and construction (see Figure 2.2). His pieces mirror the ways in which new technologies have simplified the construction and craft of both fashion and architecture and resulted in replication of designs, forms, and structures. Miyake's work has also been described as occupying a unique role in forging closer connections between a number of disciplines, including art, industrial design, and architecture, to piece together what has been called "visual clothing," clothing that involves intense engagement with the body and space. As early as 1960, Miyake challenged that organizers of the World Design Forum, held that year in Tokyo, as to why fashion design was not included in a conference featuring architectural, industrial, and graphic design. The discipline was eventually included but the experience highlighted to Miyake how clothing design was viewed at that time in Japan as "merely dressmaking or something nonessential. Clothing design was by nature ephemeral" (Miyake 2006: 5). In a similar way Rei Kawakubo, the founder of Comme Des Garçons, recurrently challenges fashion convention by producing asymmetric, "architectural,

Figure 2.2 One long length of fabric, many different dresses. Photo: © Remy de la Mauviniere/AP/Press Association Images.

sculptural objects" (Mores 2006: 141) designs that are radical in structure and form, extending beyond the realms of normative fashion. She argues that she likes it when something is *off*—not perfect. The enigmatic nature of her garments once resulted in her opening a completely empty boutique. She conceives of "interventions in space" based on architectural principles rather than those of garment construction and in so doing "links fashion and architecture in the most invincible way—making one so invisible that it vanishes into the other" (Mores 2006: 15). Kawakubo doesn't intend for her clothes and stores to be separately commodified but, rather, tries to create a complete space environment, where the inter-relatedness between the intellectual content of the individual garment, the conceptual themes behind the collection, and the spatial representation of this through her architecture are one single expression (Quinn 2003: 50). Helmut Lang's work similarly explores the spatial connections across scales, focusing specifically on the porous boundaries between inside and outside the body, and the evocative and sensory registers that clothing hits. Lang suggests that interior desires rest on the surface, as if worn on the body. He embeds repressed and formerly hidden feelings and emotions within the supposedly unreadable surface of clothing (O'Neill 2001: 42). In his collaboration with Jenny Holzer for the Venice Bienale for example, the cadences of language were explored and echoed in Lang's tracings of routes on fabrics, as if drawing a survival map of the city onto the body (Wilcox 2001: 6). In a provocative expose of the olfactory stimulus of clothes on skin Lang argued "I smell you on my clothes…I smell you on my skin" (Lang and Bienale 1996). Most notable for probing the boundaries between bodies and buildings is Hussein Chalayan, described as an austere, intellectual, architectural designer (Steele 2001: 51), whose designs are inspired by religion, isolation, and oppression. "Space is central to his vision: clothing is an intimate zone around the body, architecture is a larger one" (Steele 2001: 53). Chalayan has revolutionized the form and function of clothing by addressing how the body relates and reacts to the built environment. Chalayan traces the fabric of urban space through clothing and produces garments that appear architectural. He suggests that

> everything around us either relates to the body or to the environment. I think of modular systems where clothes are like small parts of an interior, the interiors are part of the architecture, which is then a part of an urban environment. I think of fluid space where they are all a part of each other, just in different scales and proportions. (Chalayan 2002: 122)

Deconstruction and post-fashion: Clothing as social and political statement

For a number of theoreticians and practitioners alike, the coming together of architecture and fashion opens up a whole range of progressive possibilities regarding the unfolding of urban space, offering alternative visions of inclusion, openness, and the spontaneity of spaces of assembly (Sorkin 2005: 119). In certain ways fashion has always been political—from gendered historical constructions of appropriate attire (Brooks Young 1937) to the political–social movements of the 1960s and 1970s that sought to politicize appearance as part of a broader politics of difference—and fashion has been anything but trivial (Edwards 2007). Fashion space is far more than surface carapace or commercial craft.

> We think about it, talk about it, wear it and perform it. The ubiquitous space of fashion takes shape at precisely the point where traditional definitions of public space—as an urban site, a physical place, a democratic arena—fail…Fashion space provides sites for curiosity, exploration and resistance, routinely deconstructing image and object. (Quinn 2003: 34)

The spaces of fashion have the potential to probe the locus of economic power and to critically question processes of commodification and consumption. A number of fashion designers have used their collections and spaces as a means through which to make broader statements about temporality, regeneration, and reuse. In the following examples I draw on recent examples of designers who have worked explicitly with questions of space and time in order to draw out the more progressive possibilities enshrined in contemporary consumption. Together the works discussed below offer a much-needed break with the hierarchy and pace of much contemporary fashion which has been described as a discipline and a practice "on the brink of exhaustion … fashion was bleeding to death while the pace of its productions sped up. Intravenously fed fashion editors stepped forward with spiked heels heavier than their pencil-thin legs. In the middle of this haemorrhage of creativity and feeling, Margiela offered for us all a tourniquet" (Saillard, 264).

One of the most well-documented exemplars of how fashion and architecture have combined to conceptually question contemporary urbanism is Rei Kawakubo's brand Comme des Garcons. Kawakubo's creation of garments by knitting together past motifs and patterns or by turning old garments inside out for re-use raises a number of questions about value determination in fashion and underscores the valorizing potential of second-hand use and exchange (Gregson and Crewe 2003). The intentional flaws and monochrome palette contrasted starkly with the power dressing glamour of the 1980s fashion scene. Her use of knitwear as a "sculptural piece full of holes" (Sudjic 1990: 10) provides an astute social commentary on the redundancy of hand-crafted garments in an era of machine-made precision. This parallels the brand's use of architectural reconstruction in formerly decayed urban space. Kawakubo argues that she "thinks forward by looking backwards, recycling old things to make them new" (Kawakubo 2001 in Wilcox: 158). The opening of the Comme des Garcons guerilla store in 2004 was a particularly noticeable example of the emergence of "parafunctional spaces" (Papastergiadis 2002: 45) in which creative, informal, or unintended functions overtake officially designated uses. The "store" was located in a redundant bookshop in Berlin and was difficult to distinguish from the surrounding squatted premises. Designed by the German architect Christia Weinecke, it captured the rhythm of local culture, using old water pipes, industrial wire, and factory railings to hang a rapidly changing stock and advertising solely through "underground" media on the internet and via harsh and grainy black and white posters (Mores 2006: 149), whose "Guerilla Rules" slogan is itself wonderfully contradictory. These temporary stores look to "find the cracks in the wall … of corporate culture" (Mores 2006: 149), sell garments with no price tags, change their stock every few weeks, and disregard any notions of spectacle. These deconstructed, liberating, crude spaces emerge and then disappear as quickly as the clothes they display.

Maison Martin Margiela's stores and collections similarly disrupt the conventions of fashion space and suggest a number of possibilities based on recycling, reclamation, and reuse. Margiela argues that while existing spaces or clothes may outlive their original purpose, it is still possible to reappropriate them, as Mower describes: "While others have made a big noise about sustainable sourcing in recent times, Margiela's been practicing it for years" (2008: 598). When we gaze at, purchase, or wear a Margiela piece, we are interacting with an object that appears to have already lived one life: "The garment is conceptually permanent because its temporary quality is part of its look. It is a picture of life after the fact, even before it happened. What moves me most is that this tear, or burn, or misfit, feels unique, as if it were customised for me" (Beecroft 249). This metaphor of re-use, abandonment, and decay extends to Margiela's use of space. He draws parallels between second-hand or abandoned clothing and derelict urban areas that he terms wastelands or warzones. He creates heterotopic spaces by staging fashion shows in the midst of liminal, interstitial, or relic spaces—an abandoned plot in Paris' 20th arrondissement in 1989, a derelict car park near Barbes in 1990. Margiela also explores the congruence between clothing and architectural principles through the mechanics of his garment construction. He sees the garment as architecture that "fits out" the body and was an early pioneer of deconstruction, which he deployed conceptually and materially to dismantle fashion's conventional syntax and aesthetics. He reverses sartorial techniques by turning garment construction literally inside out so that many of the garments appear as if their construction is still in process, with raw unfinished seams and pins left in place (Figure 2.3).

This is part of a broader interest in processes of aging, wear, and decay: some of fabrics are made to decay, others are hand-silvered to artificially create a patina of age. Some are treated in order to appear covered in layers of dust while others still are fabricated from old garments. Here we see how Margiela's philosophy about age, craft, repair, and reclamation chime perfectly with contemporary concerns about the environmental and economic impacts of the fast fashion system and the race to the bottom, and with emergent movements engaged in craft, upcycling, and slower forms of creating and sustaining fashion (Fletcher and Grose 2012). Margiela explains that he "loves the idea of recuperation. I believe it is beautiful to make new things out of rejected or worn things" (Margiela in Hodge et al. 2006: 35). Through his work Margiela is revealing the possibilities of creating new identities for existing spaces and clothes through a broader revisioning of the processes of use, wear, recycling, regeneration, and reclamation. Like the new generation of Japanese deconstructionist designers whose work influenced mainstream design more broadly in the 1980s and 1990s, Margiela explored the aesthetic of "wabi-sabi" in his designs to signify beauty that is imperfect, impermanent, or unfinished. This strategy stands in stark contrast to that of the global branding tactics adopted by many large fashion houses and reveals

Figure 2.3 Margiela Jacket with seams. © author's photograph.

Margiela to be a master of contradiction and to be particularly adept at assuming an oxymoronic identity by building a powerful global brand on invisibility and anonymity: That it is Margiela's fashion that must do the talking is illustrated quite literally in his AW2000-01 collection where a dress, suspended on a simple coat hanger and on a stage flooded by spotlights, is besieged by a flurry of hands carrying microphones: "The image not only radically dismantles the politics of the celebrity cult but also attests to the House's fascination with the vulgarity of stardom and the divaesque" (Debo 2008: 5). Margiela is also notable for his obscurity. He has actively withdrawn from the public eye and stands out by his absence. "This withdrawal has become the 'signature' of his brand" (Grumbatch 2009: 56). He has never been photographed, doesn't do press interviews, and refuses to have his name or personality used to brand his products.

> This anti-branding stance suggests that it is the garments that are important rather than the creative designer himself. His invisibility is captivating, absence brings him into sharp relief. His immateriality is material. Deploying the white label is simultaneously self-effacing and self-affirming. The four white tacking stitches are immediately "read" by those in the know as Margiela's signature. (Holgate 1999 Harvey Nichols Magazine)

The selection of store locations worldwide is further testament to Margiela's progressive vision of fashion and its spatiality. His is a brand built on desire and discretion, as evidenced by the selection of the locations for the MMM stores worldwide:

> they are never located along a main avenue or a prominent shopping street. Rather, a discrete location—often a side street or an alley—receives preference. Furthermore, the stores are not designated by means of glaring logos or conspicuous signs. This seemingly non-commercial strategy is reinforced by the display windows that rarely show clothing ... Instead of clothes it is MMMs ubiquitous use of different shades of white that vies for the attention of the passers-by. These stores do not cry out for our attention but simply survive in the sanctuary of byroads that ward off the busy shopping lanes where major labels compete in the wooing of consumers. (Debo 2008: 7)

The impact of Margiela's fashion project has been quietly and understatedly dramatic, as Debo argues "No other fashion house has had quite the same impact on our conception of fashion and its underlying system, as well as our views regarding fashion and history, craft, commerce, authorship and innovation" (2008: 3). As the brand evolved, alongside the emergence of a range of high-profile international celebrity designers, Margiela's anonymity became both louder and ever more interesting to the media. He is an "arch non-corporate anti-brander…(the blank white labels) whose operation is actually branded through and through, from the whitewashed walls and secondhand furniture of his shops to the lab coats of his staff and white canvas shopping bags, right down to the cotton envelopes to which press communiques are stitched" (Mower 2008: 98). Margiela's concept is one that requires the consumer to think, reflect, see possibility, and not rely on a corporate brand message or readymade total look. Rather, it "demands the participation of the customer, expecting consumer creativity and interpretive labour" (Debo 2008: 7) (Figure 2.4).

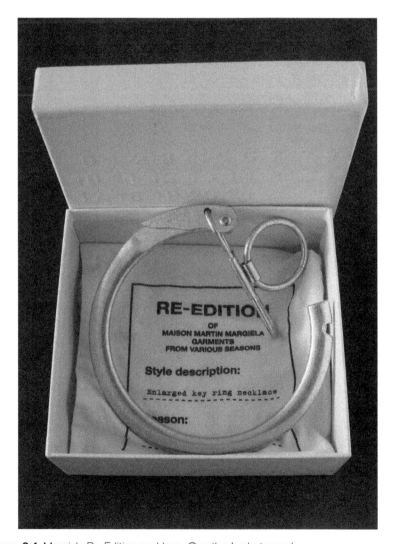

Figure 2.4 Margiela Re-Edition necklace. © author's photograph.

The example of London-based designer duo Boudicca is particularly instructive in relation to the political and social power of fashion. Drawing on literature, art, music, and film, Boudicca's overriding project is one of social documentation, aiming to reveal both "the beauty and the vanity of modern life, the anger of another, the fake lies we are told and the truths we forget … Boudicca strive to see a future of people wearing clothes that express a person's feelings and emotions to the world they exist in. Not clothes as escapism, but of expression" (Platform 13). Boudicca uses exquisitely crafted garments as a means to explore contemporary social issues. Like Margiela, Boudicca is keen to explore and reinterpret conventional methods of fabrication and tailoring through practices of deconstruction and reconstruction. Garments are seen by the duo as being emotionally charged and sensory. They speak to broader cultural tendencies and invite the audience and the wearer to reflect on urban isolation and the potential impact of the internet and new technology on human experience (author's interview). Two projects illustrate this particularly well. The *System Error* SS1999 collection included an "Embrace Me Jacket" that had visible pockets at shoulder height that enabled people to hug the wearer (Ryan 2012: 50). Another design, the Solitary Dress, was slashed at the sides so that the wearer could hug herself, again a reference to isolation under contemporary urban conditions: "as their work attests, Boudicca perceives fashion as a viable forum for critical dialogue on socio-political issues" (Ryan 2012: 59). This radical fashion reshapes the notion of body and design, challenges perceptions, and pushes boundaries (Zhang and Benedetto 2010). As these examples testify, the emergence of innovative and radical fashion is challenging the political and social role and profile of the sector in powerful ways. Fashion is an outcome of multiple agents, institutions, and practices that intersect and it is in many ways a barometer of change in a rapidly evolving world.

As the examples illustrate, fashion reflects and communicates many of the economic, political, environmental, and aesthetic attitudes of the moment (Gill 1998). New–old construction methods and digital design have enabled technical innovations in image production and ushered in new forms of visual representation in art, fashion, and architecture. Contemporary fashion is forming new relationships with digital technology and creating radical structures that have not been seen before; digital technology provides a new and alternative suite of visual and structural effects for designers to use (Quinn 2009). This new generation of fashion designers thinks beyond past limitations, inventing structures that are independent of the existing designs and are taking fashion in completely new directions; the work of these innovative designers has created a new visual language. Their work looks back to the future and involves a suite of new possibilities of construction, installation, and representation, forming new alliances with both science and the arts.

The socially conscious label "Vexed Generation" has created countercultures of resistance against the urban condition and exposed the injustices inherent in neoliberalism. Since the company's inception in 1994, their London-inspired street wear has symbolized social, historical, and political urban struggles and encouraged clientele to "break out of the plastic-cage of mass consumerism" (Mansvelt 2007: 104). Through a range of hoods, collars, zips, concealing masks, and parka coats, their weather-proof garments cover most of the body. They therefore render social surveillance redundant, allowing wearers to attain social anonymity and providing them with protection. Their parka coat in particular was designed as a critique of excessive surveillance systems since the wearer could cover their face and effectively make CCTV redundant. The garments ironically also allow wearers to reveal more of themselves, to be who they want to be by virtue of being covered, hidden from the scrutinizing eye of others: "because we are now alienated and unrecognised we have the freedom to re-invent ourselves" (Evans 2003: 281). Many of their garments are capable of giving "voice to an inner self that is often imprisoned in everyday life" and subsequently encourage freedom of physicality and perception within cities (Destefani 2006: 17). In broader terms their clothes embody the difficult urban condition of 1990s London where the Criminal Justice Act and the government's implementation of poll tax reforms led many to question their own powers in terms of freedom of expression, the right to demonstrate and to assemble. In terms of their "store" design, Vexed Generation used space to make a series of political and social statements about London's urban environment in the mid-1990s. Their first "shop" featured a glass box, similar to an incubator, in the middle of the floor. Small slits were cut into the walls surrounding the incubator display unit so that customers could peep in, reach in, and feel the clothes, but not remove them. The outside of the space was left under decades of grime and the only way for passers-by to see inside the shop was via a black-and-white CCTV monitor that relayed what was going on inside the shop. There was thus no need for staff or security inside the shop and by placing the shop under the surveillance of passers-by Vexed Generation inverted conventional surveillance tactics and in so doing made a broader political statement about excessive surveillance, the erosion of civil liberties, and individual freedom. Their work reflects very well the difficult relationship between civil liberties and security, consumption and repression, anonymity and visibility, freedom and fear in the contemporary city.

The final example of the powerful combinatorial potential harnessed by clothing and architecture is the work of Luca Orta. Orta refutes the premise that clothing and shelter are separate entities and uses her work to highlight the ugly social reality of contemporary urbanism where dazzling retail and residential spaces coexist with a rising problem of homelessness. Through a series of projects Orta addresses the structural social conditions that leave some individuals marginalized or rendered invisible in our city spaces. She describes the plight of the homeless as "tangible invisibility" and follows their traces as they "literally melt and disappear into the margins and framework of the city" (Orta 2003). She sees no distinction between the aesthetic function of art, architecture, or fashion and its political, institutional, or economic function and creates garments that can be both worn and quite literally inhabited. Her project entitled "Refuge Wear" occupies the territory somewhere between architecture and fashion and explores notions of community, shelter, and social networks through the construction of modular garments that protect the wearer from the elements but also connect them to at least one other person (see Figure 2.5). Using the principles of fashion

Figure 2.5 Lucy Orta Refuge Wear. © Lucy Orta, London/ADAGP, Paris and DACS, London 2016.

Orta creates wearable shelters and interconnecting survival sacs. It has been argued that Orta's work operates "like a scalpel in social consciousness, peeling back the skin of indifference to expose the ruptures soothed by unawareness and indifference" (Quinn 2003: 158). Like Vexed Generation, this work emphasizes the individuals' right to occupy public space without fear or stigmatization.

Orta's Refuge Wear is transportable—the very antithesis of the built form but emblematic of the contemporary city that compels mobility. Significantly Orta's work offers the capacity to move beyond the idealism of contemporary art spaces such as galleries and flagship stores and moves instead into mundane and ordinary spaces thus making broader statements about the politics of consumerism and the inequalities and exclusions that characterize the contemporary city (Orrell 2007). Her work is a powerful means through which dwelling and wearing enable a broader questioning of spatial politics, identity, collectivity, and belonging. The centrality of the subject (the wearer) underscores the way in which "It is not possible to conceive a garment without the body...the empty garment...is death, not the body's neutral absence, but the body decapitated, mutilated" (Barthes 1967). And so it can be seen that once we strip the aesthetics away from fashion and architecture one is left with two much simpler equivalents: clothing and shelter. The common denominator between these two words is protection. Each protects our bodies from the elements of nature and society. In this way fashion and housing are becoming pseudo-synonymous—near twins (Mcluhan 1994: 120). "There are many spaces in architecture now that are neither solid, nor void, nor in between" (Koolhaas 2000).

Reflections

This chapter concludes with an evaluation of the significance of convergent practices in fashion and architecture for broader debates about urban form, function, and practice—about how we imagine, inhabit, and represent the contemporary urban condition through our clothing and buildings. Clothing and architecture overlap to fashion the contemporary city. Yet both are about far more than retinal stimulation, fabrication and fantasy, the spectacular or the superficial. Rather, they articulate our experiences of being in-the-world and strengthen our sense of space and self (Pallasmaa 2005: 11). Buildings and garments comprise part of a broader spatial landscape that defines and delineates the relations between private and public, and social space and intimate space. As the examples above have demonstrated, a number of contemporary designers are using deconstructionist designs, experimenting with asymmetry, bodily form and (de)formity, old and new, deformation and reformation in order to raise urgent and prescient questions about time, space, skill, desire, and design. The pioneering creatives discussed in this chapter understand the connections and assemblages between disciplines and they meld craft and material to fashion new kinds of garment for new sorts of spaces—the aesthetic opposite to the celebrity-endorsed "guilt-buttoned logoland all around them" (Groom 1993). In part, this is in order to make a critical intervention into concerns about growing consumerism, disposable fast fashion, and the loss of craft. Both fashion and architectural design reveal the constraints and possibilities of materiality and both transform the status of the surface (Wigley 2001). On a microscale, fashion represents the construction of individual identities by mapping the physical bodily form. On a larger scale, these layers of wrapping, threading, sewing, folding, pleating, and draping of garments provide theoretical frameworks for architects to create buildings as both material and emotional spaces, solid yet sensuous (Sidlauskas 1982). Both disciplines reveal the inseparability of a work and its context. The creative envisioning of fashion space as economic, political, and cultural practice, that is, as material *and* representational capital, ultimately reveals the impossibility of severing buildings from being, fashion from urban form, inhabitation from fabrication. Fashion and architecture are critical elements in the creation of city spaces; they are the material autographs of contemporary design and communicators of what our urban fabric is and may become. Thinking about fashion and architecture takes us to the heart of key questions about the contemporary city. First, fashion and architecture, like the city, are multilayered. They are also double-sided: characterized by new forms of constraint and new possibilities for more active, progressive, and creative intervention in the production of habitable and hospitable cities. Second, architecture, like clothes, touches us, is intimate. Clothing and buildings have the agentive capacity to be "life-enhancing" (Monatgu 1986); they address all of our senses simultaneously and can be the very locus of memory, imagination, and reference (Pallasmaa 2005). As I have tried to argue here, we live, feel, inhabit, and embody both fashions and buildings. Buildings and clothes are performative elements of everyday life. They produce emotions, sensory experiences, feelings, and engender memories. Architecture, like clothes, touches us, is intimate. Thinking about "wearing" buildings and imagining architecture as clothing may offer profound new ways of visualizing and inhabiting architectural discourses and practices, as sensory, emotional, lived. For when we feel buildings, we become attached to them; they hit all of our sensory registers. Buildings are alive, they have agentive capacities—the shock of warm skin hitting cold metal; the creak of the wooden floor; the revulsion of one's naked flesh reflected in the changing room window. Like the memories enshrined within our special clothes (the great night out, the worn-in worn-out jeans), buildings too are sensory spaces that hold personal memories and feelings; they become associated with moments in time, even with time itself. The intimacy of clothes and buildings goes far further than their touch; it is an external representation of inner intentionality and personhood in aesthetic form (Gell 1998; Wilcox 2001: 1).

Note

1   Again the alleged impasse between the two disciplines is in part an intellectual tactic, a caricature that glosses over the long historical associations between the two. A number of highly influential fashion designers including Balmain, Paco Rabanne, Tom Ford, and Gianfranco Ferre themselves originally trained as architects.

3
FAST FASHION, GLOBAL SPACES, AND BIO-COMMODIFICATION

In 1997 Nguyen Thi Thu Phuong died while making Nike sneakers in a factory in North Vietnam. She was struck in the heart by a piece of shrapnel that flew out of a sewing machine and died instantly.[1]

In August 2006 a 22-year-old Uruguayan model died of heart failure, allegedly as a result of starvation, while participating in a fashion show during Fashion Week.[2]

In August 2008 the summer Olympic Games were hosted by Beijing, China. The Olympic Games are the most effective international corporate marketing platform in the world.[3]

What unites these seemingly unconnected events that span continents and decades and speak of both death and celebration, the individual and the crowd, labor and leisure? The answer, as I go on to demonstrate below, is the global significance of the fashion industry and the contradictions that lie at its heart. These events reveal how the geographies of fashion connect people, places, practices, and objects in ways that are scarcely imaginable. Think for a moment about some of these connections. From the sweatshop worker making premium branded sportswear for the Beijing Olympics, to the clothes-hanger models on the catwalk prepared to die for their careers, to the unemployed young designer fresh from college who dreams of a highly paid job in the fashion industry that is unlikely to ever come to fruition, to underpaid and overworked shop assistants in the global north, and to us, the consumer, faced with the constant anxieties about what to buy, where to shop, what to wear, and how to wear it. It would appear that there are a great many fashion victims, all connected by the invisible threads binding this global system of garment design, production, retail, consumption, and wear (Bhattacharjee et al. 2015; Chamberlain 2016). It is tempting to see the fashion commodity chain as a series of discrete and distant places each with their own specific economic and social geographies (international designer hubs, global production sites, retail stores).

In many ways this has been a spatial construction that has suited big business well. It has enabled brand managers and designers to seduce fashion consumers into paying hugely inflated prices for branded goods while masking the global inequalities that lie at the heart of the international fashion industry. In a classic example of the international division of labor, global companies in an increasingly borderless world have been able to use wage differentials in order to derive competitive advantage. Fashion is arguably capitalism's favorite child and "the transience woven into the fabric of free trade zones is an extreme manifestation of the corporate divestment of the world of work which is taking place at all levels of industry" (Klein 1999: 229). Klein discusses with precision and persuasion how the violation of basic employment, and indeed, human rights has become standard practice in globalized garment supply chains. The recent history of the garment industry encompasses not simply a relocation of the geographies of employment from developed north to global south, but a simultaneous reordering of the moral obligations owed to workers in garment-producing factories around the world. The violation of wage, child, health, or safety law is the product of a concentrated and powerful clothing retail sector that scans the globe in search of vulnerable, desperate workforces that can be super-exploited in the neoliberalized world order that seeks to extend the social and economic distance between employer and (hidden) employee. Anita Roddick, the founder of The Body Shop tells how

> money without borders leads to sweatshop exploitation of the world's poorest. Industry after industry seems perfectly happy to use sweatshops and the globe is quickly becoming a playground for those who can move capital and projects quickly from place to place. When business can roam from country to country with few restrictions in its search for the lowest wages, the loosest environmental regulations and the most docile and desperate workers, then the destruction of livelihoods, cultures and environments can be enormous. (Roddick 2000: 7)

While some economists would argue that any job is better than none for those who live in the global south, such a "better than" argument (Krugman and Venables 1995) can be challenged with remarkable ease: "the 'better than' argument is a slippery slope – working in a sweatshop is better than picking through a trash heap, which is better than prostitution, which is better than bonded labour, which is better than slavery, which is better than death. So by Krugman's logic, two cheers for slavery?" (McIntyre 2006: 4). Moreover, the excessive attention paid to distant sweated labor practices within the fashion industry has masked a number of other inequalities, asymmetries, and connections that begin to scramble many of our trusted assumptions about the taken-for-granted distinctions between production and consumption, near and far, us and them, now and then.

Drawing on a range of commodities (jeans, t-shirts, trainers, handbags) and organizations (Primark, Zara, H&M, Hermes, Louis Vuitton) the chapter critically reflects on commodity fetishism, value, and the ways in which global flows and processes enable the creation, exchange, and consumption of fashion. It reveals how the most highly priced fashion commodities may be socially and culturally the least desirable, if their production depends on exploitative, unscrupulous, or toxic practices. It argues that while many people in global north own more items of clothing than any other commodity, they also know the least amount about their clothes:

> I checked the labels on my eggs but not on my t-shirts. I didn't know the significance of fibres like polyester, nylon or elastane of which so much of our clothing is now made. I knew nothing about garment construction nor could I recognise quality ... one need not have the sharpest fashion acumen or know a single thing about clothes to accumulate massive amounts of them. (Cline 2013: 5)

It explores the misplaced value of fakes and the liminal, hidden, and fictitious worlds of counterfeit fashion. The chapter asks the reader to come on a journey in search of some answers, to explore the secret geography of our clothes. This is a journey that connects people, places, and objects together in ways that are scarcely imaginable. It is a journey that spans scale, from the world to the body, and traverses from here to there and everywhere in between. Fashion is one of the most global and the most intimate of commodities. It is both the world and the body. It is both mundane and extraordinary. And of course we all wear clothes. But do we think enough about where our clothes travel around the world, through farms, fields and factories, oceans and air, into shops, homes, wardrobes, bodies? And how often do we reflect upon who made these clothes, where and under what conditions?

Significantly too, it is striking how rarely we question what our clothing is made from. So while commodity fetishism—the ways in which consumers are persuaded not to reflect on the hands of the makers of their clothes—has been an important focus of geographical enquiry over many years, this chapter argues that a new form of geographical *dissociation* is in the making, one that asks the consumer to reflect not simply on "who made my clothes?," or "where were they made?," but to question what our clothes are made from and to understand how contemporary capitalism has so adeptly disguised from view not just the geographical and social but also the biological origins of our clothes. Taken together, these questions of geographical association and dissociation underscore the complexities of the geographical biographies of commodities. If our clothes could talk, what geographical stories would they tell? Where do our geographical imaginations take us when we hear the word fashion? Perhaps it takes us to spectacular flagship stores in global fashion cities such as London, Paris, New York, Milan, and Tokyo. Or maybe we imagine spectacular performative events such as the biannual Fashion Weeks in world cities (Duggan 2001; Evans 2003). Perhaps we reflect on how the dominant global spaces of fashion are but nodes in a much larger, richer, and highly textured and variegated fashion system that presents exciting opportunities for emergent fashion spaces that were formerly "off-the-map"—Casablanca, Melbourne, Mumbai, Shanghai, or Sao Paulo. Or perhaps we think about hidden geographies "over there," the distant sweated labor practices that shore up this vast global industry or the sentient animals that are farmed for their skins, feathers, and fur. Somewhere in our geographical imaginations we sense the growing presence of China on fashion's world stage as both a production and a consumption "super-power." China's contribution to world clothing trade is undeniable: exports were valued at $164 billion in 2014 and it accounts for 38 percent of the world market for garments. The next six lead exporters combined (Turkey, Bangladesh, India, Vietnam, Indonesia, and Mexico) export just half of China's total output (China Customs Statistics 2014). We might also wonder about the provenance and authenticity of "designer" goods and on the spaces through which the trade in fakes travels.

The key point made in the chapter is that a critical geographical understanding of fashion needs to break away from existing, static (and constraining) dualisms between, for example, global cities and "the rest," Western and non-Western fashion, core and periphery, human and animal. If we begin to think about relationality and about spatial connections we see that the discrete fashion spaces we might at first imagine ("over here" and somehow socially, economically, and morally "acceptable," or "over there" and quite the converse) begin to unravel, collapse, and reveal some curious and troubling geographies at work. If we adopt this more relational conceptualization of space the centrality of journeying or mobility becomes instantly apparent. Clothes have lives or biographies. They are made, born, fashioned, and differentiated in a variety of ways. They are sold, retailed, advertised, and consumed/reconsumed/recycled/disposed of. The life of a garment involves movement through space and time during which it adds values and meanings of various forms. Clothes are therefore inherently geographical objects. We can usefully conceptualize consumption, exchange, and value via the metaphor of the journey, as one moment in a much longer series of person–object encounters.

Mapping fashion's geographies

The collapse of the Rana Plaza building in Bangladesh in April 2013, the worst disaster in the history of the fashion industry, was also the most graphic display of its failure to ensure the most basic of workers' rights.
(War on Want 2013)

In the quotation above, War on Want demonstrates that the geographies of fashion reveal the stark disparities between different actors and spaces within the clothing supply chain. In order to unravel some of these connections we need to travel around the secret world of fashion. Let us pause for a moment at the first stop on our journey, at a large discount store called Cromwell's madhouse in a provincial British city. Piled high are endless pairs of branded Lee Cooper jeans. The jeans sell for £19.95—cheap for a global brand—and include a label instructing the consumer to "wash inside out separately." Curiously, the label tells us nothing about the geographical origins of these jeans, and I suspect few of us would spend much time thinking about where the product was made, nor by whom. Clothing labeling is a legal, if profoundly misleading, mechanism through which manufacturers creatively interpret the World Trade Organization's "rules of origin" (ROO) in order to circumvent quotas imposed by the United States and the Europe. As global brands enter into ever more tortuous sub-contracting agreements with overseas producers they can actively use space and global complexity to create a production system that is sufficiently intricate as to make the application of ROO extremely difficult. Current ROO legislation is both highly technical and very obscure. The qualifying criteria include "substantial transformation" at the labeling site which is itself an inherently subjective concept. In practice garments that are finished, labeled, and/or packaged in the destination location can be labeled as "Made in USA" or "Made in England" (Jones and Martin 2015). As is the case with a majority of fashioned garments, the labels inside our clothes tell us far more about how to launder our garments than they do about where they were made or by whom. Yet this pair of jeans connects us, the consumer, to people and places we could scarcely imagine and reveals that we are complicit in determining the conditions of their production simply by turning a blind eye in our pursuit of cheap fashion. The retail store is one stop on a 40,000 mile journey where raw materials and components criss-cross the globe.

> The jeans arrived in a van that came up the A12 from Lee Cooper's warehouse at Staples Corner, just at the bottom of the M1 in North London…Before that they came through the Channel Tunnel in a lorry from France, and before that by boat and train from Ras Jebel in Tunisia, colloquially termed Lee Cooperville. In one of the three Lee Cooper factories in Ras Jebel 500 woman

work furiously, eyes down, muscles clenched amid the heat and noise of the huge grey factory. Each individual here functions like an automaton, hurling garments onto machines and roaring their sewing machines down seams, over and over again. There are no safety guards on the machines and the women work hard and fast and concentrate to avoid the pounding needles punching through their fingers. It is alarmingly simple to imagine how the fatal accident that began this chapter took place. The average pace is three tasks per worker per minute and there are eight lines, each with more than 60 people and each producing 2,000 garments per day. (Abrams and Astill 2001)

If this pace of work is difficult to conceptualize, the online game www .simsweatshop.com may clarify things a little. Here you can become a virtual sweatshop worker. You are invited to enter the world of the sports shoemaker. The clock ticks away while you frantically try to put the trainers together. If you work hard you will be paid your full wage. If you make a mistake you will be punished accordingly.

If we continue our journey back at Ras Jebel and investigate the geographies of jean production in more detail we see that this tiny, busy node is just one moment in a much more extensive journey for our pair of jeans. It is here that dozens of different components converge and are transformed: the cotton is grown in Benin, West Africa; the raw denim comes from Milan; the indigo with which the denim is dyed comes from Frankfurt; it is stonewashed with pumice from Turkey; the thread is made in Northern Ireland, Turkey and Hungary and is dyed in Spain; the rivets and buttons are manufactured from zinc and copper from Australia and Namibia. And these components in turn raise a whole series of questions about the real social, economic, and political costs incurred in the making of a pair of jeans: stonewashing produces several tons of powdered pumice each year that is discarded in Tunis; indigo leaches into local streams and kills plants and fish; Benin's cotton industry is haunted by corruption and mismanagement, its labor is hard, the rewards slight, and people are dying from insecticide and pesticide poisoning (Abrams and Astill 2001). A pair of jeans uses three-quarters of a pound of pesticides and synthetic fertilizers (Harkin 2007). Pollution from the copper mines in Namibia is toxic, but considering environmental and health impacts is a luxury when the alternative is no job and no income. Yet the tortuous geography that is the making of a pair of jeans doesn't stop here. This is a partial story of production. For these jeans have been designed in the United States, advertised globally, and will end up in someone's wardrobe, on someone's body, ready to begin another set of journeys and transformations in their biography: they will be worn, soiled, washed, dried, and perhaps even ironed. As Rachel Snyder argues so persuasively, exploring the complex geographies of a commodity such as jeans reveals dramatic stories about "the people in our pants" (Snyder 2008). When Snyder looks at a pair of jeans, she sees faces and ghosts. "She pictures Ganira Aliyev in red socks and ankle high galoshes picking cotton in Azerbaijan. She recalls Cambodian Ry Muong, whose right hand has no fingers apart from her thumb, sewing belt loops onto jeans six days a week" (followthethings.com, Brooks 2015; Miller 2010). But as a report on the life cycle of a pair of jeans reveals, from production to daily use, washing your jeans can cost the earth (Boeglin 2006). Machine washing, tumble drying, and ironing causes 47 percent of the eco-damage caused by an "average" pair of jeans that are worn one day a week for four years and washed every third wear at 40°C. This is the equivalent of burning 4,000 light bulbs for an hour (Boeglin 2006). And it is highly likely that our jeans will then be worn again, they will wear, perhaps tear, undergo repair, be stashed or stored, customized or cannibalized, discarded, donated, or given away (Brooks 2015). Denim "has a life and lives with the wearer…When used jeans are transported somewhere new and taken up by a second owner they will form part of a new semiotic register, made up of a group of different signs and signifiers" (Brooks 2015: 13). Here we begin to see something of the hidden lives of things and how their stories and journeys speak geographically. The vast expansion of the global denim market reveals a fascinating political-economic geography and has undoubtedly been a good double fix for capitalism, enabling the super-exploitation of global labor and the creation of a generic yet ever-changing global uniform (Guthman and DuPuis 2006). As Snyder argues "No other fabric has held the symbolic fortitude of denim" (2008) and in a number of ways jeans embody the dynamism and the contradictions of capitalism. Jeans are everywhere and nowhere, a source of both creativity and constraint, comfort and discomfort, individuality and conformity. They reveal rich historical geographies yet are very much of the here and now. Their presence in the world is both global and intimate; as a commodity form they are both mundane and extraordinary. Jeans are the most ubiquitous form of everyday attire, the most popular item of clothing in the world (Cotton Incorporated 2005) and a key referent of contemporary consumption. They are worn throughout the world by people of all ages, by the fashionable and unfashionable, by those who want to stand out and those who want to fit in (Candy 2003). It is estimated that American women own on average nine pairs of jeans (WGSN 2005) and over half of the adults in the UK reportedly "usually" wear jeans (Mintel 2007).

The UK denim market is currently worth £1.51 billion and it was estimated that 86 million pairs of jeans were sold in Britain in 2007 (Mintel 2007; Smithers 2007). And as our Lee Cooper jeans reveal, a little geographical detective work uncovers labyrinthine connections. The global maps of denim supply and retail expose our complicity in the production of deeply unequal economic geographies. Our lives are affected by and implicated in the social and economic consequences of globalization (Ramsey and Wrathmell 2009: 59–60). Exploitation will shift geographically as the hunt for a spatial fix drags different territories into global systems of provision (Brooks 2015: 252; Shell 2009). Mapping the geographies of jeans underscores above all the importance of thinking relationally about global inequalities.

Fast fashion: From Bangladesh to Manchester to a high street near you

Let us pause again as we begin the next leg of our journey into the secret life of clothes. This part of the journey takes us to the remarkable growth of value clothing retailers such as Primark, H&M, and Zara. Following the collapse of the middle market in the UK and US through the 1990s and on through the subsequent years of financial crisis, recession, and austerity, the growth of global discount clothing stores has been one of the most marked, and remarkable, features of the urban landscape. The disruptive effect of discount retailers has been profound. Spatially and socially they have reconfigured high streets and consumer behavior around the world, eating into middle market retailers who have unique selling propositions based on quality points, but with price points to match. The Irish chain store Primark is one of the most instructive examples. Primark's annual sales were close to £5 billion in 2014, having risen 17 percent during the year-ending September 2014 and it was estimated that the company could be worth £19 billion (Butler and Rankin 2014). For a retailer that has no web presence and relies solely on store sales, Primark is in many ways a remarkable success story. The recent growth has been a result of the addition of 1.4 m^2 ft of shopping space and its expansion abroad, including the opening of stores in Boston, US, in 2015, and Milan, Italy, in 2016. Primark has, in many ways, become emblematic of the "fast fashion" revolution, where a "season" is no longer winter or summer but, rather, is four or five weeks, from design, through global manufacturing to shop floor. The economic success of Primark has been astounding—in the first ten days of trading its Oxford Circus store sold one million garments (Siegle 2011). When Primark opened its first Oxford Street store in 2007 there was a frenzied stampede in which 3,000 crazed bargain hunters clambered over each other. Doors were ripped off their hinges and police were brought in to control the crowds as would-be shoppers were crushed.[4] Primark has come to symbolize many of the evils of fast fashion (Hoskins 2014: 23). The store connects children in India, toiling by candlelight sewing beads onto clothes to be sold in Primark and earning 60 pence per day, to migrant workers in deindustrialized cities across northern Britain working for far below the minimum wage in an ugly globalized supply chain (BBC 2008). There are few consumers in the global north who will not own a garment that was "Made in Bangladesh." Garments account for 80 percent of Bangladesh's exports and a cheap and willing reserve army of labor has ensured that the country is the second largest clothes producer in the world after China, a trade worth in excess of £15 billion per year. Primark is not alone of course. Ninety-seven percent of our clothes are made overseas (Timmerman 2008) and the intricate sub-contracting supply chain webs that characterize the fast fashion industry are both tangled and opaque. Primark has undoubtedly had profound impacts on the lives of consumers and the strategies of its rivals. It has effectively rebased the price of a collection of core clothing items which has had transformative and lasting effects (Ruddick 2014).

It is important, however, to recognize that "fast fashion" is an amorphous and conceptually vacuous descriptor for the range and variety of retail models within the mid–low range price points of the fashion market. The next stop on our giddying journey around global fashion sites takes us to northern Spain, home to the world's richest man (Ortega) and the world's largest clothing retailer. Zara, the Spanish chain store, operates in over 7,000 stores in eighty two countries (including over 350 shops in China) and makes in excess of 840 million garments per year. These figures are but snapshots at a particular moment in time because the groups are currently opening in excess of one store per day and have been described as an "unstoppable sales machine" with sales rising to 15.4 percent in 2015 (Bain 2016). But their rise to success has not been founded on distant global sweatshops, grotesque violations of labor rights nor long, opaque geographical supply chains. From the outset Ortega wanted to maintain his own manufacturing business in La Coruña, northern Spain, so from the very start Zara's business model was markedly different to the majority of fast fashion retailers. More than half of Inditex's manufacturing takes place either in the factories it owns or within the proximity to company headquarters in Europe or Northern Africa. Zara uses geographical variation in unusual and fascinating ways and have arguably inverted the international division of labor, locating manufacturing close to "home," using distant locations in South East Asia as style and trend incubators, rather than as reserve armies of labor, and investing in prime retail sites as opposed to expensive advertising and marketing campaigns. They argue that the neighborhoods in which stores are located often share more trends and similarities than countries do: The store on Fifth Avenue in Midtown New York "is more similar to the store in Ginza, Tokyo, which is an elegant area that's also touristic, and SoHo is closer to Shibuya, which is very trendy and young. Brooklyn now is a wildly trendy place to go, while Midtown—well, no New Yorker is actually shopping on Fifth Avenue now" (Hansennov 2012). Thompson explains Zara's process-driven innovation strategy thus: Rather than hire world class designers Zara . . . politely copies them. Then it relies on a global network of shopper-feedback to tweak their designs. Corporate HQ absorbs thousands of comments and sends tweaks to their manufacturers in Europe and North Africa who literally sew the feedback into the next line of clothes. The clothes are shipped back and the stock changes so quickly that shoppers are motivated with a "now or never" choice…It's a user-generated approach to fast fashion (Thompson 2012). Zara deliberately undersupplies many of their lines and operates a policy of limited reordering which has the effect of reminding the consumer to buy what they see when they see it, as it won't be there on their next visit. The supply chain—that rather boring metaphor for the choreographing of clothing's design, fabrication, and retailing across space—is absolutely central to Zara's competitive success. The "fast" in Zara's fast fashion model comes largely from its proximate production plants and its lightning speed response to consumer preferences—a perfect illustration of the importance of spatiality and temporality as key components in determining the success of fashion's geographies.

The real success of Zara's supply chain model lies in its geographical strategy: the generation of fast fashion, directed by global consumers, influenced by international designer firms, and produced close to home. In spite of global recession, Zara saw sales increase by just over 50 percent between 2007 and 2012 to $17 billion (Thompson 2012), employment numbers rise from 80,000 to 110,000 over the same time frame, "despite being headquartered in a depressed Spanish economy and selling predominantly to a very sick European continent" (Thompson 2012). The merchandizing policy at Zara emphasizes rapidly changing product lines, high fashion content, and an increasing tendency toward classical, minimalist, design-led garments with clean, spare lines that are excellent yet affordable approximations of runway trends. Approximately 11,000 distinct items are produced per year, compared to an industry average of 2–4,000 and designs rarely stay in store for more than one month. With their affordable prices, prime pitch locations, and sophisticated stores that draw in repeat customers, Zara has pioneered a perfect design-led-copy-cat strategy that off-sets the advantages of cheap off-shore production by investment in local, or at least proximate, production facilities, ownership of production by the lead firm, fast delivery speeds, careful attention to consumer demand and knowledge, and to the significance of retail and web aesthetics and brand message. Their high-luster website with carefully curated, crafted, and presented minimalist pieces have caught the attention of both progressive fashion celebrities and fashion bloggers globally, some of whom argue "I'm addicted" (Style blog with Kirsten Kai) and ask "why can't our closet be just like the Zara lookbook?" (Hannah Weil, Pop Sugar).

Economies of scales: Dissociation and bio-commodification

Picture a hot dusty farm in the outback of Australia, the sun beating down on a series of large concrete tanks filled with a writhing mass of crocodiles. The tanks stretch on and on, housing 70,000 factory-farmed reptiles which will get a bullet in the head once they have grown enough scales to satisfy European handbag manufacturers…In the wild crocodiles can live to be 70 years old; on factory farms they are shot at the age of three. (Hoskins 2014: 90–91)

Moving from the case of fast fashion to the very different market segment—luxury—we begin to see ways in which circuits of value are obscured—a particularly chilling example of which is described in the quotation by Hoskins above. Within contemporary geographical scholarship much attention is afforded to geographical *associations* and country of origin appellations (Made in Italy, Made in England). There is mounting interest, discussed above, in where our clothes are made, by whom, and under what conditions. Much less attention has been paid to the ways in which luxury firms employ techniques of geographical *dissociation* and encourage the consumer to not reflect on what our clothes are made of and what the implications are of the increasing bio-commodification of luxury fashion and the manufacture of luxury commodities fabricated from sentient animals (python leather, crocodile and alligator skin, ostrich hide and feathers, silk, fur). This section of the chapter argues that bio-commodification is quite literally "fleshing out" the luxury market through the commoditization of animal parts across a range of integrated spaces in the global economy. From the crocodile, fox, and mink farms of Russia, Norway, and the USA and the python farms in South East Asia, via global tanneries and manufacturing plants in China, Malaysia, Singapore, and Bangladesh, to the flagship stores of Louis Vuitton, Hermes, Gucci, and Prada in global cities, and on to the bodies of the wealthy super-rich in world fashion capitals, the luxury market actively puts geography to work in its production of high-value, high-controversy goods for global markets produced under intensive factory conditions and leaving toxic chemical wastes in its wake.

Luxury fashion, so often positioned as fast fashion's alter-ego, also has a dark geographical underbelly. A number of fashion houses are relying on sophisticated methods of "geographical dissociation" and are becoming increasingly adept at managing the "dark side" of their operations. In part this is being achieved by subtly shifting their marketing message away from the primacy of the geographical origin of production (Made in Appellations, ROO), and away from the materials used in the production of luxury commodities (skins, hides, furs, and feathers), toward the brand message and the "context of consumption" for their products (Tokatli 2013). This geographical dissociation from the places, practices, people and raw materials of production, and the assertion of the primacy of the brand, the logo and the place of consumption represents a strategy of super-commodity fetishism that actively puts geography to work.

The growth of the luxury market underscores the impossibility of severing strictly commercial or financial explanations from those that emphasize the aesthetic, auratic, and creative determinants of value and desire. This is conceptually significant as it furthers our understanding of the possible ways in which the immaterial and aesthetic qualities of goods can generate, or even determine, value (Karpik 2010). Geographical dissociation will be explored here in relation to one particular commodity—the leather handbag—which will be used as a lens through which to understand the enduring growth and increasing demand and desire for labeled luxury goods. Handbags are a particularly useful commodity through which to explore the geographies of desire and dissociation in the luxury fashion sector as they are both global and ubiquitous but also intensely personal and a key means of displaying the self. Iconic, enduring, and symbolic of both status and the brand, designer handbags have entered the popular imagination and vernacular—the "it" bag has its own set of meanings and vocabularies and is a key commodity for the display of cultural and economic capital (Bourdieu 1984). Not only is the luxury handbag sector growing, but it is a key means of tracking how luxury products hold their value. There is an emergent auction market in designer handbags, many of which sell for more than their original market price at global auction houses. One Hermes alligator bag, for example, sold in auction in New York in 2004 for $64,000. Meanwhile in Hong Kong, designer handbags are being accepted as collateral for the securitization of loans. As with other economies of singularities such as art and fine wine (Karpik 2010), the valuation process is a complex amalgam of reputation, quality, taste, distinction, and rarity. The global market for luxury leather accessories grew to represent almost 30 percent of the overall personal luxury goods market, up from 18 percent in 2003 (Exane BNP Paribas 2015), and the category has transformed business, invigorated brands, and contributed significantly to sustained periods of double-digit revenue growth at a time of widespread global recession. A number of factors might explain this. First, the success of the luxury sector can be attributed in part to the structure of the industry. It is a highly concentrated sector where market share and power is held in the hands of a few global corporations. The world's ten largest luxury companies account for 48.9 percent of global sales for example (Deloitte 2015). Second, the industry has been founded on a long history of skilled craftwork, artisan labor, and talent creation. Third, the global luxury leather sector offers attractive retail economics across a number of metrics—high margins, high sales productivity (sales per square meter), strong full-price sell-through (Solca 2015). Fourth, the handbag has long been seen as a significant marker of taste, style, and distinction that has fueled ongoing and sustained consumer interest in what have recently been termed "cost-effective status anchors" (Solca 2015). Handbags are a perfect example of "Veblen goods," the demand for which increases the more expensive they become. Veblen goods derive value as a result of conspicuous and competitive consumption: these are display goods that are consumed in order to signal wealth or prestige (Figure 3.1).

Fifth, the global luxury market is expanding vertically in order to secure control over the supply chain, traditionally in terms of skilled labor at assembly sites but more recently in relation to the sourcing of raw materials that are

Figure 3.1 Louis Vuitton handbag elevator, London, 2014. © author's photograph.

becoming both more costly and more difficult to acquire. In 2014, for example, the price of all rawhides increased by 18 percent. By buying up tanneries and vertically integrating the leather supply chain, luxury fashion houses are increasingly geographically "managing" an industry characterized by tight demand to supply ratios in order to ensure the ongoing supply of quality skins. Such corporate strategies appear to be accruing reward: the global luxury market is currently valued at $46 billion (Bain 2015). But this is a competitive and crowded category, a murky market that derives value in part through the construction of brand myths and the obfuscation of sourcing realities. While luxury designs undoubtedly hold and grow their value from the moment they are purchased and act as investment objects, the significant geographical question of interest here relates to the extent to which consumer knowledge informs investment decisions. As this section goes on to argue, the dislocation between how we and the market value luxury handbags and how their global supply chains operate "on the ground" raises some important social, economic, and environmental questions. Behind highly coveted brand messages lie altogether darker geographies. How many of us know where and from what our handbags are made and how does the commodification of animal products interface with consumer's geographical knowledge about the origins of the luxury products they are buying?

Our exploration begins with "brand Hermes" whose dedication to quality and luxury are argued to be the result of three guiding principles: craftsmanship; control over stock, inventory, and distribution; and careful management of the supply chain of raw materials. First, Hermes has been a family-run enterprise since its inception, allowing it to maintain its focus on skilled craft work; the company does not employ production lines but, rather, relies on the reproduction and management of talent within French "ateliers": "all luggage and handbag collections are handmade and typically only one craftsman will work on one handbag at a time" (Huey and Draffan 2009: 89). In an interview with Hermes for Forbes Life, Hannah Elliot asked "Why the Artisans Matter?" The vice president of Hermes quotes that their regular "Festivale des Metiers is a way for us to show some of our know-how and our craftsmen who are behind the quality and beauty of the Hermes object…The success of Hermes is based on this savoir faire. The consumer—the people who shop at Hermes—know that they are buying quality" (de Seyne 2015). Hermes has created two of the most classic and covetable handbags in the world, the Kelly and the Birkin, seen by some as "works of art": Exceptional craftsmanship, exquisite materials, and attention to detail mean these heirloom bags never go out of style (Huey and Draffan 2009: 85). Kelly and Birkin bags are rarely displayed in store, have waiting lists lasting months, sometimes years, and the price of a Hermes Kelly has had a compound annual growth rate of 13 percent over the past decade (Exane BNP Paribas 2015). Second, Hermes maintains tight control over the distribution of their products, which are only available through their own retail stores and would never appear in an outlet or discount store. They argue that "discounting would be a disservice to our clients…Keeping excess inventory out of the market is a top priority. If something doesn't sell it goes into our sample sale. If it doesn't sell there it is destroyed" (Hermes 2009). The philosophy is to protect the positioning and imaging of the brand in an attempt to guard the value of the commodity. While destroying valuable merchandise may seem counterintuitive and grossly wasteful, as a corporate strategy it is one means by which to reinforce exclusivity and protect the brand's image and integrity. Legacy is everything for Hermes. Their website exudes a sense of history, craft, and legacy—the orange font against the luxurious rainbow of soft leathers and silks is redolent and seductive, the tabs acting as tiny windows into the philosophy and heritage of the brand, the spatial allusions "placing" Hermes and "petit h," the brand's symbolic horse, firmly in France and the Parisien ateliers of Hermes. Hermes reveal the magic alchemy that creates their brand message, itself a project in the art of commodity fetishism where, through hand-craft, individualization, ancient skill, the finest materials, and most opulent spaces of display, all reference to sourcing and supply chains is effaced: "Everything that issues from the *hands* of Hermes is the product of a metamorphosis—of *matter* most of all…preciously attested by *each* of our objects" (italics author's own, Hermes 2014 'Les metamorphoses de l'objet).

Hermes' consumers can be described as "passionate investors" who are "driven purely by their passion for the product category and not economic gain; they have a very personal, emotional and interest-driven view to investment," a view which is motivated by beyond-market calculations (Mehta 2013). The passion, hunger, and enthusiasm that certain consumers feel for particular objects of desire are undeniable. They love their things, worship them, cherish them. Quite why consumer groups commit considerable emotional investments to the objects, subjects, and texts that they follow is the focus of much debate (Sandvoss 2005). The fetishistic worship of designers is revealed in the Tsuzuki photography exhibition "Happy Victims" that features one young Japanese man who describes himself as being so devoted to Hermes that he carries his 500,000 yen Hermes briefcase in a (Hermes) towel to protect it from his own sweat. High-investor, passionate consumers rely on the skill and craft that has gone into the production of their love objects to sustain desire and demand. Third, while craft, skill, and knowledge certainly play a significant role in the final assembly of Hermes' luxury leather goods, behind this public-facing celebration of French skill and artisanship lie a series of other spaces that are involved in their value chain, spaces that are legally and commercially concealed, hidden from view. There is much more to the story of a handbag than retail prices and inventory control (PETA June 23, 2015). Hermes, along with a majority of luxury leather goods houses, is exploiting increasingly exotic and rare species such as python and alligator in their search to capture value in global markets, and bio-commodification is emerging as a key means through which luxury commodities are valorized and sacralized. The demand for exotic skins is high and growing.

If we continue on our journey in this chapter and travel from the Maisons of Hermes in Paris to the Padenga factory farm in Zimbabwe we find ourselves in one of the world's largest suppliers of Nile skin (crocodile) in the world, and Hermes' key supplier. The Padenga site has a single supply arrangement with Hermes whereby the French luxury house buys every skin that the factory produces. The belly of the crocodile is used in the production of iconic Hermes handbags such as the Birkin and the Kelly. It takes three crocodile skins to produce one Kelly handbag which in turn retails for upward of 37,000 euros. (PETA 2015). A closer look at the farming of crocodiles reveals a profoundly unethical and dispassionate mode of production. In the wild, crocodiles have a lifespan of between 70 and 90 years. Mothers guard their eggs fastidiously, carry their hatchlings for many months, and stay with their young for up to three years. The fashion industry kills the animals when they reach thirty-six months, either by stunning them or, more usually, by plunging a scalpel into their spine and removing it in its entirety before grinding the brain to pith, "otherwise the nerves and everything are always twitching on the table" (Padenga Head of Operations 2015). The skins are stripped of flesh and tissue and are worked on before being treated at the Padenga-owned tannery that treats the skins for Hermes before they are shipped back to France to be made into handbags, wallets, and purses (ibid.). It might be more accurate to explore the Hermes supply chain in terms of a *harm chain* analysis rather than a *value chain* study.

Tracing the python-skin bags from Hermes flagship stores to their finishing plants in France again obscures a snakes-and-ladders geographical journey that is as complex as it is long. The forests of South East Asia have supplied Hermes with python skins worth in excess of $1 billion annually for many years. In 2004 the EU banned imports of Malaysian python over fears that the species *Python reticulatus* was becoming endangered. Two specific geographical outcomes are identifiable. First, the hunting and farming of python has shifted in part from Malaysia to other South East Asian countries such as Vietnam and Cambodia. Second, a more intricate chain of import–export sub-contracting relationships have emerged. With little political will in Malaysia to protect the python and few accurate records of the population in existence, a small number of companies have emerged in Malaysia to orchestrate the procurement and sale of python pelts from both illegal hunters and indigenous snake farms (Journeyman 2014). One company continues to export 8–10,000 python skins annually to European luxury fashion houses, a similar number as before the EU legislation came into force, but they do this via an intermediary in Singapore. Ninety-five percent of the profits of the python industry accrue to European fashion buyers, a profoundly geographically skewed harm chain that is ecologically, biologically, and economically damaging. We see here how import bans and ROO legislation become, in practice, impotent in the face of such opaque and convoluted supply chains. The Malaysian trade in exotic python skin, far from being curtailed has, rather, been rerouted via Singapore before onward transmission to Europe in a legitimate global trafficking network that uses geography in order to circumvent legislation that applies solely to certain sovereign jurisdictions. The figures produced by CITES,[5] a regulatory agency for trade in endangered species, allow us to explore this trade in "blood skins" in a little more detail. In 2009, for example, France imported 5,800 python skins from Singapore, although their shipping licenses confirmed that the original source of the cargo was Malaysia (Journeyman 2014). More recently, customs searches and seizures have increased in Singapore. Again, a clear geographical response has been mobilized in order to overcome the increasing surveillance and seizure of skins in Singapore: python tanneries, such as the Sunny International Leather Industry in Malaysia is currently exporting 40,000 pre-tanned python skins per year to Europe, this time through Turkey which has emerged as the largest global buyer of exotic skins in terms of volume (Journeyman 2014). As one Turkish import–export intermediary explained "I know which skins are Malaysian but it doesn't matter to the buyer. You don't need to know. Nobody can say 'This is Malaysian' by looking at the skins" (Journeyman 2014). Laundering contraband Malaysian python skins into Europe is, it appears, all too easy. As CITES argue,

> There isn't a traceability system right now, whether at a regional, national or international level. Such a system simply doesn't exist…This is what TRAFFIC and a number of other organisations are pushing for. We want to know whether a skin caught by one person somewhere in the world is the same skin being sold in the shop in the EU. (Journeyman 2014)

These global movements begin to reveal how the value of luxury is created, displaced, transformed, and consumed through space and time. They demonstrate how important it is to understand the range of sites and spaces that commodities travel through and suggest that "luxury" goods may be less valuable and desirable if their sourcing and supply is based on toxic, unequal, or immoral practices that come at significant environmental, ecological, economic, and social cost. This exploration of one luxury fashion house has revealed the complex connections that exist between bodies and economy, between life and capital. That which appears most priceless—life itself—is being commodified and marketized in highly disparate ways. The geographical disjunctures that emerge between, for example, the feathered geese in Louis Vuitton's Christmas window in 2014 (see Figure 3.2) and the skins, hides, and furs that its luxury

Figure 3.2 Louis Vuitton Christmas window, 2014. © author's photograph.

commodities are fabricated from articulate the profoundly unequal and unsettling global geographies that underpin luxury production and consumption in the contemporary era.

The window displays a number of geese surrounding handbags fabricated from exotic skins. The irony of the skins of rare animals that have, by alchemy and craft, been transformed into handbags, alongside an array of large display geese—traditionally resonant of Christmas (its celebration and its feasting) is not lost. The iconography of the goose nods to the perils of greed in the laying of golden eggs, providing a richly symbolic and deeply geographic set of allusions that speak to the global traffic of goods, the role of bio-commodification and bio-trade in the luxury industry, and the pivotal space of the store window in displaying, but rarely dispelling, many of the more unsettling aspects of luxury leather's supply chain.

This section of the chapter has attempted to unpack the meanings, materials, and spaces of luxury fashion. Global in reach and encompassing some of the largest global organizations, wealthiest global citizens, and most highly priced (and desired) global commodities, this is an industry that reveals significant but opaque connections—between consumers and producers, between people and their objects, between biotrade and retail display, and across entangled global spaces of supply. Taken together, the discussion offers new insights into the articulations between luxury production and consumption. It reveals both the resilient and variegated geographies of luxury and the affective capacities of luxury goods on consumers. Investment purchasing is clearly emerging as a key consumer motivation, one that appreciates how commodities accrue in value through time. Luxury leather goods are seen to hold value and meaning in ways that cheaper fashion products may not, and yet their conditions of production may be similarly dark, ugly, and tainted. As Iain Hay argues so well "luxury fever and the associated 'arms race' of possessions in which many of us find ourselves now occurs against a crumbling and putrefying environmental backdrop" (Hay 2013: 13). The discussion raises a number of questions about how sustainable and ethically attuned luxury firms' sourcing strategies are given the central significance of rare skins in their product ranges. It suggests that passionate "high investor" consumers know relatively little about the things they own, love, and desire and that theirs' may be a tainted love.

Fake luxury and fictitious value

Consumer's geographical knowledge about the production conditions, places, people, and raw materials that make up their clothes appears to be, at best, patchy. The value of luxury goods is determined via an unstable conjunction of "tangible, material things (products and commodities) with immaterial forms of value (brand names, logos, images)" (Moore 2003: 334). Brands are constructed both as objects and as signs and meanihgs. The inherent instability of the brand is "fixed" through careful corporate discourses of authenticity, craft, heritage, and rarity. Luxury brands leave behind the "dull, passive, generic, inert utility and materiality of the product" (Manning 2010:

36) and emphasize, instead, a commodity's qualities, aura, and signification. The value of luxury is entangled with economic imaginaries, perceptions of place and knowledge of good labor, care, and economic worth. When the significance of the brand is related not to object materiality but to its auratic qualities and self-referential dimensions, the creation and continuation of the luxury project is vulnerable to co-option and usurpation in unpredictable and unanticipated ways. The misplaced value of fake-branded luxury goods is a perfect illustration of the risks associated with authenticity that is culturally and socially constructed.

The "problem" of counterfeiting has allegedly increased substantially during recent years, with estimations of the counterfeit market standing at 5–7 percent of all world trade (International Anti-Counterfeiting Coalition 2014; OECD 1998). The rhetoric surrounding counterfeiting is that it is increasingly linked to organized crime, money laundering, and even terrorism (ACG 2007; AAIPT undated). Counterfeiting is seen as detrimental to legitimate businesses and to national economies. Ethical discussions about fake fashion are centered on the economic harm that the traffic in counterfeit goods brings to bear on large corporations. The most heavy-handed legislative battles against counterfeiting are carried out in the poorest parts of the world by international legislative bodies working in the interests of world's largest and wealthiest organizations—a perfect illustration of corporate greed at potential lost income peddled in the interests of international security and vague allegations of organized crime. It comes as little surprise to learn that the major counterfeited brands are Louis Vuitton, Gucci, Burberry, Tiffany, Prada, Hermes, Chanel, Dior, Yves Saint Laurent, and Cartier (Ledbury Research 2007: 9). Desperate to maintain their luxury credentials, the world's largest fashion businesses classify and position the fake as a deceptive object—the opposite of the original which boasts authorial hallmarks, signatures, and solitary craft. In suitably hyperbolic terms, global luxury firms report growing concern over the scale and quality of the counterfeit market. They argue that the emergence of high-quality "superfakes," whose inauthenticity is discernible only to the very well–trained eye, is damaging the values that are fundamental to the perception of luxury designer brands. The copy, they argue, represents an inferior craft, a failure of creativity. The fake stands as "the discredited part of the pair, the one that opposes the multiple to the singular, the reproducible to the unique, and the fraudulent to the authentic" (Krauss 1981: 58 in Craciun 2014). The threat that the copy represents to the commercial success of luxury brands was acknowledged by Veblen who argued that "the offensive object may be so close an imitation as to defy all but the closest scrutiny; and yet so soon as the counterfeit is detected, its aesthetic value, and its commercial value as well, declines precipitately" (1934: 81). It is little surprise, then, that those with the most reputational and commercial capital to lose through the copy-cat market are those who mount the highest profile and most aggressive attacks on the market:

> The grand golden doors of 500 Pearl Street, in Manhattan, have welcomed such glamorous names as Hermès, Tiffany & Co and Kering, a French conglomerate whose treasures include Gucci and Bottega Veneta. The building is not a posh hotel or department store. It is the federal court for the Southern District of New York, a favoured battleground for the decidedly unglamorous war against counterfeit goods. (The Economist 2015)

Hermes International won a judgment in the New York court that included $100 million in damages against thirty-four websites that sold fake copies of its luxury goods including Birkin and Kelly handbags (Bloomberg 2012). Similarly, in 2008 a French court awarded LVMH (Louis Vuitton Moet Hennessy) $51.3 million in damages for trademark violations by the online retailer Ebay and harm to its brand's image. The European Commission recently reported that lost sales due to fake clothes and accessories amounted to 10 percent of the industry's revenue in Europe. "This makes luxury firms shudder. They cherish their reputations for quality and exclusivity" (Antonio Achille, Boston Consulting Group).

It is argued in the following section that a more critical approach to the counterfeiting literature needs to be taken which incorporates discussions about knowledge, culture, and geography. Luxury fakes are a perfect exemplar of the paradox of value and reveal many of the contradictions that lie at the heart of the articulation of value. An exploration of counterfeit luxury reveals a great deal about the liminal, hidden, misleading, and fictitious worlds of value. It demonstrates how vulnerable brands are to exposure and how fragile their creation is. Authenticity is an elusive attribute. It is slippery and motile despite big businesses' attempts to fix or stabilize its meaning. The fake, those "brazen simulacra … expose a conceit at the core of the culture of Western capitalism: that its signifiers can be fixed, that its editions can be limited" (Comaroff and Comaroff 2006: 13). Superfakes expose with some clarity the extortionate premiums that brand owners charge and that high-investor consumers are willing to pay. They also reveal the extreme lengths that brands go to in order to preserve and protect their reputation and status. Hermes, as we saw in the preceding section, would prefer to destroy unsold merchandise than to risk its release onto the secondary market. The fake market has stripped away the garb of authenticity and revealed corporate tactics of distinction, prestige, domination, and profiteering (Craciun 2014). The quest for authenticity is marked by ironies, perplexities, vicissitudes, excesses, and even atrocities (Craciun 2014: 12; Handler 1986; Lindholm 2008). The desire for branded goods leads consumers into a "deceptive dreamworld which is no dream at all but a sales pitch in disguise" (Williams 1982: 65). The dreamworlds of consumption that Williams discusses are "not a casual fantasy or a vague desire but an inevitable corruption that results when business exploits dreams, blatant lies and subtle ones, lies of omission and commission" (Williams 1982: 65).

Fake-branded goods are an acute form of a doubly commodity-fetishized product. They are not what they claim or presume to be and thus betray both their makers and users (Craciun 2014). Who are the deceptors and who the deceived in the global luxury fashion market? Is the consumer who buys a superfake, a near identical copy, not the superior agent here? The consumer of fakes arguably outwits big business with its excessive margins, the regulatory authorities (with their eye on the corporate prize rather than the ordinary citizen), and the gloating eyes of fellow consumers, unaware that the status good they see is a copy. Fake brands are, after all, "inauthentic only in the eyes of certain people and only in certain moments or contexts" (Craciun 2014: 70). Further, in less economically developed economies, the fake may be bought by consumers who want to acquire the signifier but lack the economic capital to redress the worst excesses of global income inequality. Fakes here offer at least the potential to participate in the brand economy, without its extortion. It may be that the immorality of luxury production legitimates the fake economy. It certainly raises some important questions about the ethics and morality of the authentic luxury-branded economy that extracts extortionate surplus value from the global production of commodities.

It has been argued in this section that it is important that we think geographically about fashion value and its supply chains. Only by thinking through where, by whom, and of what our clothes are made can we understand the value of fashion. In the case of luxury leather products, the real costs of production are global in scale and reach. The circuitous routes of production and supply that underpin both fake and authentic commodities mask the realities of social, economic, biological, and ecological exploitation. As Siegle has argued, leather goods are the "rocket fuel" for the rapidly expanding global fashion business. "The fact that they are made from the skin of a beast is incidental. Presently around 290 m cows are killed every year from a global herd approaching 1 billion. Projections tell us that in order to keep us in wallets, handbags and shoes, the industry needs to slaughter 430 m cows annually by 2025" (2016). The realities of bio-commodification and the traffic in animal skins to furnish the luxury fashion industry, real and fake, are deeply troubling. The geographies at play are disguised and hidden in this deception economy where the brand hides all traces of production and distribution.

Skins are bought and traded across the world, from Ethiopia to Brazil, processed into the soft, buttery leather we associate with upscale European-made accessories. Nearly half of the global leather trade is carried out in developing countries—from Ethiopia to Cambodia and Vietnam—where, despite a backdrop of exploitation of animals and humans and the extraordinary level of pollution caused by unregulated tanneries and processors, the pressure is on to produce more. (Siegle 2016)

This is in spite of a seminal Greenpeace report in 2009, Slaughtering the Amazon, which made a direct connection between leather and environmental destruction. The report revealed that the Brazilian cattle industry is responsible for 14 percent of the world's annual deforestation. Meanwhile the leather-production zone of Hazaribagh in Bangladesh has been declared "ecologically dead" and one of the world's "Top 10 Toxic Places." It is important that we challenge the normative discourses around quality, craft production, and deception at all levels in the fashion chain, both "authentic" and fake. Good fashion value must rely on both materiality and signification, on economy and culture. Corporate lawyers and state agents might attempt to place certain objects and their makers as outside legality; this is merely an exercise in classification and abjection. It has little grounding in the moral economies and supply chain ethics that underpin the global fashion system, both original and fake. Legislation may attempt such classification; those with geographical knowledge about the dark underbelly of the global fashion industry must refute them. The deceptive economy—narrowly applicable to counterfeits, may, in fact, be a perfect descriptor for the global fashion industry more widely. Falsification, secrecy, and deception apply in equal measure to the luxury-branded economy as to markets in fake commodities.

Reflections

This chapter has mapped out the complex relational scalar geographies of fashion. It has revealed the gaping disconnect between dreams and commerce and desire and business. It has argued that while it is tempting to see the fashion commodity chain as a series of discrete and distant places each with their own specific economic and social geographies, it is important to acknowledge that scales are not stacked on top of one another in discrete layers. Scale is generated by distance and unequal power relations and these geographical scales need to be brought into simultaneous view. The chapter has argued that the strategy of commodity fetishism via forms of geographical association and dissociation is a spatial construction that has suited big business well. It has enabled the fashion industry to bring certain spaces and places into high relief while masking the global inequalities, abuses of labor standards, ecological damage, and environmental catastrophes that underpin the industry. It has allowed consumers to be seduced into paying vastly inflated prices for branded goods and for capital to extract enormous profit. It has revealed too that there is seemingly a disconnection between what people allegedly care about and how they fill their wardrobes. At one end of the market, we continue to buy more clothes that have short lifetimes. A "season" is no longer winter or summer. It is 6 weeks from design to shop floor, and probably not much longer in our wardrobes or on our bodies. But value retailing and fast fashion isn't necessarily fashion democracy. It can also be a manifestation of consumer ignorance where we are encouraged not to think about the murky, circuitous supply routes of fashion and the demands this puts on garment workers in cheap– cost off-shore locations. But would higher price points have any material effects on global labor or environmental standards? While supporters of the current form of globalization often defend the "neoliberal" trade regime as one that favors consumers by keeping prices low, such arguments carry little credence given that the wages of garment workers account for 1–3 percent of the retail cost of clothing. Moreover, it is argued here that a majority of consumers would dearly like to pay more for their clothes if they believed it would make a material difference to those who produced them. And if only they could afford to. A majority of contemporary Western consumers may be doing all that they realistically can under increasingly precarious economic conditions at home and away.

Meanwhile at the luxury end of the market, firms are tightening their grip on supply chain networks and on their retail distribution channels, both online and off-line. Such tightly choreographed organizational control over the entire luxury value chain has some important geographical implications. Unlike the case with fast fashion companies who use the global division of labor primarily to drive down costs, luxury firms are in the midst of a significant wave of vertical global acquisition activity in order to control the value chain more effectively and thus to manage and protect both their reputational capital and, most critically, their most ethically and environmentally damaging activities. Vertical integration and the acquisition of global tanneries and animal factories ensure that firms can protect their carefully crafted brand identity from the prying eyes of the market. The chapter has revealed a profoundly polarized fashion market that has, at its heart, a series of geographical inequalities and dislocations that, together, ensure that scale is relational, that power and control is increasingly concentrated in the hands of a few global fashion corporations, and that the value chains that underpin the "fast," the "luxury," and the "fake" ends of the market are spatially skewed, and economically, socially, ecologically, and environmentally toxic. An important challenge in developing a critical geography of fashion is to capture the multitude ways in which markets conceal social and economic information and relations.

More broadly the fashion industry seems to perfectly reveal the contradictions inherent in the projects of neoliberalism and globalization. As social and political functions are gradually shifting to the corporate sphere a number of prescient questions are raised in relation to the role and authority that consumers have in markets, and the extent to which the presence, practice, and regulation of markets might be influenced by workers, NGOs, trade unions, and governments. First, as geographical knowledge about fashion's inequalities becomes more widespread, a requirement for firms to deliver social value in addition to generating financial return is likely to grow in significance: "Publically available environmental profit and loss statements, such as Kering's, measure a firm's environmental footprint throughout its supply chain and calculate its monetary value" (Deloitte 2015). Such accounting methodologies hold the possibility at least of providing greater transparency to stakeholders who are calling for more joined-up "triple bottom-line" accounting approaches that bring into focus the social, financial, *and* environmental implications of fashion's global activities. This shift toward conceptualizing fashion in terms of a "harm chain" rather than a value chain approach may go some way toward ameliorating the very worst consequences of fashion's global activities. Second, there are, it seems to me, a number of ways in which consumers-as-agents might participate in fashion in more productive and participatory ways. These rely on the importance of thinking, seeing, and acting relationally, and conceptually require that we free up our bounded notions of the organization, consumer, commodity, and place. When consumers acknowledge the profound geographical inequalities resulting from the globalization of fashion, they may use their economic and cultural capital to resist the worst excesses of the free market. This is particularly exciting in that it opens up new possibilities for more ethical and equitable systems of provision. The economic and political significance of fashion is increasingly giving consumers unprecedented power as global citizens. Significantly, these alternative ways of thinking and acting about global fashion emphasize the very real possibilities that we as consumers have for exerting our agency. As a whole range of recent forms of consumer mobilization such as *No Sweat*, *Buy Nothing Day*, and *Students Against Sweatshops* have revealed, consumer activism, boycotting, and buy-cotting can have significant economic and political ramifications. Equally, tactics of brand jamming and adbusting that refigure corporate logos and images have the potential to raise ethical questions about "big fashion" in highly persuasive ways. The streetwear brand Homies, a clear allusion to Hermes, borrows and repurposes imagery from iconic logos and designers to make a satirical parody about branding, value, and logo. The crafty iterations of brand names on his streetwear designs including Feline and Ballin, Paris, question the price and value represented by the fashion logo. The Fashion Revolution movement is one particularly significant example of how people can connect globally and mobilize for change. The movement grew out of the tragedy of the Rana Plaza factory collapse in Bangladesh on April 24, 2013, in which 1,133 people died and another 2,500 were injured, making it the fourth largest industrial disaster in history. That's when Fashion Revolution began. It is now active in over eighty countries and believes that positive change can happen

> if we all think differently about fashion and demand better. We want a cleaner, safer, fairer, more transparent and more accountable fashion and textiles industry. We want fashion to become a force for good. We believe in an industry that values people, the environment, creativity and profit in equal measure. Knowledge, information, honesty. These three things have the power to transform the industry. And it starts with one simple question: Who made my clothes?

The mobilization of consumer, activist, NGO, and corporate interests to work together in the interests of a fairer and more transparent fashion industry reveals the possibilities and potential for doing fashion differently (Figures 3.3 and 3.4). As McIntyre argues, "It **is** a small effort to develop a moral response to human indignity. It **is** a partial response to a global problem and it can, in some times and places, concretely improve the material living standards, solidarity and freedom of some of the most exploited people the planet" (McIntyre 2006: 8).

Figure 3.3 I made your clothes. © Fashion Revolution.

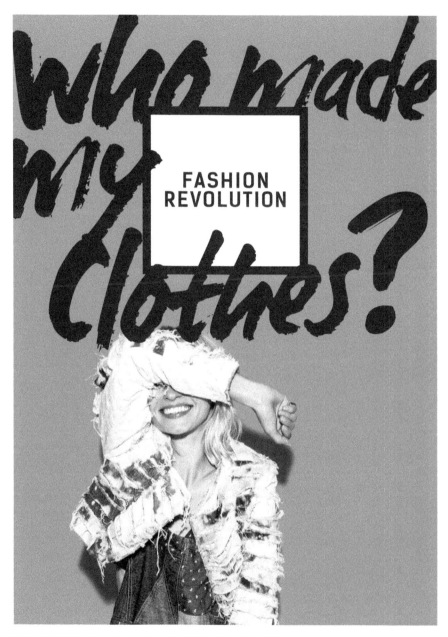

Figure 3.4 Fashion Revolution day. © Fashion Revolution.

Notes

1   McIntyre (2006).

2   BBC News (2006). Is ultra-thin going out of fashion September 27, 2006.

3   Playfair (2008)—an organization lobbying to clean up sportswear production in the run-up to the Olympics.

4   Freeman (2007).

5   CITES is the 1973 Convention on International Trade and Endangered Species of World Fauna and Flora.

4

SLOW FASHION AND INVESTMENT CONSUMPTION

A product has the less soul, the more people participate in its manufacture. (Simmel 1957)

As writers such as Simmel, quoted here, have often acknowledged, the spatial division of labor that underpins much of the garment supply chain can result in clothes that lack meaning and history. This chapter focuses on the temporalities and spaces of fashion, looking specifically at models of slow luxury fashion, craft, quality, and knowledge. The conceptual basis for the discussion lies in an industry founded on a lowering of quality and a future based on fast, cheap, throwaway fashion produced under distant, exploitative work conditions (Crewe 2008; Siegle 2011). Although fast fashion has been a key strategy in the industry's attempt to maintain competitive advantage, it is also widely acknowledged to be economically, socially, and environmentally unsustainable (Brooks 2015; Brown 2010; Fletcher and Grose 2012; Hoskins 2014; Minney 2011; Siegle 2011). While the global supply of cheap, fashionable clothes may have been a perfect competitive strategy for fashion retailers, it brings with it set of social, economic, and environmental conditions that are altogether more troubling. While the fashion industry has been remarkably adept at heading off environmental and social censure, it has also enabled the creation of both dirty, ugly business practices and giddily accelerated cycles of consumption with long and often invisible production footprints and short (and equally invisible) consumption lifetimes. The volume of clothing purchases has increased by over a third in the past decade, largely because of the growth in cheap, fast fashion. As a result waste volumes are high and rising (Allwood in Lean 2007: 16). Consumers are buying more than they need and cheap prices are fanning hasty, thoughtless, and at times needless consumption. The faster the fashion moves, the more toxic is its effects, and globalized production systems are threatening a range of geographical spaces, from cotton fields to sweatshops, high streets to landfill sites—not only are our homes becoming filled with barely worn garments but a volume of clothing and textiles equivalent to approximately three-quarters of purchases is buried in landfill in the UK each year (Cline 2013; Hoskins 2014). The longer term implications of these tendencies are of note both economically and theoretically. Cost, value, and worth of objects have become confused. Why do we buy what we buy? How do we begin to understand object value? Do we care any longer about our clothes? What now informs our consumption practices? How aware are we that the life cycle of garments in terms of production, consumption, and use is being rapidly accelerated, that clothes are shoddily and hastily constructed, their post-purchase lifetime intentionally truncated? Disposable fashion is unsettling, objects become expendable, things feel impermanent, and consumers become restless awaiting the next quick fix, a fix that ultimately rarely satisfies. We are left hungry, wanting, desiring the next purchase. And as long as consumers continue to be seduced by cheap, fast clothing, mass market retailers will continue to tread the path of least resistance and churn out cat-walk copy designs made by the world's poor, for sale on a high street near you within weeks of their runway launch.

In reaction to the increasing unease generated by fast fashion and its outcomes, two dominant responses are identifiable in both theory and practice. First, there has been a growing intellectual and industry-driven focus on sustainable or eco-fashion (Brown 2010; Fletcher and Grose 2012; Minney 2011; Siegle 2011). Second, there has been a more politically and socially driven focus on fashion production through recycling, reuse, crafting, mending, knitting, and repair. Growing discontent among certain groups of consumers with the business operations of some retailers means that alternatives to the harried cycle of fast fashion are increasingly being sought and there is a growing interest in "geographies of making" (Carr and Gibson 2015). The social and economic relevance of the craft renaissance is "far more complex than the cliché of the middle-class mummy hooked on crochet" and "speaks to a more visceral and socially urgent need to reconfigure the nature of work" (Brooks 2009). Knitting, for instance, has been argued to be an effective means to critique capitalism and its exploitative supply chains and labor practices, and as a way to forge alternative identities, communities, and ways of living and doing (Buszek 2011; Greer 2014). While knitting has often been framed as a gentle craft, one intimately connected to the home, domesticity, nurture, and care, it has also been seen as an active craft that knits thought and desire together, telling stories of texture, tactility, and wearing. Knitting is also one means of inserting agency, power, and creativity into the production of clothes as it connects labor, production, product, and consumption in ways that are rarely evident in the contemporary globalized fashion industry (Gauntlett 2011: 245). It "produces the means and conditions through which alternative ways of living can be imagined and shared, and practical examples for change defined and materialised" (Hackney 2013:

187). Fashion craft has a long history of being used as a social and political tool and has an important gendered history as Parker argues "women have sewn a subversive stitch—managed to make meanings of their own in the very medium intended to inculcate self-effacement" (1989: 215). This "new materialism" (Simms and Potts 2012: 1) is characterized by "a more deeply pleasurable, and also respectful relationship with the world of "things" (Simms and Potts 2012: 1). An important body of work is thus emerging that explores the practices, networks, meanings, and values bound up with amateur making with a view to understanding how the "maker-movement" might speak to the interests and priorities of different social groups (Carr and Gibson 2015; Gill and Lopes 2011; Hackney 2013). Gill and Lopes (2011), for example, explore how we might value material things that are "already made" as opposed to the new and novel and thus develop new more economically, environmentally, and socially sustainable consumption models.

In the following discussion I offer a third alternative vision of future fashion based on a rather different set of reflections as to how fashion production and consumption might redress and counter the more deleterious aspects of cheap fast fashion. The argument for durable, crafted fashion is persuasive and engages us, just as the fabrics and clothes about which I speak do. The argument gains added validity as it has, at its heart, a commitment to a return to skilled production, using quality materials to fabricate products that are locally made. On social, environmental, and employment grounds this alternative fashion future based around slow fashion and shorter more transparent systems of supply begins to gain credence. Additionally, the argument offers a new conceptual insight into what fashion value is, where it might lie, and how it might be created and maintained. Given that fashion has for so long been seen as trivial, excessive, hedonistic, and egocentric, it may at first sight appear to be an easy target for critique during critically difficult global economic times. If fashion is seen as an unnecessary luxury, consumers should surely regulate and monitor their consumption, become frugal, discipline their consuming bodies: stop shopping? That is, of course, one possibility. But here I want to argue for a return to a different relationship between fashion and consumption in which we see our clothes as long-term investment pieces that speak of durability, love, attachment, quality, and craft. Under this theorization we shift the locus of fashion value away from notions of "value for money" and toward an understanding of the ecology and material culture of our garments which so often accrue value because of our own personal investments in them, our connections to them, their histories, geographies, and our memories of their wearing. Fashion need not be fast, cheap, and disposable and a more sustainable fashion future is possible if we buy fewer, but higher quality pieces that will endure, garments that we will adore, cherish, will wear for many years, and keep for many more. This vision of future fashion is based around slow pace, craft, quality, reputational capital, knowledge, and longevity. Significantly in terms of geographical debate, the arguments forwarded here work with a very different set of spatialities and temporalities to those characterizing the fast fashion production model. In the fashion model proposed below, production systems are locally embedded rather than globally footloose and mobile; they are slow rather than fast; materials are traditionally crafted and garments have intentionally long consumption lifetimes rather than being "disposable" quick fashion fixes. These new–old ways of doing fashion are both competitive but also underscore the role of durability, craft, and the management of sustainable and design-led supply chains.

The proposed "slow luxury" model argues that modes of production can act as levers of the imagination: just as the ugly conditions that (usually young, usually female) sweatshop workers labor under in cheap cost locations weigh heavily on consumer's minds, so too can more equitable and durable visions of production inspire us, connect us to garment creators, makers, and designers. Here I argue for the inestimable value of cultural specificity, history, craft, and skill that globalization and fast fashion will not and cannot erode. Two examples are drawn on to explore the spaces and times that slow fashion inhabits, both with long and fascinating historical and geographical stories to tell: the tailoring cluster of Savile Row, London, and the production of Harris Tweed on the Hebridean Islands of Scotland. Together they reveal how the place of production can be a space of engagement, a space where the mythical alchemy of the product takes place. Good products are worth the wait, they develop slowly and last, weaving together reputation and history, valorized through their cultural, historical, and geographical roots. This, I suggest, offers the potential at least for a reworking of fashion's times and spaces. It reveals how locally embedded production systems offer a counter to globalized fast fashion systems and explores the significance of place, time, skill, embeddedness, and agglomeration in the generation and survival of successful fashion spaces. The chapter raises a set of broader conceptual questions about how the competitive qualities of tradition, craft, and locality can endure and adapt to a rapidly changing international environment.

Handmade, hand-touched: The evocative geographies of crafted fashion

Slow luxury fashion reveals a very different way of understanding the customer and managing a business based on decreasing the physical and social distance between fashion producers and consumers. It enables a greater awareness of the real cost—and value—of clothes. The consumption of crafted garments places crucial importance on the precise materials from which they are made, their social, economic, and historic reasons for being, and the way that we interact with them through our senses (Aynsley et al. 1999). Crafted, quality systems of supply offer both creative and economic power and acknowledge that much of the value of the garment is linked to territory, history, cultural specificity, and the places of its production. While the UK may have lost the global battle for cheap clothing supply, we have demonstrated that "we can win the battle of quality, credibility, and ideas" (Hieatt 2013: 12). Rather than cutting costs by outsourcing production and severing the ties between producer and consumer, slow fashion actively pursues non-exploitative and sustainable supply chains that reconnect the consumer with where their clothes originate and enroll the consumer in the production process and the knowledge systems that underpin it. Clothes that are beautifully made with care, sensitivity, and skill are special, precious, valuable. Special garments have a soul, a meaning and an authenticity. They generate deep desire based on knowledge and aesthetics rather than price, saturation, and duplication. Fashion value originates in part from our knowledge about the hands that crafted it and the memories ingrained within it from use, wear, love, and emotional attachment (Crewe 2011). In turn, evocative objects have the potential to invert the economics of value and price, supply and demand by decoupling a growth in profit from increased material flow. Extending the life of clothing builds symbolic worth into systems of value determination. An increased emphasis and active promotion of durable style and design classics encourage consumers to consider moving toward the purchase of fewer, higher quality, seasonless pieces that are crafted to last: "Slow burners work harder for your money than frivolous fashion and allow for a more conscientious kind of consumption" (Fletcher in Britten 2008: 16).

Fashion-conscious consumers are increasingly aware that their purchasing decisions can have a dramatic impact on employment, industry, and economy in the UK and are prepared to pay higher price points for garments that are crafted to last, using short, transparent supply chains and locally sourced materials and are designed and produced domestically by some of the most skilled craftspeople in the world. Further, through such considered consumption, they are actively supporting domestic garment production and world-class training provision that the UK offers for designers and makers that will help to ensure the reproduction and transmission of this vital skills base. Such consumption practices empower consumers and provide them with a real sense of agency to effect change through what they buy and from where, on the basis of their knowledge about supply, production, use, and value. In short, slow fashion offers the potential at least for the formulation of radical new perspectives on the production and consumption of fashion. It reveals that fashion can and is being done differently. "If fashion is about ingenuity and innovation, this is a good time for the industry to draw on these qualities and return to measuring fashion in terms of something other than quantity" (Siegle 2008). The quality, frequency of wear, and length of use thus transform both the economics and value of clothing. The close relationship between fabric, creation, crafter, and customer is central to the generation of quality clothing. Crafted garments are non-anonymous, they are authenticated and reveal the value of slow clocktimes and long lifespans. In this context luxury can be redefined and seen less in terms of excess and the needless and more in terms of thoughtful, quality consumption. Luxury can be "refinement not ostentation, communication not proclamation" (Kapferer and Bastien 2009). The connection of craft to time is one of its essential elements. Slow garments are both of the moment and design classics—timely and timeless, carefully crafted through painstaking design, beautiful materials, and personal connection. Evocative garments are worth the wait and reveal above all that the material pleasure and symbolic expression of identity through fashion can be compatible with a more politicized, socially conscious consumption ethos (Pietrykowski 2004: 309).

Appreciative consumption: The spaces and times of crafted clothing on Savile Row

London's Savile Row is a short street in Mayfair with a long history of bespoke tailoring and quality craft. While Savile Row has been the subject of journalistic and historical attention (BBC 2009) there has been little critical geographical research to date on this iconic center of British tailoring (although see Breward 2003). Yet "From Savile Row to Shoreditch, from Bond Street to Brick Lane, British menswear has never been more dynamic or indeed more successful" (Jones 2013). Savile Row has faced a number of challenges in recent decades that chime perfectly with the broader trajectory that the global fashion industry, discussed in the introduction, has followed. At various points in time it appeared that this industrial quarter almost disappeared from view and vocabulary. The specific threats to this mode of production include the rise of the ready-to-wear casual market in the 1970s, a relaxing of formal dress codes in the corporate workplace through the 1980s, and most particularly in the fashion-forward creative industries, the emergence of looser tailoring pioneered by Italian companies such as Armani, and more recently the global recession and falling consumer spending. The sustainability of their market has also being called into question as both the traditional customer base and the skilled workforce of Savile Row are aging. The Row faces difficulties recruiting and retaining apprentices to maintain and continue its bespoke tailoring skills base and has struggled to compete for young workers who—at least until the latest recessionary crisis—favored the city over the clothing industry as a career option. In addition, Savile Row is facing a number of broader global threats and several of the firms have been taken over by large multinational investment businesses that bring a very different set of knowledges and expectations about fashion futures and their spatial depth and reach. Finally, the space of Savile Row is also being challenged by a range of new entrants including ready-to-wear suit retailers, "celebrity tailors" such as Ozwald Boateng and the highly contentious arrival of the American casual youth-wear brand Abercrombie & Fitch in 2008, all of whom may shift or dilute the profile and long-standing reputation of the Row. And yet in spite of these very real threats and pressures, Savile Row continues to be a center for crafted, high-quality garment production and customization.

The endurance of the fashion model that characterizes Savile Row, in spite of seemingly insurmountable economic, cultural, and social pressures that it faces, suggests that quality, luxury consumption, and high value-added competition continue to be important components in certain spaces for particular groups of consumers. This section of the chapter explores how this locally embedded production system is responding to the broader socioeconomic threats outlined above and evaluates the key factors that begin to explain the enduring—and increasing—appeal and success of a fashion agglomeration that is committed to an economy of regard that places slow production, domestic sourcing policies, consumer relationships, and the life of clothes at its heart. It is argued that the development and survival of competitive fashion spaces may be explained, at least in part, through an appreciation of the importance of place, time, identity, skill, reputational capital, agglomeration, and particular sets of knowledge-based consumption practice. The particular example of Savile Row raises broader conceptual insights into how the competitive qualities of the "Made in England" brand, with its long and credible history of skilled, high-quality production of crafted garments, rich in symbolic value and with global consumption appeal, can offer a very real alternative to the outsourced production of cheap, disposable fast fashion garments. After many years of falling employment, margins, prices, and sales in the British fashion industry, there are emergent signs that "Made in Britain" may be regaining the kudos and respect it endured for much of the early post-war period. Long associated with a certain kind of quality, design, and luxury, British fashion is estimated to employ almost 70,000 people (BFC 2014). London fashion and design in particular has a long history, from the swinging sixties, punk and Cool Britannia through to its renewed status as the leading international center for the global fashion industry. London is a world center of creativity and design talent and has some of the most renowned fashion educational institutions in the world with unrivalled reputations. There is a renewed interest from industry, governments, policy-makers, and publics to manufacture high-quality garments in the UK and a clear vision that the future for British fashion production must be to compete on quality, design, and specialization rather than price. This is the UK's comparative, competitive, and long-established advantage. London Fashion Week is one route through which emerging British fashion talent is taken to market. It attracts in excess of £100 million of media coverage and showcases some of the most forward-facing, design-led talent that has emerged and continues to emerge from UK Fashion Schools and educational establishments. The London Collections: Men in 2013 included the highly respected and widely reported Savile Row collective that showed in Spencer House and confirmed both the iconic status of Savile Row and key role that London plays in incubating and developing new fashion skill and talent. More overtly, perhaps, the reintroduction of the Wool Awards and Wool Week at London Fashion Week brought the crofters and weavers of the Scottish Hebrides, the tailors of Savile Row, consumers, and the global media together in a live spectacle during which Savile Row was grassed over so that flocks could safely graze—a literal juxtaposition and clear spatial manifestation of the transparency of supply chains at work.

London has arguably always been the spiritual home of the sartorial man: its menswear has been seen as both innovative and timeless; it is both understated and yet unrivalled in its attention to detail. In recent years London has enjoyed renewed levels of international success and is very much setting the pace in terms of emerging talent that is both design-led and commercial, producing garments that are ageless and work well on men of all ages. A Savile Row suit has retained a traditional understanding about quintessential fabrics and cuts that are read as a distinctively British version of style that really works: "The suit is the default wardrobe setting; the most successful garment in the history of fashion and is wholly and indivisibly a British invention…A suit says authority, learning, expertise, manners, probity, efficiency, trust and a certain formality; all attributes traditionally thought of as British" (Schofield 2011). The Savile Row suit has successfully maintained a powerful grip on definitions of Britishness in the postwar era. Tailors on the Row work with clearly identifiable aesthetic, beautiful fabrics and with domestic sourcing policies and short supply chains. Savile Row is gaining in vision and visibility, its tailors are supremely competent in construction and with a new confidence and directional sense of design. In a global marketplace, a Savile Row suit can be Englishness personified. The new generation of designers are revealing a convergence between the long-held quirky, fashion-forward, edgy London style and the more Savile Row–establishment sartorial reading of fashion. London has a classiness and a quality but with none of the bland corporate styling that typifies Italy, for example, with suits that could have rolled off a machine (Grant 2010). There is a depth and maturity to London menswear that can only come through time.

> The point about Savile Row tailoring is that it takes a long time and you build on it and you develop your skills over years and years and years and you don't jump from one season to the next. That's why people like McQueen are so fabulous because he trained on Savile Row. And then went to Givenchy.

It's those sorts of journeys that produced the sort of magic that they did. And John Galliano similarly. That's the pleasure of London as a city in that side-by-side we have that tradition of tailoring and we have that bright street style too. (Grant 2010)

That many of the UK's most successful designers began their careers on Savile Row is testament to the key role of the apprenticeship schemes and training associations in attracting new entrants into the fashion sector and developing their skills bases. After seeing an advertisement on television highlighting the shortage of apprentices in the tailoring business, Alexander McQueen told how he walked into Anderson and Sheppard on Savile Row and was hired on the spot (Knox 2010: 7). His natural talent with chalk and scissors allowed him to quickly conquer classic cuts and shapes and develop his personal style, eventually moving further down Savile Row to work at Gieves and Hawkes.

The micro-geographies of the tailoring houses along Savile Row also hint at reasons for their longevity and ongoing patronage. They are both, and at the same time, retail spaces, design studios, training sites, and micro factories. The exterior architecture of the tailors' stores along the Row is grand, imposing and hints at its patriarchal and colonial history of privilege and secrecy. The uses of the row are protected by restrictive covenants that have ensured a long history of conservatism, discretion, and mystery. A quiet rumpus followed the introduction of the first see-through shop windows on the Row in the 1970s, and in the 1990s the introduction of an elegant flower box outside the store caused a scandal. It wasn't until 1992 that Saturday opening was first introduced by Richard James, revealing how the street, its appearance, and covert regulations formed part of the tailor's identity. Beneath this external architectural façade of conservatism and respectability lie the complex geographies of craft, design, and fabrication. Given that the cheapest space on the Row is on the lower floors, it is not surprising that the pressers, steamers, cutters, finishers, and tailors are going underground, living a below-stairs existence. The warren-like spaces below street level are hives of activity comprising workrooms and studios whose tools remain the same as they have done for decades: scissors, needles, chalk, shears, fingers. The teaching of tailoring is intimate and organic, a craft passed on without books or manuals, almost by osmosis, although the investment required to sustain the apprenticeship system is considerable: it requires a minimum of five years for a junior tailor to acquire the basic skills of the trade, and many more to reach the exacting standards required by the slow and precise rhythms of work and the meticulous coordination of hand and fiber. Other hidden spaces include rooms of archived fabrics, bespoke samples, and the marked-up patterns of Savile Row's customers over many decades: Fred Astaire, Cary Grant, Jude Law, Daniel Craig, David Beckham, and Michael Gambon, the labels identifying their individual identities carefully hidden from public view.

The Row reveals a long and rich tradition of quiet understatement and self-effacement that belies exquisite materials, faultless craft, and flawless finishing. A Savile Row suit is assembled using thousands of hand stitches that join cloth to linen and cotton interlinings and linings, with edges and button holes all finished by hand too. It is hardly surprising, then, that a Savile Row suit is in every respect a slow garment. Once the body has been measured and the customer has selected a bolt of cloth, the pattern is "bespoken" for and the fabric theirs. Aware of the value of provenance, customers can select a suit made with "record bale" wool whereby they know who owns the individual sheep that provided the wool for the suit. Each suit requires between 35 and 40 individual body measurements before the pattern is drawn up to make a blueprint of the customer's body that is uniquely theirs. A suit is made specifically for an individual and is cut and stitched by hand. The tailor–client relationship is built up over time and is based on trust, discretion, and confidentiality—customers develop personal relationships with their tailors. The suit will take up to three months to create and will require at least half a dozen fittings. There is certainly no instant gratification involved, but the quality and craft of the suit is worth waiting for. In a world so dominated by faceless mass production, the tailors of Savile Row recognize that handmade, craft, tradition, and individualization can be powerful counters to cheap disposable imports. These are garments that will be loved, cherished, and will last many lifetimes: "It is your labour inside a suit. It's in your heart" (Everest 2008). A Savile Row suit is created slowly and without damage to the planet, it weaves social relations through time and space and through the generations: "When Henry Stanley finally tracked down Livingstone in the heart of Africa, the good doctor was still wearing the tweed trousers he set off in from London some four years before" (Norton & Sons). One suspects that these clothes will never be landfill. As Patrick Grant of Norton & Sons argues "We just make beautiful, simple men's clothing that lasts for years. I'm fed up of disposable clothing. People buy too many clothes—we should buy fewer things, but better things … there are easy ways to buy cloth but no easy ways to produce beautiful and unique cloth" (Grant 2010). Grant insists on using only the best British materials and craftspeople and personally sources his fabrics, including Harris Tweed, on his frequent sourcing trips to Scotland. Savile Row tailoring is fashion as both product and process, a blending of time, skill, precision, and place. It uses highly specific techniques of salesmanship and selling, careful and understated forms of visual display and product design that avoid overt marketing, labeling, or policies. This is a fashion system where you won't find discount deals, logos, or sales; it is careful, considered local production for extensive and discerning global markets built on repute and reputation. It is in such spaces that the "mythical overlap of styles forged new and challenging identities" (Breward 2003: 580).

Capturing land and life in cloth: Crofting, crafting, and the making of Harris Tweed

There is probably no other British cloth with as rich a fashion history as tweed, and Harris Tweed sits at the pinnacle of this heritage. (Hills 2011)

Harris Tweed is like no other fabric on earth, as Hills argues above. It is borne of its environment, is organic, hand-crafted, and defined by time. Tweed is a place, an imaginary as much as a fabric. It is also undeniably British:

> Tweed is a parable. A stereotype of Britishness. We are tweedy. Tweed is taciturn and hardworking, sturdy, dependable, loyal. Tweed doesn't get soppy or go limp … I have a bit of a thing for tweed. I love its feel and its smell. I love that it's rough but homely, that it has the ability to deflect the elements with a jaunty nonchalance. Tweed is like a game terrier; always pleased to see you, always wants to go out, always optimistic … It is the perfect balance of utility and panache, and it is my secret vice. (Gill 2011)

It is also the only fabric that has its own legislation. Eight thousand patterns are patented and protected by the Harris Tweed Act of Parliament. The Act allows the authority to promote and maintain the authenticity, standard, and reputation of Harris Tweed and includes final quality inspectors who check that the cloth is perfect with no snags, uneven surfaces, or wool discoloration. Each piece of cloth is labeled with the trademark orb logo and a series number and each meterage of fabric has uniquely identifying "passport information" on it (Platman 2011) that encodes who has woven the cloth, the pattern used, and the date it was produced. Harris Tweed cloth can only be produced by weavers who live on the Hebridean Islands, and as consumers are increasingly wanting to know who made their fabrics and garments, where, how, under what conditions, the Tweed provides no finer confirmation of the virtues of local production for global markets. Unlike a number of other "luxury" products that are increasingly made under brutal working conditions paying poverty wages,[1] Harris Tweed retains its entirely local production base and the island crofters here are quite literally weaving the fabric of emotional connection: "The long, barren archipelago on the far north west tip of Europe is home to every dyer, blender, carder, spinner, warper, weaver, finisher and inspector of Harris Tweed" (Harris Tweed Authority 2012). The Harris Tweed archive dates back well over 100 years and is a timely reminder that, in spite of increasingly long, distant, and unknown supply chains across much of the fashion industry, Harris Tweed retains its strong sense of provenance and bears the personality of the weaver and the croft in which it was fabricated, acting as a powerful repository of information for tailors and customers alike who are increasingly concerned about the origins of the garments they buy. Like the skills base that remains along Savile Row, the fabrication of Harris Tweed is a skill that takes many years, if not generations, to hone: the grading and sorting of wool into different quality levels is a highly skilled activity that is still done by hand and eye; shearing is still a bodily encounter between farmer and animal.

Like Savile Row, Harris Tweed has a long and rich history. In its earliest days it was dyed using lichen and woven by hand. It was adopted during the reign of Queen Victoria for its seeming indestructibility in the wild (Brown 2009: 15) and became a staple fabric for the production of robust and hard-wearing jackets for many years. "Britain's story, its image, is wrapped and warped in wool. Wool can be woven into a gallimaufry of cloths... but the greatest of all, for which the grandest sheep can aspire to give the coat off its back, is tweed" (Schofield 2011). Harris Tweed has successfully steered a long symbolic history that speaks of both the establishment and its alter-ego: anti-fashion. One of the earliest pioneers to subvert the traditional, class-bound, and patriarchal associations of Harris Tweed was Vivienne Westwood who spearheaded the use of the cloth by the punk movement in the 1970s. Westwood dressed the Sex Pistols in Harris Tweed, has used it across a number of collections including the AW 2010/11 Prince Charming range, and adopted a motif very similar to the orb as her corporate logo. A number of iconic British designers have worked with the fabric as a central component in their tailored collections. Margaret Howell recently argued that

> weaving on hand looms creates a depth and complexity of texture that can't be imitated by a mechanical process. Its very nature—the resilient wool, the flecks and herringbones in earthy colours—reflects the landscape, climate and skills of the people that produce it. I've always been attracted by its authenticity and chose Harris Tweed when designing my first winter jacket and overcoat. I've used it ever since. (Howell 2012: 124)

Harris Tweed is, argues the Savile Row Tailor Timothy Everest, "an amazing institution" (2009: 14); "No-one can match it anywhere in the world" (Wylie 2009: 14). The relaunching of Woolmark Prize, originally awarded to Karl Lagerfeld and Yves Saint Laurent in the 1950s, is testament to the industrial, policy, and design status again afforded to wool, and mill production increased by 12 percent in 2011 (Fisher 2012).

Although the industry was in a precarious position during the 1980s and 1990s, due to a lack of investment, a shortage of skilled workers who wanted to enter the industry, and shifts in fashion and taste, the handwoven fabric is currently enjoying a surge in production and sales and is now the Western Isles' largest private-sector employer and generates approximately £10 million for the local economy per year (Carrell 2012). In part this resurgence has been the result of an initiative headed by a former Labour Energy Minister Brian Wilson who explains how "The objective was to create a new generation interested in it. The great thing is you're selling something which is truly genuine. It's not like spinning a story around something that doesn't exist. It's completely genuine: the distinguishing features of Harris Tweed are both quality and heritage" (Wilson 2012). One of the greatest successes in recent years has been the transformation of the image of the brand Harris Tweed into a young fabric that appeals to a new generation of consumers. Harris Tweed's client list now includes "just about every serious designer. Every fashionable designer is now working with Harris Tweed" (Wilson 2012). Jaggy Nettle, for example, has produced a range of hi-top trainers in Harris Tweed that are stocked alongside Prada and Louis Vuitton in boutiques in New York, Tokyo, and Milan: "I chose Harris Tweed because their clothes are not designed for one season or one trend, but to last" (Lee 2012 in Carrell 2012).

Like Savile Row, the production system that underpins the creation of Harris Tweed has a long and revered history, one that is again rooted in the specificity of place and the skills of people. The isolated crofting communities who produce Harris Tweed are embedded in the islands, and see themselves as "all one family, all working as a team, everyone helping each other" (Mary Ann Macleod in Platman 2011). The crofting communities that tend sheep and weave are an integral part of this landscape that provides much of the inspiration for the color and texture of the cloth. The purple and lavender hues of heather on moors and braes, the purple and green moss in springtime, the clear blue northern skies and bright blue seas and lochs form the very basis of the fabric, cloth, and land woven together. The colors and qualities of Harris Tweed are unparalleled by any other fabric through a combination of the inspirational landscape in which it is crafted, the ability for the wool to adopt a dazzling array of dyes, and the blending, spinning, and juxtaposition of yarns during the weaving process (Hills 2011: 123). The designs woven on the islands are carefully blended to the changing needs of fashion and style direction in terms of color, density, and weight but the colors of the landscape are always intertwined, an ever-present constant motif. This is a fabric that has gained its legitimacy through quality production nurtured from heritage, skill, and craft. Harris Tweed speaks of landscape, place, and origins; the cloth evokes heather-colored heaths and glens, mountains, rocks, sky, water, shoreline, pebbles, moors. Its colors and textures speak of its place of fabrication, not in laboratories or dyeing factories but in crofts and farms and rural mills. It looks and smells like the land. It captures land and life in a fabric.

Reflections

This chapter has revealed that fashion can and is being done differently. Buying without regard makes little sense, and the model of cheap, fast production via the off-shoring of production and the race to the bottom of the market is becoming less convincing economically, environmentally, and socially. The fashion system outlined here is based on appreciative consumption and embedded, active networks of supply and production. It offers a counter to the dominant narratives that suggest the inevitability of a low-cost global fast fashion industry and offers the potential at least for the formulation of radical new perspectives on the production and consumption of fashion. By focusing on time, place, skill, and quality, the examples drawn on here reveal the very real possibility of growing a slow, design-led, domestic fashion system that has global reach and highly visible and transparent supply relations. Most significantly, the arguments forwarded here have important implications for existing debates about designing for durability in which, to date, product longevity has been considered solely in terms of an object's physical endurance.

The concept of slow fashion developed in this chapter extends the notion of durability beyond its conventional interpretation to a consideration of fashion value as created through history and place, skill and craft, object quality, memory, and attachment. Our clothes "speak" to us through the memories that we associate with them. Instead of viewing the meaning of particular designs as fixed and given, by looking at the process of evocation it finds an open and continuing dialogue between things, their makers, and their consumers.

This approach argues for a revaluing of materials and materiality in the determination of quality and for appreciative consumption of products that we love, that engage our hearts and minds as well as our bodies and flesh. The importance of the materiality, surface, depth, construction tactility, and fit of garments has been very much ignored. This chapter foregrounds these effective qualities of clothes and directly engages with the clothes that are the material subject of study. In short, durability and the long biographies of garments are just as much about our connections to our things, desire, love, attachment, and memories woven into the very fiber and fabric of our clothes as it is about their physical durability. Fast fashion is widely acknowledged to be economically, socially, and environmentally unsustainable. One response that is considered here is the growing intellectual and industry-driven focus on sustainable, eco-fashion or crafting and knitting as new forms of activism and resistance. The chapter also consider a rather different set of reflections on how the fashion industry might redress and counter the more deleterious aspects of cheap fast fashion. It considers a very different model of fashion production and consumption based around slow pace, craft, service, reputational capital, knowledge, and longevity. Significantly in terms of geographical debate, these arguments work with a very different set of spatialities and temporalities to those characterizing the fast fashion production model. In this alternative business model production systems are locally embedded rather than globally footloose and mobile; they are slow rather than fast; materials are traditionally crafted and garments have long lifetimes and provenance rather than being "disposable" quick fashion fixes. The chapter evaluates the role of identity, image, skill, reputational capital, and agglomeration in the development and survival of successful fashion spaces. The chapter raises broader conceptual questions about how brand value can be created and maintained under conditions of economic austerity and rapid globalization.

Note

1   See, for example, the documentary *Schiavi de Lusso (Luxury Slaves)* about the 2,500 predominantly Chinese fashion workers in the Tuscan town of Prato, Italy.

5

LUXURY: FLAGSHIPS, SINGULARITY, AND THE ART OF VALUE CREATION

In recent decades there has been significant interest in the geographical underpinnings of retailing and consumption. In parallel, an important body of work has emerged from the disciplines of organizational strategy and marketing on brands and branding as key mechanisms in creating commodity meaning (Arvidsson 2006; Holt 2004; Lury 2004). A third strand of work has focused on the design of shopping space (Goss 1993, 1999) and, more recently, on store architecture and innovation (Barreneche 2008; Crewe 2010, 2013; Curtis and Watson 2007; Dean 2003; Manuelli 2006). While this latter work has developed our understanding of the significance of form, function, interiority, and technological innovation in the creation of new retail spaces, it has been less well attuned to the visual and material cultures of retail space and has rather side-stepped the broader cultural, social, and political implications that fashion space has on cultural consumption, fashioned identities, and subjectivities. Further, the relationships between fashion retailing space and creative collaboration in the creation of commodity value have received limited attention. This chapter advances understanding of these relationships by analyzing the role of luxury fashion retailing, display, and consumption as a remarkably enduring and resilient feature of contemporary capitalism and a key component in the creation of brand and commodity value. The luxury fashion industry is an empirically significant but theoretically neglected area of scholarship and one with a pronounced geography that requires scrutiny. On first reading, the notion that fashion value might lie in the realm of luxury production and consumption may appear both contentious and unsettling at a time of global recession, austerity economics, and very real economic hardship. On a number of levels (personal, political, economic, intellectual) it is a difficult challenge to mobilize an argument in favor of luxury production and a return to quality consumption in an age of austerity and it brings with it some degree of unease. However, to deny the significance of the luxury fashion sector is to ignore a key global competitive force, a shaper of desire and a source of employment and economic development, albeit not without a dark and largely invisible side.

In order to develop these arguments theoretically the chapter conjoins three bodies of literature that together help to better understand how luxury fashion value is created and maintained under conditions of market expansion and accelerating globalization. First, drawing on studies of value from an economic sociology of markets perspective, many derived from Dewey's seminal work on *The Theory of Valuation* (1939), (Aspers 2010; Beckert and Aspers 2011; Karpik 2010; Stark 2011; Velthuis 2011; Zelizer 2011), the chapter explores the strategies that are adopted by luxury fashion houses in order to maintain aura and grow their markets while retaining brand value and signature under increasingly complex global conditions.[1] There are evident tensions between the continued expansion and growth of luxury retailers and the premise of luxury brands being exclusive (Kapferer 2012). The drive for desingularization as a means to distinguish and valorize the unique (Karpik 2010), together with the financial interests that accompany the mass production of fashioned commodities, are significant forces that threaten brand valorization, uniqueness, and aura, a tendency that echoes Benjamin's early works on the demise of authenticity in an age of reproduction (Benjamin 1936). Drawing on devices and techniques that suggest metonymy, luxury labels have created an economy of qualities whereby a finish, logotype, or print evokes the essence of the brand. Fashion's luxury products cannot be valorized or financialized by conventional methods because they are "multidimensional, incommensurable and of uncertain or indefinable quality" (Karpik 2010: 24). As a result of their uncertain and highly subjective valuation, markets such as luxury fashion are necessarily equipped with "judgment devices," such as labels and brands, that provide consumers with sets of knowledge with which to make consumption judgments (Arvidsson 2006; Karpik 2010).

Second, the chapter adopts an explicitly cultural economy approach to the study of fashion value that underscores the impossibility of severing strictly commercial or financial explanations from those that emphasize the aesthetic, creative, and immaterial determinants of worth and desire. Powerful performative and affective affordances are enshrined in contemporary fashion space that help to explain its enduring competitiveness. In order to understand fashion value it is thus imperative to explore the spaces in which fashion is displayed, consumed, exhibited, and performed and thus to understand how fashion markets are ordered, regulated, and maintained in space and through time (Aspers 2010; Breward 2003; Breward and Gilbert 2006; Crewe and Davenport 1992, 2003, 2008; Entwistle 2009; Potvin 2009). Financial pricing devices must be understood in conjunction with social and cultural mechanisms as intricate parts of circuits of commerce (Zelizer 2011). One powerful strategy has been the pursuit of an aggressive logic of differentiation based on the aesthetic qualities of commodities. In order to construct themselves as rare and desirable while simultaneously catering for the demands of more inclusive and larger markets, luxury firms are conjoining the creative and commercial elements of their business and are emphasizing the symbolic and immaterial qualities of their brand. Brands thus become repositories of meaning, a means of conveying distinction and value (Arvidsson 2006; Bourdieu 1984; Lury 2004; Simmel 1904). The luxury fashion market is a sharp illustration of the powers of aesthetic capitalism in the contemporary era in which luxury is increasingly traded in symbolic terms rather than being a sector defined by high skilled and artisanal craft production and by a fixed geographical manufacturing identity (Tokatli 2012, 2013, 2014).

Third, and emerging out of early work on the experience economy (Pine and Gilmore 1999), the chapter draws on recent theories of display, visuality, and space and develops these to explain the power, pull, and reach presented by the visual aesthetic of the luxury retail store. Fashion has always been both sartorial and spatial and consumption spaces really do matter. They produce a sense that there is something more, some more intense experience or a wider horizon to be found (Quinn 2003: 35). The tactics employed in the design and creation of retail space are themselves a representational strategy that frames and influences the visual and material experiences of fashion (Potvin 2009: 2). The store is never simply a visual backdrop but actively engages the consumer's imagination and shapes our experiences, understandings, and perceptions of fashion. Space is a practiced place because bodies move in and through it and in turn enliven and transform it (De Certeau 1998: 117). The fashion store thus becomes a locus of the performing subject and a point of connection that bonds and conjoins the creator, commodity, and embodied consumer (Potvin 2009: 2). By incorporating visuality into an analysis of luxury retailing we bring the sensory and the material into simultaneous view (Rose and Tolia-Kelly 2012). This approach attests to the simultaneous range of scopic regimes experienced in fashion space that involves both seeing and experiencing, the body and the psyche. As Quinn argues so effectively "the fashion system is premised on visuality; a concept essential to the consumption of fashion but often underestimated in interpretations of it.... Visuality is not the same as sight; it occurs when visual media and sensory perceptions intersect, where gaze meets desire" (2003: 21). Visuality is a key component of contemporary aesthetic capitalism, characterized by a confluence between commercial imperatives and cultural tastes and practices (Assouly 2008). It captures the affective and sensory powers of signs, symbols, and images, the iconography of the contemporary city, and is a key means through which we experience and understand it (Foster 1988; Mirzoeff 2006). Visuality and visibility are, argues Potvin, "the conceptual glue that binds space with fashion.... Space thickens fashion, it extends it, attenuates it, grounds it, while fashion adds texture, colour and life to space" (2009: 6–10).

In adopting such an approach it becomes possible to conceptually rework our understanding of the place of fashion and to develop a far richer insight that acknowledges both the commercial and the affective and material affordances offered by fashion images, spaces, and performances. Such a cultural economy approach to the study of luxury markets acknowledges the significance of moving beyond strictly economic calculations of value and problematizes the notion that geographies of production and "Made In" appellations are the key locus of value creation. The chapter first analyzes the scope, scale, significance, and geography of the global luxury fashion market. It argues that a set of alliances between global fashion firms, their creative directors, and contemporary artists are emerging as a central strategy in the making of current consumption space in the particular case of flagship stores in global fashion cities (Breward and Gilbert 2006).[2] Building on recent work by Currid (2007, 2012) and Hawkins (2013) it is argued that the collaboration between art and fashion opens up a means to critically explore how representational worlds are brought into being and offers new ways to understand how creative activity can be rooted in (and reflective of) broader social, economic, and cultural concerns. Significantly, this approach inserts the practices of consumption into the analysis of retail space, offering insights into the affective dimensions of consumption during and beyond the moment of purchase. The discussion then moves on to focus on the much-neglected role of the shop window as a key site for the display of luxury goods. Fashion houses have become increasingly concerned with how the product and the brand are visually communicated to the customer via store window displays, which have become significant interfaces that bring the consumer, fashioned object, and store together to the point where the store window has become a "key instrument of many retailer's communication strategy" (Kerfoot et al. 2003; Sen et al. 2002: 277). Significantly, the creative collaborations and shop window installations discussed here are centrally engaged in the creation of retail environments that speak directly to key contemporary geographical questions about time, space, sound, vision, longevity, transience, and environment. The implications of the analysis are explored in the conclusion.

The geographies of the luxury fashion market

The growth of the luxury fashion sector and its highly uneven geographies is currently little understood. What is clear is that the luxury market has displayed remarkable resilience in the face of global recession and the slowdown in consumer spending. The UK luxury fashion sector, for example, is forecast to almost double in size from £6.6 billion to £12.2 billion between 2012 and 2017 (Ledbury Research and Walpole 2013). At a finer level of granularity, a number of luxury fashion houses are continuing to grow in spite of the difficult economic climate—Burberry for example has seen global revenues triple (2006–2013) and opened their largest Asian flagship store in April 2014, using store openings as a way of raising brand awareness among Chinese customers (Sharman and Robinson 2014), and the French fashion house Yves Saint Laurent reported a 59 percent increase in annual sales during 2013 (Butler 2013). The rate of growth has been driven by a variety of factors, including a desire on the part of consumers for more responsible investment purchasing, a renewed interest in the creative capacities of experiential retail spaces, and an increase in the number of high-net-worth individuals with the emotional desire and economic capital for luxury-brand consumption (Bourdieu 1984; Capgemini 2013). The super-rich, it has been argued, "are amongst the most powerful actors shaping environmental futures," the runway spending at the top has been a virus that, to one degree or another, has all of us in its grip (Davidson 2016: 341–2).

One of the most significant reasons for the dramatic and sustained growth of the world's largest luxury fashion conglomerates[3] is geographic expansion, particularly in China but in a range of other emerging markets too. Luxury fashion firms are actively using geographical variation as an organizational expansion strategy that is both driving, and driven by, luxury consumption. The appetite for luxury consumption is particularly apparent in the emerging economies of China, India, and Brazil and more generally in Asia and the Middle East (McKinsey and Co 2013; Shukla 2012; Tynan et al. 2010). The resurgence in the acquisition activity of luxury brands by investment firms in Asia and the Middle East, and by luxury conglomerates such as Louis Vuitton, Moet Hennessy, and Richemont since 2011, is further testament to the buoyancy of the sector and to the apparent immunity of high-end branded products to the more deleterious effects of global crisis. Luxury firms are responding to the growing global demand for luxury products, particularly in emerging markets, through engaging in dramatic international store-expansion strategies. They are also maintaining scarcity and continually raising their prices at significantly above-inflation rates: "Think of it as an exclusivity tax...this is something really extraordinary" (Herships 2014). It is predicted that 85 percent of all luxury retail stores will be opening in emerging markets over the coming decade (Shukla 2012: 576). Strong growth figures are particularly reported in China, which offers enormous opportunities for global luxury brands and is predicted to become the world's largest luxury market by the end of 2013, worth £16 billion (McKinsey and Co 2013). The Chinese luxury sector continued to grow in spite of the global recession and now accounts for 25 percent of the global market, making it the second largest luxury consumer market after Japan (Zhan and He 2012: 1452). Rapid urbanization and growing wealth outside China's largest cities are driving the emergence of new geographic markets for luxury in China, and global brands such as Louis Vuitton, Gucci, Coach, and Burberry are all expanding into third-tier Chinese cities in order to take advantage of continued rising demand (Kapferer 2012).

The consumption of luxury goods in China is projected to rise from 12 percent in 2007 to 29 percent by 2015 (Zhang and Kim 2013: 68) and Chinese customers are expected to buy in excess of 44 percent of the world's luxury goods by 2020 (CLSA Asia Pacific). Rising GDP in emerging middle-class markets has increased the demand for luxury goods (Kapferer 2012). Particularly in China, middle-class consumers are being targeted as key consumers for whom luxury products are seen as aspirational commodities, a key means through which to increase social status via their associations with affluent, cosmopolitan Western lifestyles given the relaxing of social mores that previously sanctioned excessive displays of wealth (Zhan and He 2012: 1453; Zhang and Kim 2013).

Within this complex tapestry of global retail investment and variegated consumption practice, two specific developments within luxury markets are apparent that have pronounced implications for the geographies of the sector. First, there has been a notable global shift in the geographies of luxury production, with a number of fashion houses outsourcing production to offshore locations including China in the case of Burberry and Prada (Bloutin Artinfo 2011; Pyke 2015). The example of Gucci is particularly instructive here. The Italian heritage of the brand was formerly secured and promoted by the "Made in Italy" appellation. Since the 1990s production has been met through increasingly complex supply chains including the offshoring and outsourcing of production to China, Turkey, Vietnam, and Romania for cost-related reasons (Reinach 2005; Tokatli 2014). In order to manage this "dark side" (Holt 2004: 6) of their operations, Gucci subtly shifted their marketing message away from the primacy of the geographical origin of production toward the "context of consumption" for their products (Tokatli 2014) and, in the process, both highlighted the significance of the retail store as a key geographical site for the production of the brand image and redefined what counts as "place" in a more relational and unbounded manner (Tokatli 2013: 239). This was an adept move that enabled Gucci to maintain their luxury credentials and aura by blurring the lines between country of origin (or manufacture) and brand origin—which "can be thought of as the country a brand is associated with by its target consumers regardless of where it is manufactured" (Shukla 2011: 243). Such developments begin to blur the boundary lines between luxury and mass markets and problematize the definition of luxury products which traditionally created and maintained exclusivity and value through transparent "Made In" labeling, craft production, quality, and scarcity. It is, in short, a skillful obfuscation of the places and means of production in what amounts to a strategy of super-commodity fetishism.

Second, there are tensions between the continued expansion and growth of luxury retailers and the premise of luxury brands being exclusive and rare (Kapferer 2012). In order to construct themselves as exceptional and exclusive, while simultaneously catering for the demands of more inclusive and larger markets, luxury firms are conjoining the creative and commercial elements of their business and are emphasizing the symbolic and immaterial qualities of their brand while also maintaining scarcity of supply and artificially inflating prices (Herships 2014). Central to this strategy are the ways in which luxury organizations actively put geography to work in their creation of value. One way of achieving this in the wake of globalization and geographical expansion is through the symbolic and authoritative presence of the flagship store. It is to this that the chapter now turns.

Flagship stores: Scaling fashion's luxury spaces

Central to the evolution of the luxury market are the ways in which retailers actively put geography to work in their creation of value. Key to this business strategy is the role of the flagship store which stands as a highly prominent spatial manifestation of the brand. One way of achieving a strong geographical presence, in the wake of increased global markets and complex geographical expansion, is through the symbolic and authoritative presence of the flagship store. The flagship store acts as the material expression of the brand and offers a place of seduction and desire. For the retailer, a flagship store serves to showcase the entire brand story to the consumer under one roof and to make use of all of the tools available to highlight the brand statement and philosophy. The luxury flagship store's origins can be traced back to Paris' Couture and ready-to-wear Ateliers, which were multilevel buildings (consisting of offices, workshops, and a shop on the ground floor). These "Maisons de Mode" acted as the creative hearts and brains of the brands (Barreneche 2008) in which collections would be both produced and consumed (Nobbs et al. 2012; Tungate 2008). As the number of luxury fashion producers increased, this format spread from Paris to the cities of London, New York, and Milan (Nobbs et al. 2012). In the past decade, as this store format has trickled down to the middle and mass market, luxury brands have evolved to cater for today's ever discerning customer (Tungate 2008) by creating differentiated branded experience (Nobbs et al. 2012). This has resulted in the development of the "uber" or "mega-flagship," in which key dimensions of stores are enhanced to become larger, improved, and more memorable (Nobbs et al. 2012). Examples of these top level flagship stores include Louis Vuitton's "Global Maisons" and Prada's "epicenter" stores (Passariello and Dodes 2007). "These stores are characterised by their large scale, cutting edge architecture, offering of cultural events" (Nobbs et al. 2012: 923) and, increasingly, a technologically mediated spectacular consumption experience. Situated in prestigious retail sites within global cities,[4] flagship stores represent a key means through which luxury fashion houses internationalize (Fernie et al. 1997). Located in luxury enclaves to increase exclusivity and prestige (Doherty and Moore 2007), these luxurious streets of style "form communities of affluence which appear to support and feed-off each other in terms of their sense of exclusivity and style" (Nobbs et al. 2012: 931). Situated in prestigious retail sites within global cities, flagship stores represent a key means through which luxury fashion houses internationalize (Fernie et al. 1997).

These clusters of luxury stores are quite literally "economies of icons" (Sternberg 1999) where brands are enshrined in exclusive spaces and products are displayed as "treasures," behind glass, in sleek cabinets placed delicately on pedestals and directly lit—echoing the artistic tradition of exhibition space. Just as in a museum, distance is maintained between the viewer and the object (Dion and Arnould 2011)—touching is strictly forbidden. The space is "intimidating. It is done on purpose … you shouldn't feel like anybody can participate in that world" (Herships 2014). The presentation of products through mechanisms typically derived from museums and art galleries, and the sacralization rituals performed by sales assistants not only assists in maintaining exclusivity and sacredness but also creates a consumption experience that is ultimately just as important as the creation and display of rare and expertly crafted products. Consumers in flagship stores can expect to be met with a consumption experience intended to epitomize the company ethos and immerse the consumer in a complete branded experience (Kozinets et al. 2002), thus imprinting the consumer experience, not just the product (Fionda and Moore 2009). It is in this way that luxury retailers expand the notion of luxury as being above and beyond ownership to encompass the sensory experience of luxury (Roper et al. 2013). This is no more apparent than in the flagship store where the highest levels of investment correlate with the highest levels of experience, interaction, performance, and spectacle (Fionda and Moore 2009). At one level, this translates into a form of experiential service where the consumer is both indulged and engaged with the consumption experience. For example, in the Cartier flagship store in Paris customers can create their own made to order perfumes (Nobbs et al. 2012) and in the Louis Vuitton flagship in Tokyo customers can join a private club where they can browse products while sipping champagne (Bingham 2005). At another level, this manifests itself as a form of immersive experiential retailing that creates an all-encompassing brand lifestyle experience that extends far beyond merely purchasing fashion items. For example, the flagship Chanel store in Tokyo has its own restaurant that is intended to evoke the elegance of Coco Chanel, and the spirit of the Chanel brand, through the delicate white, cream, and black color palette and the use of Chanel's iconic tweed for its interior furnishings (Atwal and Williams 2009). At the Dolce & Gabbana flagship store in London there is a traditional Sicilian barber where male customers can have a shave and a haircut while Kenzo in Paris offers a massage service (Nobbs et al. 2012). These offerings are designed to create luxury, hedonistic, pleasurable, multisensory consumption experiences that are "affect-rich" (Dion and Arnould 2011: 503) and enable consumers to "interact with and touch the brand" (Nobbs et al. 2012: 926).

That luxury shopping is spectacle, theatre, and performance, and performativity is nowhere more apparent than in the Burberry flagship store at 121 Regent Street, London. Opened in 2012, this is a space that is intentionally experiential: it brings the runway to the store, the catwalk to the shop. The store is tactile, visual, aural, immersive. The consumer is drawn in and whirled around along grand staircases where the wooden interior design coexists and coalesces with the most innovative virtual worlds, products reflected and reflecting, interiors melting into exteriors. Mannequins bear gifts, products are packages, an opulent covering for the unknown commodities inside that lie hidden, enticing, waiting to be discovered. Boxes and bags, draped in ribbon and rained upon by cascading gold leaves, are redolent, enticing. The sheer scale of the store and its architecture reveal its place within this city of signs. Crucially, Burberry have transformed and enlivened conventional in-store structures and strategies through their use of digital technologies. In addition to hosting live concerts at their flagship Regent Street store, by for example the Kaiser Chiefs and Jake Bugg, Burberry developed a "Runway to Reality" in-store event that included the live-streaming of its Spring Womenswear Collection across a number of digital platforms. Burberry Regent Street has used disruptive digital technologies to create an immersive multi-sensory environment that bridges the online–offline experience: RFID (radio-frequency identification) chips inside garments bring product information to consumers in innovative ways as the chips trigger RFID-enabled mirrors to become digital screens which in turn display information about production, craft, and catwalk footage. At set times a choreographed "digital rain storm" is synchronized across the store's 50 speakers and 100 digital screens, starting as a gentle shower and building into a downpour with a climactic thunder crack shown on every screen and echoing in every space, simulating the iconic London downpour and exposing customers to an immersive sensory brand experience (Figure 5.1).

The flagship store is a key site for the constitution and representation of contemporary consumption. A magical space of possibility where culture and commerce merge and meld, the flagship store is the physical manifestation of the soul and signature of the brand. Flagship stores act as powerful spatial landscapes that set the stage in the contemporary city for the performance of everyday life. They serve to develop the global reputation and presence of the brand, to leverage brand status and awareness, and act a means of communicating and enhancing the image and personality of a luxury retailer's brand identity (Nobbs et al. 2012: 921). Once placed in its flagship setting, a brand draws meaning from architectural form. These forms are indexical symbols of the world of art. The flagship brand store becomes an "autonomous presence" (Habraken and Teicher 1998: 233) contributing to the brand's persona "at least as much through connotation as it does explicitly" (Kozinets et al. 2002: 28). The flagship store is often referred to as "the brand cathedral" as it acts as an emblem of the visible and tangible power of the label, paralleling the ways

Figure 5.1 Louis Vuitton, London, 2015. © author's photograph.

in which the cathedral is seen as the geographical emblem of the power of the church (Cervellon and Coudriet 2013: 874). Flagships clearly demonstrate power and prestige though their status as visitor attractions that elevate and enhance the eminence of the city in which they are located (Nobbs et al. 2012) and become tourist destinations that are commonly frequented by "non-traditional customers of the brand" (Nobbs et al. 2012: 923).

Flagship stores are founded on significant financial investment and are considered crucial to a brand's marketing communication process and reputation. The intention of the stores is to maintain and embody the image and symbolic capital of the brand, rather than exclusively generate profit (Doherty and Moore 2007; Kozinets et al. 2002), with stores commonly not being required to show a typical return on investment. Flagship stores are used as a key entry-to-market strategy in emerging markets in the early stages of luxury retailer's business development as a method of gaining direct entry into, and demonstrating commitment to, foreign markets (Doherty and Moore 2007). Flagships are intended to powerfully impose themselves onto the exclusive streetscapes in which they are located (Figure 5.2).

Figure 5.2 Gucci Store, London, 2015. © author's photograph.

Brand names are embossed on store fronts, buildings, and canopies to tangibly and visibly superimpose the brand upon the urban landscape. Similarly, flags displaying company logos hang authoritatively from the store fronts, a stark mechanism through which to quite literally brand the city. The brand flags allude to the notion of expedition and colonization, suggesting that the brand has physically and metaphorically marked its territorial claim on the exclusive retailscape. The territorial claim of the flagship is further reproduced through the imposing nature of the size of flagship stores which are intentionally larger than their non-flagship counterparts to serve "as a physical manifestation of their premier status" (Nobbs et al. 2012: 932). The inclusion of "unproductive space" (Nobbs et al. 2012: 932) in prime retail locations emphasizes the excessive wealth and prestige of the brand and therefore their luxurious and exclusive characteristics (Figure 5.3).

The art of designing a luxury store is an exercise in communication, in making concrete the imaginative energy and creative power of artists and designers. In part this is achieved through architecture and visual design and display that both embody and build the brand. Exclusivity, exceptionality, and prestige are reflected through the positioning of flagship stores "in historic structures or landmark buildings" (Nobbs et al. 2012: 926) and through the blurring of art, architecture, and retail in elaborate store spaces "which themselves are conceived of as works of art" (Dion and Arnould 2011: 511), increasingly designed by star artists and architects commissioned by luxury retailers. Notable examples include Renzo Piano who designed for Hermès, Frank Gehry for Louis Vuitton, and John Pawson for Calvin Klein (Crewe 2010; Doherty and Moore 2007: 280). Flagship fashion stores iconicize the city not merely through the surface features of glamour and glitz but via their shared understanding of the affective power of space, form, materiality, and color (Antonelli 2007).

Chanel is an instructive example of how the elements of color, material, and light fuse to capture the essence of the brand and quite literally project it onto the cityscape. Coco Chanel long recognized the affective and symbolic affordances enshrined in color. From the "little black dress" that has become a fashion classic, to her use of the black sans serif logotype throughout her store and product designs, Chanel understood well the timeless aesthetic appeal of achromaticity. The Chanel Store in the New York, designed by Peter Marino, reveals the sensual and captivating power of color and light. While the exterior resembles a white cube, the interior surfaces are uniformly finished in high black gloss and have hundreds of tiny back-lit perforations randomly cut into the surface. The effect is magical and enchanting. The visual collision of white light and black gloss is a tantalizing example of the achromatic chic and monochromatic materiality that has characterized both fashion and architecture for many decades (Ojeda and Mccown 2004). In Marino's Chanel store in Tokyo, Japan, the interplay between white and black, light and dark, is again revealed

Figure 5.3 Ralph Lauren Store, London, 2015. © author's photograph.

to dramatic effect through the use of technology, color, and textures. Through a fusion of ceramics, glass, and iron, the store reveals an exterior surface that is illuminated by 700,000 LED backlights. Built as part of the building's skin, dynamic videoscreens enable luxury-brand building in its most literal form (Crewe 2010). Chanel can project an infinite number of corporate images and texts onto the streets of the city.

This dramatic use of mediatecture through cladding buildings with visual, branded screens changes not only the aesthetic of the city but also the way in which buildings occupy space. The building itself, through new technological architectures and sensory stimuli, becomes a representational feature of both architect and brand. It is the materialization of luxury. The architect Rem Koolhaas for Prada has argued, somewhat controversially, that global expansion via spectacular flagship stores can be employed as a means of stretching, bending, and perhaps permanently redefining the brand. When the flagship is recast as an epicenter store it can become a device that renews rather than dilutes the brand by counteracting and destabilizing any received notion of what Prada is, does, or will become. The epicenter store acts as a conceptual window, a space of anticipation, spectacle, desire. Next-generation flagship stores have the potential to be simultaneously perceptual and physical, symbolic and material.

Window wear: The art of the street

Alongside architectural prowess, another key instrument through which luxury retailers communicate strategy is through their store fronts (Sen et al. 2002: 277). Store entrances and windows communicate between the interior and the exterior of the store and bring dreams and fantasy into tangible view. The signs, symbols, and products displayed in flagship store windows "play a key role in defining global fashion culture and in charting its discursive space" (Shinkle 2008: 1). The symbolic power of window design can be spectacular and is designed "to reflect the essence of what the store represents, its product range and symbolism" (Pereira et al. 2010: 2). Shop windows tell "stories about ourselves and the desires that drive us" (Moreno 2005: 8). They are "mirrors that reflect the faces of our time" (Portas 1999: 8). Windows communicate desire and dreams, they build brands and shape consumption. In an era saturated by the screen and ways of looking and seeing (Turkle 1995) it is curious that shop windows have been so neglected in critical consumption literature. The alchemic properties of glass have transformed retail space in a number of dramatic ways. Glass is a solid liquid, a magical paradox, which links the real world outside to the world of luxury inside. A display surrounded by windows, the most efficient type of temporary staging of expensive goods, is a neglected focus in discipline of retailing, yet one which plays a crucial role in consumption and culture. Historically windows were little more than a means of introducing light into a store. In medieval times, large arched unglazed windows were used by shopkeepers to draw attention to their wares (Manco 2010). As glass-making methods improved, so too did display techniques. The first shops with transparent window displays appeared in the Netherlands at the start of the nineteenth century and began the process of communication between the street and the store, the merchandiser and the consumer, interior and exterior (Pevsner 1976).

Initially store windows were small and functional, but as shops grew larger and department stores evolved, windows were transformed into selling tools and the importance of windows grew in direct proportion to their size (Portas 1999). By the early twentieth century the potential role that store windows could play as performative, spectacular spaces was acknowledged: "The best window displays aspire to imitate the theatre by framing and illuminating the commodities and mannequins in a carefully arranged scenario in order to imbue them with the captivating qualities of the theatre" (International Correspondence School 1912). In more recent decades store window displays have become a unique form of advertising and are the first point of contact between the store and the customer. Thus "the pane of glass separating the object of desire from the shopper forms an imaginary screen not unlike the mirror, a surface for receiving and reflecting" (Oswald 1992) which highlights the complexity of this space. The multifaceted dimensions of shop window displays remain undertheorized considering their importance and significance in contemporary consumer culture. The shop window provides a space for image makers to experiment and challenge notions of physical display (Arnold 2001). Contradictory messages haunt fashion imagery in the store window as in many other commercial spaces, and tensions between the commercial and aesthetic, financial and creative placing of fashion, shape the forms and modes of display (Arnold 2001). Windows are both an "outward projection of what can be found inside the shop and yet also relay a whole series of more subtle and unconscious messages". Shop windows have developed into forms of art themselves and produce some of the most interesting imagery within fashion culture. They are a space for making, assembling, displaying, and performing fashion—a co-production place that reflects contemporary consumer culture: "Although they are ephemeral, they mark the seasons, record a moment in our politics, our characters, our fantasies, our times. If they persisted, boxed carefully away, they would provide rich artifacts for future archaeologists" (Moreno 2005: 8). A display window, like film, can be a space for the creation of desire. Store windows are liminal spaces that can bring dreams and fantasy into reality. They are at once inside and out—for looking and seeing. They are simultaneously spaces of reflection and contemplation, such that "the store window is the physical mediator between products and consumers, between stimulus and shopping decisions and between the store's fantasy and street reality" (Cuito 2005: 5). "It is what each person chooses to take away from the windows that is significant: looking without buying may make us richer in more ways than one" (Moreno 2005: 14). "The label itself is not enough; it requires to be housed in a space equally endowed with the potential to elicit reverence and pleasure, a coveted destination" (Potvin 2009: 247). Selfridges is an excellent illustration of the ways in which store windows can challenge conventional commercial signals and raise questions of a more socially attuned and provocative nature (Figure 5.4).

Figure 5.4 Selfridges × Katie Paterson window. © MJC Courtesy of the artist.

The collaboration between Selfridges and the Scottish artist Katie Paterson in 2013 is a particularly apposite example of the ways in which store windows can act as spaces for reflection and contemplation—in much the same way as the iconic Vexed Generation stores in London's Soho did in the 1980s and 1990s. In an unlikely move Selfridges, one of the world's largest and busiest chain of department stores, launched a collaboration that centers on silence, mindfulness, mediation, and anti-branding. Its "No Noise" campaign urged customers "to seek out moments of peace and tranquillity in a world that bombards us with information and stimulation" while capturing "the western world's focus on detoxing, decluttering, bettering oneself and finding greater well-being so commonplace at the start of a new year" (Selfridges 2013). The installation was launched officially with a 500-strong mass meditation session led by former monk Andy Puddicombe in the London store's ground-floor beauty hall. The campaign included the reopening of Selfridge's "Silence Room," which had been closed for ninety years, and was redesigned to provide a quiet sanctuary for those who wanted to take some time out from shopping and relax. The store also opened a "Quiet Shop" that offered customers debranded products such as Levis and Marmite, stripped of their logos and branding and wrapped in the distinctive yellow Selfridges bag, minus the logo. The conceptual complexity of this particular Selfridges window-display communication reveals the potency and currency of contemporary intersections of culture, fashion, and art. One of the window displays was stripped back to gallery-style white walls displaying one Selfridges shopping bag with no logo and no products on display. No Noise is an initiative that goes beyond retail by inviting the consumer to reflect on the power of quiet, to see the beauty in function, and find calm among the crowds. As Selfridges states:

and who wouldn't have lifted her [sic] dear, distracted head from her mobile device to contemplate the significance of the No Noise windows earlier this year? The No Noise campaign … was a comment on the fact that, in a world of 24/7 information overload, simplicity and serenity are the greatest luxuries. For one of the world's largest department stores, a palace to consumerism and the desire for more, it was a provocative exercise in debranding. (Selfridges 2013)

The series of window displays created by Katie Paterson ask the viewer/ consumer to contemplate time, space, and the environment—key questions for geographical enquiry. One of Paterson's window displays was called "Light Bulb to Simulate Moonlight" that comprised a set of light bulbs that, combined, would provide a person with a lifetime supply of moonlight (see Figure 5.5). Not only was this an installation that encouraged the viewer to think beyond the moment of purchase, but it also raised broader questions about the temporal cycles of night and day, about energy supply and sustainability, use and reuse—again key contemporary geographical questions.

Figure 5.5 Katie Paterson's "Light Bulb to Simulate Moonlight" installation, Selfridges, London, 2013. Photo © MJC Courtesy of the artist.

In another of the windows the consumer could view the "100 Billion Suns." This comprised a confetti canon that was set off each day at 12 noon and burst 3,216 pieces of tiny colored paper into the store window. Each piece of paper represented the color of a gamma ray burst—the brightest explosions in the universe that burn with a luminosity 100 billion times that of our sun. Again we see here how the store window is far more than a space for commodity display but, rather, is a spatial spectacle that enrolls the viewer/consumer into a performative event that in turn encourages contemplation about space, time, and their relationality. Powerful aesthetic affordances emerge when we bring the background to the fore and arouse contemplation rather than just consumption. Store windows not only reflect and anticipate some of the most exciting developments in consumer culture but also prompt more philosophical and conceptual questioning. As these examples demonstrate, shop windows are in a constant state of flux, reflecting pace and change, energy and creativity. The question that critics continue to pose is whether the display of affective objects in affective spaces that are the result of a fusion between artists, fashion creatives, and space, is anything more than hypocritical/hypercritical gimmicks that exploit "art" in what amounts to little more than a gestural critique of consumerism that is in fact masquerading as simply another means of driving markets and fueling consumerism itself. But as the examples above illustrate, these new alliances reveal how the space between fashion and art—*ma* in Japanese—is drawing closer together in far from trivial ways. "Collaborating with contemporary artists brings a new kind of creative fecundity to the product. It forces creativity that is different to that typically found in fashion" (Carcelle 2007). The collision between the two practices in the spaces of the fashion store reveals the significance of visuality and affective affordance in consumption, framing the consumer in a new role as active participant and interpreter rather than merely passive receiver of prescribed sales messages. This is significant as it emphasizes new relations and subjectivities and opens up new opportunities for how we understand and theorize retailing and consumption in space and time. Foregrounding the "personal and public, material, imagined and visual experiences of the subject with its objects of desire…the spectator is active, that is, as the inevitable scopophilic participant in the display of fashion, the engaged interpreter of what is seen and, finally, the fashionable interloper" (Figure 5.6).

Flagship stores have highly design-focused and luxurious shop fronts that intentionally exude style, sophistication, exclusivity, and luxury. This is exemplified by the flagship luxury stores on London's Bond Street where the colors white, black, and gold are a key motif and recurrent theme. Black and white have long been key signifiers of fashion, taste, and style, and gold is symbolic of luxury, expense, and prestige. Store fronts and windows exude elegance and exclusivity through the communication of the store interior and brand essence to the public space of the street outside. The Louis Vuitton store in Roppongi,

Figure 5.6 Burberry Store, London, 2015. © author's photograph.

Tokyo, for example is constructed of more than 20,000 glass tubes that are expertly arranged to form a vast pixelated screen that transmits changing images of the Louis Vuitton logo and motifs.

Similarly, the Louis Vuitton store front in Seoul is blanketed by a translucent mesh over its façade with the intention of mimicking the fabric that is used to cover the iconic Louis Vuitton travel chests (Curtis and Watson 2007). It is via such mechanisms that shop fronts become melded as part of the architectural and artistic structure of the flagship store. Seducing the street outside through imagery and advertising, the glass shop window brings dreams and fantasy into

Figure 5.7 Chanel Store, London, 2015. © author's photograph.

reality by linking the "real" world outside to the world of luxury within (Bingham 2005). Window displays produce a sense that there is something more, some more intense experience or a wider horizon to be found. Store windows act as a powerful spatial landscape that sets the stage in the contemporary city for the performance of everyday life, acting as theaters of signs and symbols in which representation is not the opposite of materiality but rather its alter-ego, a space that both constitutes and reflects commerce and culture, transaction and imagination. The luxury flagship window expresses worlds of excitement, luxury, and indulgence that are intended to be highly visual and inviting. However, in contrast to the high visibility of the shop windows, and the products displayed there, is the relative (in)visibility of price tags. Hiding the prices of products in shop windows is a common tactic employed by luxury retailers to invest both the products and the associated brand with an air of exclusivity and expense. This offers entry into a secret world of privilege and exclusivity for whom the price of goods for sale is not a concern. The invisibility of product prices in shop windows is thus a way in which to simultaneously flaunt the products for sale in store while providing an invisible barrier to entry. It further elevates the products into a beyond-market status, valuable, priceless. Similarly, the selective and exclusive entry into luxury retail spaces is physically, as well as symbolically, significant.

Although flagship stores are located on the public space of the street, they are highly securitized, patrolled, and surveilled. This is particularly apparent in real the doorways of luxury retailers that are always closed, symbolizing the gateway "between the mundane (the street) and the sacred (the brand universe)" (Cervellon and Coudriet 2013: 875). These gateways are guarded by uniformed door staff who play a shifting role between doorman and bouncer: welcoming "desirable" customers into the store, while simultaneously intimidating others by their mere presence. And yet this is a kind of servile labor that one might not associate with luxury: their job is long and boring and consists largely of standing, waiting, doing nothing, looking the part. Like the prominent goods with no price tags, here are highly visible workers who remain largely invisible to consumers—door staff, butlers, the servants to the retail brand. If granted access into the store through its physical and symbolic gateways, the notions of exclusivity, rarity, and expense are further emphasized throughout the retailing tactics employed to encase the products for sale with auratic-like qualities. This is achieved through the display of products as "treasures" displayed behind glass, in sleek cabinets, placed delicately on pedestals and directly lit—echoing the artistic tradition of exhibition space. Just as in a museum, distance is maintained between the viewer and the object (Dion and Arnould 2011)—touching is strictly forbidden. This creation of spaces of display is an additional means through which luxury brands to legitimize their power (Cervellon and Coudriet 2013: 880) and emphasize the sacredness of the products and ultimately the brand. The rarefied positioning of goods is further endorsed by sales assistants that act as brand ambassadors (Cervellon and Coudriet 2013: 869) and touch products with precaution and care as part of a carefully choreographed "selling ceremony" (Cervellon and Coudriet 2013: 869) which is designed to confer the superiority of the sales person over the customer, the product over its price. It is through such rituals of careful commodity handling that a form of symbolic dominance is enacted over the consumer. This creation of spaces of display is an additional means through which luxury brands to legitimize their power (Cervellon and Coudriet 2013: 880) and emphasize the sacredness and scarcity of their brand. Collectively, these examples of spatial tactics employed by flagship stores demonstrate the importance of the physical and symbolic space of the store to luxury retailing.

In flagship stores, the expertly designed and architecturally impressive shop spaces, sacralized product displays, carefully manufactured service encounters, and consumption experiences collectively create a powerful stage for the creation and reproduction of the brand. Flagship store designs are as much about creation and art as about sales and persuasion; their effect on the brand and the city is one of communication as much as it is one of commerce. Flagships are a symbolically efficacious form of branding. These physical exemplars of brand power expressed and embedded in the flagship store are difficult to replicate on a virtual platform online (Jackson 2008; Okonkwo 2009). Therefore, despite the rise of extensive online retailing, the flagship store remains an important medium for communicating brand messages, asserting retailer dominance, and maintaining "auratic power" (Cervellon and Coudriet 2013: 869) in an ever increasing virtual retailscape. The maintenance of their auratic power is increasingly important as luxury retailers continue to compete in global markets, particularly in emerging economies and in new luxury markets where the symbolic resonance of the brand may not yet be well established. It is in these conditions of global expansion and competition that luxury retailers must maintain their brand dominance and enchantment.

This section has revealed that brand aura, value, and signature is fixed and manifested spatially by flagship stores, which act as physical beacons, embassies, and embodiments of brands, in which luxury is increasingly defined and appropriated in symbolic terms rather than merely being a sector defined by high-skilled and artisanal craft production. The flagship store is a tactic employed to give geographical presence and a physical sense of exclusion, power, and rarity in an increasingly expanding and inclusive luxury market. At the microscale the flagship asserts brand dominance and symbolic sacralized power through exclusive shop spaces, selling rituals and experiential retailing. At the macroscale flagships act as global markers of brand strength and commitment to new markets through asserting their dominance in an increasingly globalized luxury marketplace. The flagship store can therefore be seen as a tactic employed by luxury retailers to give a strong geographical presence and a physical sense of exclusion, power, and rarity in an increasingly expanding and inclusive luxury market. The flagship store acts as the material expression of the brand that offers a place of seduction and desire. Store spaces act as powerful signifiers, windows on fantastic worlds, and a geographical landscape that sets the stage in the contemporary city for the performance of everyday life, acting as theaters of signs and symbols in which representation is not the opposite of materiality but rather its alter-ego, a space that both constitutes and reflects commerce and culture, transaction and imagination. Flagship stores function as microeconomies of icons where brands are enshrined in exclusive spaces. More broadly this analysis has revealed that a close interrogation of luxury flagship stores opens up a space to critically explore how new representational worlds are brought into being and offers new ways to understand how creative activity can be rooted in (and reflective of) broader social, economic, and cultural concerns. Luxury fashion and its complex geographies act as an early warning system for major cultural transformations. This requires that we need to better understand the means and mechanisms for sustaining luxury brands which in turn depends on exploring more critical approaches that engage and question the desires and demands for commodities with a high ratio of intangible value in order to more fully understand their affective capacities and emotional reach (Figure 5.8).

Figure 5.8 Alexander McQueen, London, 2014. © author's photograph.

When fashion and art collide: The contemporary artist and the fashion director as a creative project

For far too long fashion and art have been viewed as disparate disciplines, warring factions that are technically and philosophically opposed. Fashion is popularly understood to be fickle, transient, superficial, and largely driven by popular culture (Castle 2000; Mores 2006; Sudjic 2001; Wigley 2001). Fine art, in contrast, is viewed as timeless, rarefied, considered, and elitist (Oakley Smith and Kubler 2013; Ward 2008): "We think of art appreciation as erudite, but an interest in fashion is considered airheaded" (Gregory 2014). Fashion is routinely criticized for its perceived lack of content and ephemeral nature in spite of the skill, craft, and artistic rigor demonstrated in both the design and the display of luxury fashion. Art, it has been argued, "has historically been exalted as the more noble and intellectual pursuit in comparison to fashion, which was regarded as a primarily commercially motivated form of expression" (Oakley Smith and Kubler 2013: 12). Certainly art and fashion have been seen to exist in separate, discrete, constructed categories, wherein art represents something valued as an object with longevity while fashion is seen as a commodity with accelerated cycles of production and consumption. "Art is normally aligned with meaningful intention and thus meaningful engagement, fashion is generally regarded as momentary and meaningless" (Ward 2008). Of course these broad generalizations fail to acknowledge the long-standing intersections, dialogues, and creative crossings between the worlds of fashion and art which demonstrate that the alliances between art and fashion are in many ways nothing new (Tokatli 2011). From Elsa Schiaparelli's collaborations with Salvador Dali in the creation of the lobster-print gown fabricated from silk organza and synthetic horsehair to Yves Saint Laurent's planar shift dresses that resembled Mondrian's canvases, the special relationship between the same-but-different worlds of art and fashion has always been commercially lucrative (Gregory 2014). What is striking now are the ways in which the boundaries between art, visual culture, fashion, commercial commodities, and the meaning of consumption have become increasingly blurred and opaque in recent years. Art historian Isabella Graw has argued that "The borders between the system of "fashion" and the art world are increasingly permeable, the transitions increasingly fluid…. Today fashion principally operates not just latently within art, it is irrevocably becoming part of it" (2010: 137).

Emergent partnerships between fashion designers and artists are raising new questions about the similarities and synergies between the two practices of art and fashion: the notion that an artist's creativity and authenticity could be jeopardized by corporate fashion collaboration now seems rather precious and naïve (Gregory 2014). This chapter contributes to this debate through interrogating the practice and significance of a number of collaborations between art and fashion (Oakley Smith and Kubler 2013: 10), recently described as a "mutual appreciation society" (Gregory 2014). The Italian fashion house Fiorucci was arguably one of the first to grasp the significance of the hybridization of art and fashion. Marc Jacobs for Louis Vuitton has argued that "every time we try to do new things, it feels like we're doing Fiorucci" (in Mores 2006: 60) and Vivienne Westwood has argued that Fiorucci is "the teacher of us all." He collaborated with some of the most subversive artists and pioneered the mobilization of street art onto the fashion scene by, for example, covering every surface of the Fiorucci store in Milan in graffiti overnight. "The artistic contamination of which Fiorucci was so fond found expression in communication, architecture, graphics and merchandising" (Mores 2006: 69). Thus while art works and genres have long been associated with luxury production and retailing, recent developments have brought fashion creators and artists into much closer and more productive dialogue via longer-standing project-based collaborations (Girard and Stark 2002; Grabher 2002).

The American sociologist Howard Becker's book *Artworlds* (1982) is theoretically instructive here. Becker examines the cultural contexts in which artists produce their work and emphasizes collective activity and the joint contribution of a number of people in order to produce a work of art or fashion. The artist's position is that of the indispensable figure in the center of a large network without whom the work could not have been accomplished (Grabher 2002). The alliances between art and fashion are in part an attempt to bond the product of the fashion retailer to that of both "high" and more contemporary street art and thus to enhance the status of the product. This is particularly apposite in the contemporary period as the traditional crafted production of luxury fashion goods gives way to mass production methods. The drive for desingularization, together with the financial interests that accompany the mass production of fashioned commodities, are significant forces that threaten brand value (Harnett 2014). One powerful strategy to dissipate this tendency has been the pursuit of an aggressive logic of differentiation based on aesthetic qualities, most notably evidenced by the spectacular alliances between fashion and "art in general and with contemporary art in particular" (Karpik 2010: 163). Karpik's originality model includes a diversified set of products, including art and fashion, that are increasingly defined by aesthetic criteria. Crucially, their practice (and place) of commodity production becomes less significant and may indeed be industrially produced: their value increasingly lies in their aesthetic credentials and brand allure. A number of luxury organizations have redefined themselves as not simply producers and retailers of commodities but as cultural aficionados whose creative directors act as guarantors of cultural credibility. A number, including Marc Jacobs for Louis Vuitton and Miuccia Prada have, in the process, "elevated themselves to the role of insightful intellectuals" (Tokatli 2014: 6). Marc

Jacobs for Louis Vuitton was a particularly directional force in promoting luxury fashion as an artistic cultural enterprise. Well known for his "self-identification as a postmodern fashion designer, and for his self-conscious understanding of his role as a cultural arbiter in a global world" (Tokatli 2014), Jacobs understands very well that the "creativity of designers is rooted as much in their ability to pick up on cultural currents and popular culture as in their own 'thinking repertoires'" (Tokatli 2014). Creativity emerges from immersion in and engagement with a suite of cultural practices that require collaboration and co-creation.

The example of the global luxury retailer Louis Vuitton is instructive here and is a clear illustration of the ways in which alliances between artists and fashion firms are emerging as a key means of "placing" fashion and maintaining commodity aura in an era of off-shoring and the global outsourcing of production. In 2005 it took 20–30 craftspeople eight days to produce a Louis Vuitton bag. The high price for the item could perhaps have been justified on the basis of its skilled, craft production and consumers undoubtedly bought into the concept of the value, aura, and singularity of artisan production (Aspers 2010; Karpik 2010). This valorization of commodities and consumer's visuality of them became altogether more problematic when the company shifted toward the mass production of their goods, accompanied by front-page headlines such as "Louis Vuitton Tries Modern Methods on Factory Lines" (Passariello 2006). As one means to justify the high price of mass-produced items Louis Vuitton's collaboration with a range of super-artists, including Takashi Murakami, Richard Prince, Yayoi Kusama, and Stephen Sprouse, is undoubtedly an aesthetic investment in the immaterial and symbolic definition of the brand. Many of these collaborations have themselves become iconic and are consumed by some as investment pieces that will accrue value through their lifetime and become collectable pieces in their own right. The Louis Vuitton art collaborations have helped to define the brand's value and shop space, both structurally and conceptually. These alliances go some way toward fixing the consumer's imagination on retail space and serve as a key means to enhance and extend the cultural value of the brand.

What is striking about contemporary retail space, particularly in the luxury branded sector, is how value is created not just (or not at all) in relation to the high quality of raw materials and the craft and skill involved in their fabrication but in relation to their immaterial qualities; value is increasingly seen to lie in the codes of meaning enshrined in commodities through processes of dematerialization, commodity fetishism, and the elevation of the retail store and commodity aesthetic as key creators of value. By adopting a cultural economy approach to fashion it becomes possible to see how aesthetic valorization thus becomes an increasingly important component in the making of luxury fashion markets (Aspers 2010). Collaboration with artists is thus argued to be a key means through which brand value is created and maintained. The boundaries between high art and popular culture are beginning to fray and new partnerships are being created. Fashion ceases to be art's "Other" but begins to vie for equal status (Geczy and Karaminas 2012: 3). While art and luxury fashion have always been intertwined, what is new and innovative in the contemporary era are the multiple ways in which these collaborations are emerging. Art and fashion, as a number of scholars have recently argued, are rarely discrete ideas and practices but, rather, are joint players in a complex aesthetic firmament that together shape and make markets (Currid 2007, 2012; Hawkins 2013; Karaminas 2012; Oakley Smith and Kubler 2013; Rantisi 2014; Steele 2012; Webb 2012; Yeomans 2012).

The global luxury brand Louis Vuitton is again a forerunner in many of more notable recent art-fashion collaborations (Castets 2009; Edelman 2012; Golbin 2012; Pasols 2005). It has been argued that "No other fashion house has wielded as much influence on the work and reputation of an artist in the way Louis Vuitton cultivated its highly visible relationships" (Saillard 2009: 71). The partnership with the cartoon-print artist Takashi Murakami in 2002 involved printing Murakami's soft toy images over Louis Vuitton's feted monogram, a logo central to the fashion house's closely protected authenticity. The result was both a radical artistic gesture and one of the house's greatest commercial successes. "By aligning with contemporary art, fashion affords itself a criticality that it lacks. This criticality can then be acquired, literally, by the buyer, in a knowing gesture of cultural and economic mastery, turning a shopper into a collector" (Oakley Smith and Kubler 2013: 16). In the case of this particular collaboration, "the distinction between commercial product and high art was blurred in a truly Warholian gesture when the artist later incorporated the paintings and sculptures he had produced for the house into his solo gallery exhibition" (Oakley Smith and Kubler 2013: 17). As the fashion house themselves argued in relation to the Murakami monogramoflage: "Our collaboration…has been, and continues to be, a monumental marriage or art and commerce. The ultimate cross-over— one for both the fashion and art history books" (Geczy and Karaminas 2012: 9). Murakami accurately pitches his promiscuous style of artistic spectacle as a product of a specific, interpenetrating alignment of economy and culture, a perfect exemplar of cultural economy at work.

The project undertaken jointly between Vuitton's Creative Director Marc Jacobs and the artist Olafur Eliasson in 2006 was another example of their pioneering approach to collaboration in both business (economy) and aesthetic (cultural) terms. The team created a site-specific store installation that challenged the tropes of retail design and display and actively enrolled the consumer in the production and interpretation of the space—visuality at its most stark. The *Eye See You* lamp installation blocked the consumer's view of every commodity in the window in every Louis Vuitton store worldwide—an audacious move during the feverish Christmas holiday consumption period. Resembling the pupil of an eye, the sculpture comprised a low-pressure sodium lamp that produces a strong monochromatic yellow light (see Figure 5.9). The image is illuminating,

Figure 5.9 Louis Vuitton × Olafur Eliasson's "Eye See You." © Olafur Eliasson 2006.

spectral, and vibrant and creates a dialogue and connection between the interior of the store and the exterior viewer, flooding the street with light as darkness falls and so transgressing the physical and psychological boundary represented by a commercial window display. The installation was viewed by millions of pedestrians and "Eye See You" became part of urban streetscapes around the world for the duration of its showing, combining the conventional notion of window shopping with the visual experience of looking at art.

The emotional and affective charge of the window design is engaging and powerful. By representing the eye, quite literally, we see how this collaboration questions the very nature of the shop window as a space for looking at commodities. In a striking inversion of the gaze, the 350 Louis Vuitton windows display nothing but the illuminated monochromatic pupil of an eye, watching, following, surveilling. The eye light is so bright that it is difficult to look at and the remainder of the window is shrouded in blackness. In this daring switching of the relationship between viewer and viewed, the consumer sees nothing. The eye sees you. The installation, as a metaphorical eye with an indifferent and/or aggressive relationship to moving viewers, effectively speaks to a number of conceptual debates about the gaze, the relationship between watcher and watched, consumer and store, surveillance and social control (Modigliani 2007). The relations between art and fashion provocatively reveal how, on the one hand, fashion can "transform places and spaces, adding, deferring or altering the identity of the environment, while, on the other hand, it can increase the cultural cachet of [an artist]" (Potvin 2009: 5).

> What is absolutely new and avant garde is that fashion designers and visual artists will co-author a single, collaborative work of art in which their contributions are perfectly integrated: both craft and concept a joint enterprise from the start. Whether blatant, referential or allusive, this exchange of ideas continues to be a work (of art) in progress. (Webb 2012: 11)

Contemporary artists and their relations with fashion designers thus become a key means of making and defining markets. The collaboration constitutes a real axis of aesthetic invention. The nature of art and fashion practice and their aesthetic status become interwoven and combined in order to preserve aura and ensure the continuation of their status as markets of singularization (Karpik 2010). Both groups of agents have evolved into cultural impresarios, and an appreciation of their work is increasingly connected to being part of a collective, as opposed to consumption being an individual, aesthetic experience. Contemporary artists are increasingly comfortable to work alongside fashion creatives as "imagineers" and to frame their work according to the specifications of fashion houses. It would appear that the emergent fashion-art fusion is capturing a complex set of contemporary cultural developments—on the one hand, the alliances reflect the increased mainstream currency of contemporary art and a popular hunger for meaningful consumption experience; on the other hand, this tendency is in turn bound up with the need for artists, and the institutions that support them, to reach out and see and be seen as more than rarefied collector's pieces. Fashion and art are together key cultural actors in the fabrication of contemporary urban space and are simultaneously reflections and representations, both constantly in the process of presenting and interpreting the contemporary geography of the fashioned city. Both art and fashion translate a dream into a material form. Thus "the differences are less in the objects of fashion and art, since both are aesthetic creations for which judgement is always subjective, but the places of exchange—social, economic, linguistic—that they occupy" (Geczy and Karaminas 2012: 5).

Reflections

At one level this chapter contributes to social scientific research on luxury fashion markets by revealing the increasing significance of creative practice and retail design and display. At another level the argument presented has demonstrated the fundamental importance of geography and space as key mechanisms through which to explain the enduring growth of the luxury fashion sector. Significantly, and in contrast to many new economy prophets who imagined that physical stores would become a "dead weight", global luxury stores appear to demonstrate the enduring power and potency of the physical retail store that has the capacity to recast luxury in line with shifting global consumption practices. This is important given that luxury fashion and its complex geographies are an extraordinarily resilient feature of contemporary capitalism and may act as an early warning system for major economic transformation. This requires that we better understand the means and mechanisms through which luxury brands grow and develop. It further depends on exploring more critical approaches that engage and question the desires and demands for commodities with a high ratio of intangible value in order to more fully understand their affective capacities, emotional reach and ongoing commercial success.

Through the analysis presented the chapter makes two significant conceptual contributions. Firstly, while art, fashion, and luxury have always been intertwined, recent decades have revealed that contemporary notions of luxury, quality, and added value are quickly combining with the immaterial qualities of retail design, display, atmosphere, and experience. This is engendering a shift away from the significance of the materiality and origin of luxury objects per se to toward their aesthetic pull—as evidenced by the original etymology of the word, aesthesis, meaning sensation. The chapter explores the uneasy alliance between the two practices and the tensions that unfold between integrity and authenticity, commercialism and craft, medium and message in the creation of contemporary retail spaces. In so doing the piece offers a more critical reflection on the worlds of art and fashion and draws attention to the many ways in which the two practices are coalescing around a set of practices that enshrine value in the spaces of retailing and consumption as much as in the place of origin of goods. Conventional accounts have argued that "art and fashion inhabited different modalities of presentation and reception"; they had different uses and were subject to different responses within both monetary and aesthetic economies (Geczy and Karaminas 2012: 5).

Within extant social scientific research, cultural objects have conventionally been classified in terms of their varying properties in a system of categories of goods relative to one another (Bourdieu 1989; DiMaggio 1987). The cohtribution of this chapter is to argue that the boundaries between art, fashion, creativity, and what is institutionalized as such have been breaking down or at least becoming more porous in recent years. This is conceptually significant as it furthers our understanding of the possible ways in which the immaterial and aesthetic qualities of goods can generate, or even determine, value (Karpik 2010). The contemporary alliances between artists and fashion houses are an exemplar of a market of singularity that is characterized by the primacy of competition by qualities over and beyond economically determined competition. These are aesthetic markets where the issue of quality, value, and worth lies beyond purely economic explanations or pricing regimes (Beckert and Aspers 2011). The important point here is thus that the particular nature of the luxury fashion market requires that we theoretically integrate culture, creativity, aura, and allure in ways that take us far beyond price-based determinants of value. Cultural objects, in both the art and fashion worlds, carry multiple meanings which in part shape their value. The adoption of a cultural economy approach to fashion markets allows us to interrogate the geographies and politics of creativity that are emerging through fashion and art's fusion and collusion and to explore how new creative practices of design and display are impacting on regimes of commodity valorization in very important ways.

The chapter has argued that this is a critical moment for the mixing and melding of genres and for hybridizing art and fashion (Lipovetsky and Manlow 2010: 110). The creative practices explored here "engage a whole suite of relationships between bodies, materials and matter, technology and objects that are a source of creativity's subject, place and world-making potentials" (Hawkins 2013: 6). They represent a key means of making and shaping value and reveal the significance of visuality, singularity, and judgment in determining commodity and brand meaning and value. This orchestration of fashion through artistic collaboration in store also provides a critical space for reflections on the workings of commercial and creative practice and offers insights as to how, together, these may offer new ways through which to theorize value, aura, and the ordering of markets (Beckers and Aspers 2011; Karpik 2011; Stark 2009). The alliances and convergence between art and fashion are in part the product of the rise of the creative director as a key agentive figure in the production and reproduction of luxury spaces and markets—a collision of craft, commerce, and cultural production that requires detailed scrutiny given the central role it plays in the creation and determination of value. The art of designing a fashion space is an exercise in communication, in making concrete the imaginative energy and creative power of artists and designers. It is also a key strategy in foregrounding the space of consumption while masking the intricate shifting global geographies of luxury production. In an increasingly integrated, mobile, and volatile world, the creation of retail spaces is one means through which to communicate the concerns of our lives in motion with urgency and power. As Hawkins has argued to great effect, and as the examples explored here too reveal, the geographies and economics of creativity are "not just a way of making a living but also about making lives" (Hawkins 2013: 3); they reveal the critical potential of fashion space to address key concerns of contemporary geographic enquiry—sight, temporality, day, night, sustainability. Fashion space has both cultural and economic power and potential. This is geographically critical in furthering our understanding of the economic, social and political dimensions, possibilities and tensions of creative practices (Hawkins 2013: 5).

Second, the chapter develops current understandings of the globalizing nature of the luxury industry and argues that the luxury fashion store remains a pivotal feature in a world where retail markets are more fragmented and diverse than ever before (Kozinets et al. 2002); it is a space where dreams are created and fantasies fulfilled. Fashion has always been framed by the use of image and display and is characterized by an ongoing compulsion to create ever-more striking images (Arnold 2001: 56). Images play a key role in defining global fashion culture and in capturing its discursive power (Shinkle 2008: 1). Brand identity and consumption spaces, as the discussion has revealed, are fundamental to the fashion industry and instrumental in a variety of forms to the global fashion culture of the twenty-first century, not least in dramatic in-store collaborative installations. The chapter has demonstrated that the micro-geography of the shop window is a key (and much neglected) site for the constitution and representation of contemporary consumption—a space of possibility where art and fashion, culture and commerce, design and desire merge and meld. Store windows act as a powerful spatial landscape that sets the stage in the contemporary city for the performance of everyday life, acting as theaters of signs and symbols in which representation is not the opposite of materiality but rather its alter-ego, a space that both constitutes and reflects commerce and culture, transaction and imagination.

Notes

1 The empirical focus of the book is on the eight largest luxury fashion organizations— Louis Vuitton (LVMH), Hermes, Gucci, Prada, Chanel, Burberry, Fendi and Coach— and on global "flagship" spaces of display such as Selfridges and Harvey Nichols.

2 There remains a pronounced geography in the distribution of flagship stores in global cities that agglomerate in, for example, Bond Street/Sloane Street (London); 5th Avenue/Madison Avenue (New York); Rue du Faubourg Saint-Honore/Avenue Montaigne (Paris' Triangle D'Or); Via Manzoni/Via Montenapoleone (Milan); Harumi Dori (Ginza)/Aoyama Dori (Tokyo); Queen Street/Canton Road (Hong Kong).

3 Hermes, Kering, Richemont, and Louis Vuitton Moet Hennessy have, for example, all grown tenfold in the past two decades.

4 Bond Street/Sloane Street (London); 5th Avenue/Madison Avenue (New York); Rue du Faubourg Saint-Honore/Avenue Montaigne (Paris' Triangle D'Or); Via Manzoni/ Via Montenapoleone (Milan); Harumi Dori (Ginza)/Aoyama Dori (Tokyo); Queen Street/Canton Road (Hong Kong).

6

POSSESSED: EVOCATIVE OBJECTS, MEANING, AND MATERIALITY

I hate when people say they don't care about clothes, because it's a lie... We are always asking for something when we get dressed. Asking to be loved, to be fucked, to be admired, to be left alone, to make people laugh, to look wealthy, to say I'm poor, I love myself. It's the quiet poem in the waiting room, on the subway, in the movie of our lives. It's a big fucking deal. (Core, L in Heti et al. 2014: 24)

This chapter explores the role of possession in determining the value of our clothes. In the quotation above, Core argues that our clothing choices reflect who we are, and would like to be in the world. Drawing on this, the chapter contends that the boundaries between cost and value, between acquisition and ownership, between memory and materiality, and between object and possession are both blurred and mobile (Edensor 2005a, 2005b, 2005c; Hetherington 2004). As this book has argued throughout, the value and meaning of fashion is mutable and mobile, it is also relational and scalar. This chapter argues that clothes derive value in part from our relationships with them. In addition to addressing the relational journeys that underpin the geographies of fashion, it is important to understand that the biographical histories and geographies of clothing, and their connections to people and places, really do matter (Belk 1988; Jarrett 2006; Miller 2009, 2010). In the following discussion I argue that value and significance can be seen to reside in the most unlikely of places and may emerge through everyday practices of wearing, caring, loss, and remembering as well as through more conventional processes of production and purchase (Baudrillard 1997). Value lingers and endures. Drawing on Koptyoff's work on the eventful biographies of things (1986), this chapter explores the ambiguities of value that are attributed to different categories of good. Valuations and categorizations are slippery and elusive. Inconsistencies between and within categories of goods ensure that questions of value, meaning, and worth remain mutable in time and space and open to accidental interpretations. However much we try to organize, manage, and orchestrate our consumption, clothes can be resistant or unruly, misbehave, or be freighted with feeling of sadness or loss. Our possessions can haunt us and evoke memories that we would rather have remained hidden. Our connections to our clothes reveal untold significance. Our most valuable possessions are so often those with the least market value. They are quite literally invaluable—above and beyond the market. The chapter focuses on the role of possession and memory in the creation of fashion value and explores to what extent fashion value is a function of the brand, the designer, an object's age, authenticity, or social relations. Why do we keep clothes we no longer wear? Why do the biographies of things matter and why is it so difficult to dispose of certain garments, to erase them? The chapter explores the elevated moral and sentimental status of certain objects and argues that what a garment is and what it means depends on how, where, why, and when we see it; value is inseparable from geography. The chapter frames fashion value through questions of possession, ownership, and use. It has long been recognized that things are forever engaged in the process of becoming, but clothes are in many ways a particularly acute exemplar of this, a unique category of good. It is argued that the key to understanding the secret of value may lie less in the realm of supply and demand curves, nor even in product design or aesthetics, but in the auto-topographical potential of goods and the relations between objects and subjects. Our clothes are extensions of the self: we use them to signal to ourselves and others who we want to be and where we want to belong. And long after we're gone they become our legacy. Some might even say our essence lives on in what once we made or owned (Jarrett 2006: 560). Things embody different kinds of personal meaning and in turn they define who we are to self and others. There is no meaning inherent in things themselves—things derive meaning from human relationships. The chapter argues that fashion value and significance may reside in the most unlikely of places and may emerge through practices of wear, use, and memory as well as through more conventional processes such as production and purchase. The discussion emphasizes the importance of clothing as social practice and highlights that fashion value is always mobile and contingent; it is always a process rather than a revelation or a moment. Value lingers, endures, and can be stubbornly resistant. When a garment is purchased it begins to record its own individual story. Clothes are repositories of accumulated sensory biographies. Clothes have memories stored, layered, deposited within them and it is through the excavation of use and wear that consumption value may emerge. Crucially this layering of meaning and memory through use cannot be replicated or created by producer firms. It relies on the connections between the commodity, the consumer body, and space.

The chapter makes two broad theoretical points. First, it argues that different categories of good have widely varying status values and underscore the role of possession and memory in shaping clothing value. Second, the chapter emphasizes the importance of the auto-topographical potential of things in understanding value creation and destruction. Our possessions and our commodities may be two very different things; variable categories of meaning and value are ascribed to objects as a result of our personal connections to them. We bestow intensely passionate and possessive feelings onto some of our things. Our understandings of value and possession are profoundly shaped by our often quiet, hidden, or routine interactions with our stuff. Spectacular insights can emerge from the seemingly trivial and banal (Bennett 2004). Enchantment can reside in the most mundane of objects (Brown 2001, 2004; Davies King 2008; Glenn and Hayes 2007; Turkle 2007; Watson 1992). The key to understanding the secret of value may not be in the realm of supply and demand curves, nor even in product design or aesthetics, but in the auto-topographical potential of goods and the relations between objects and subjects. Things are tie-ins: signs of social bonds (Goffman 1971). The value of a thing is irreducible to numerical or monetary worth but, rather, rests in its social history and geography, in the traces of wear and use embedded within it, and in the particular category of good (Gregson and Crewe 2003; Gregson et al. 2007). Value is entwined within the social, cultural, temporal, and geographical specificity of things. What something is and what it means depend on how, where, why, and when we see it. Our objects have meanings stored, layered, deposited within them, and it is through the excavation of memory that value may emerge. The theoretical question then becomes how we might capture the different mediations through which the subject experiences the object and vice versa (Miller et al. 1998: 5). How, why, and where do things become captivating, meaningful, enchanting to us and might this take us some way in cracking the code of value-meaning?

Breakdown

This section of the book explains the ways in which our clothes may unwittingly encapsulate value in beyond-market terms. As Dalgety argues "Like most people, my most important possessions are worth nothing. And everything" (2001: 13). The chapter first examines one particular artistic installation, Michael Landy's *Break Down* project, that explores where value remains once everything is lost. Landy's inventory of destruction exposes just how much our possessions continue to haunt us, even when their material presence in our lives has gone (Hetherington 2004). His experiment in disposal reveals the hugely variable status of different categories of good and the elevated moral and sentimental status of certain objects (gifts, private personal possessions such as letters, photographs, clothing). It reveals the role that meaning-value plays determining significance. In February 2001 Michael Landy, a British artist with a long-standing interest in questions of waste and consumerism, created a "production line of destruction" on which he itemized, listed, and then destroyed every possession he owned in a two-week public performance. The event, called "Break Down," was the end point in a three-year project undertaken by Landy that aimed to question the meaning of consumerism and the value of possession and to examine society's romance with consumerism. Landy wanted to reflect on the life of things after we've finished with them, to classify the material presences of things, and to think about destinations of the discarded and about our lives without belongings. Landy's project is used here to make three substantive points. First, the installation underscores the ways in which destruction can reveal a great deal about value. Landy argued that his exploration of the meaning of consumption via practices of destruction has had ramifications that have changed the rest of his life. Apart from having to manage the daily routines of life without a passport, driving license, photographs, an address book, phone, or credit card, Landy had to come to terms with who he was. What had really mattered and why? How much of his life depended on what he owned? What memories did certain objects trigger and why? Significantly, it emerges that it is not merely "things" but things in motion that illuminate their human and social context and in turn their value (Appadurai 1986: 5). *Break Down* encouraged witnesses and spectators to "follow their own associations and to wonder how much of what it is to be human is in what we own" (Cumming 2001). By reversing the logic of commodity fetishism and returning objects to their preproduction state on a production line of destruction, Landy encourages the viewer to make connections, to trace commodity chains backward, and to think about who made these things? And where? What are the spatial and temporal relations between us and the makers of our things? The connections between origins and final destinations are quite literally prised apart, thrown into sharp relief, exposed. While at first glance the space appeared to be a factory making things with people hard at work, on closer more sustained inspection visitors realized that it was in fact a process of careful, meticulous destruction, yet one that is every bit as complex as that of creation. Above all the project reveals the way in which objects come alive and accrue meaning through their interactions and transactions with people (Komter 2001). Second, this example reveals the significance of different categories of good in the creation of value. Landy's itemization and classification of things produced a personal, symbolic hierarchy of goods. Distinctions between sentimental and market value emerged with startling clarity. Landy acknowledges that he made emotional choices when dispatching his possessions to the shredder. Certain categories, such as electrical goods, were relatively easy to dispose of. Others, such as private letters and fragments of fabric, were far more difficult and stirred more complex emotions. The symbolic and personal meaning of different categories of goods was profound, and their hugely variable biographical profiles offer some important clues into the locus of object meaning. Evocative objects leave their traces behind and continue to exist in the shadowy hauntings of our memory, if not in their original material form. *Break Down* was the culmination of three years of object sorting, classifying, and logging. Landy categorized every item he owned. Landy himself acknowledged the personal profundity of the project and said that he was asking questions about consumption that would have ramifications for the rest of his life and would force him to confront, evaluate, and reflect on which possessions, if any, really matter: "I thought about me being one of many millions of consumers and somehow at some point we begin to create our own biographies from the things we own or possess" (Landy in interview with Lingwood 2001). The private, personal, and irreplaceable artifacts that hold memories of relationships, encounters, and attachments are often our most meaningful possessions. Their presence can activate memories and reveal the material significance that objects play in affirming social relations regardless of their market value or worth. Clothes are a particularly significant category of good. Like perishables and electrical items, clothes are so often seen as easily disposable. For Landy, however, the memories and histories woven into many of his clothes elevated them to a more significant position in his system of values. He destroyed the things he valued most last, and his father's sheepskin coat was one of the most difficult objects to part with; he "wanted someone to take it away but they didn't" (Landy quoted in Cumming 2002). He argued that "the sheepskin coat was there on the conveyor belt from the first day and it just kept travelling round and round … Over those two weeks the coat became my Dad in a way" [Landy quoted in Lingwood (2001)]. "I'm going to kill the operative who destroys my dad's coat … The coat assumed a kind of totemic significance during the show and was one of the losses that weighed particularly heavily on Landy" (Cumming 2002). He revealed that "destroying that will feel a bit like disposing of my dad" (Landy quoted in Withers 2001: 189). A number of Landy's other items of clothing reveal the auto-topographical nature of clothes and underscore the complex ways in which garments narrate personal histories and geographies. They tell about the school he attended, the gifts he received from whom, and where they were purchased, the friends he partied with, all tiny pieces of a biogeographical journey. Clothes are intimate. We wear them and feel them and leave our bodily effects on and in them, trapped between the fibers. Our clothes become us. We inhabit them, and they tell stories about us: where we bought them; when, where, and with whom we wore them; the places we went; the stains from the party, the rip from the fall as marks of value not distain. They touch us and reveal significance and memory-value. Clothing is an object in the space between self and surround, a second skin, porous, absorbent, soaked in memories and steeped in stories. Undoubtedly the exercise prompted some to think about their possessions and the meanings within them. What would Landy select as the final possession to be destroyed and why? What will his first purchases be after *Break Down* and why? How do we feel when there is nothing left? The project revealed quite clearly to Landy himself where value lies. It is not in his car or electrical items, but hidden, concealed, and tucked away in the most unlikely places: "Every now and then I'd pick something up from the conveyor belt and I'd think 'ah, yeah' and then have to put it back down again. Some things can never be replaced. And they are probably the hardest to get rid of" (Landy 2002). Evocative objects leave their traces behind, the loose ends of consumption that linger and haunt, in numerous material and immaterial states.

The second example drawn on is the Belgian designer Margiela, who actively explores the role of the brand and the label and logo in determining value. His clothes carry no labels or identifiable logos and are seen to derive value from their craft and their exposure of key tailoring details: "MMM is candid about beauty. Its beauty comes from faults, burns, rips, memories of the past, dreams, tragedy. This beauty is surreal, asymmetrical, has no gender, no status. It is not sexist, is not luxury, is not money, is not class" (Beecroft, 2009). Value here lies in the biogeographical stories that clothing tells, the connections it has with its wearers, and the histories woven through its threads. The quiet cult consumer who wears Margiela understands the vulgarity of many contemporary designer brands and may be making an alternative set of consumption choices that actively resist the branding, opulence, and grandeur of celebrity fashion:

> MMM avoids celebration, buckles, gold and logos but conveys humour and substance, new ideas, abstraction, social provocation, happiness, beauty. By referring to classic bourgeois clothes that are altered, turned inside out or upside down, MMM forbids the reification of ideals by embedding them in their ghosts … once we wear it ripped, out of size or out of gender we give these faults meaning that create a fundament for the new …. True beauty is bare. It … shows us that it is ephemeral. We fall in love with its imperfections and fragility. (Beecroft 2009: 250)

Third, the chapter draws on an example taken from a seminar class with final-year undergraduate students that I have run for many years. In the seminar I ask them to think about and discuss their three most "valuable" possessions, the things that they would rescue above all else if their house was burning down, the objects in their lives that mean the most to them. With startling regularity their discussion revolves around objects that have relatively little "economic" worth: few, if any, mention branded clothes, expensive electrical appliances, furniture, or art. Perhaps this has something to do with their stage in the life cycle: the majority are under 21, living in shared student accommodation, and may thus not have accumulated much by way of material possessions. But I suspect that age isn't the defining feature here. Rather, I suggest that the things that matter to these undergraduates matter to many others too. For their significant objects have little to do with design, branding, market value, or price. The majority talk about photograph albums, CD or vinyl collections, a gift from a friend or lover, something bequeathed by a deceased relative. In one sense this is slightly curious given multimedia technologies and new means of data storage. Few, for example, mentioned their laptop or memory stick. For me this endorses the significance of the materiality of the object in value creation. It also underscores the significance of temporality, the biography of things and social relations in explaining why things matter. Things have "no meanings apart from those that human transactions, attributions and motivations endow them with … we have to follow the things themselves, for their meanings are inscribed in their forms, their uses, their trajectories. It is only through the analysis of these trajectories that we can interpret the human transactions and calculations that enliven things" (Appadurai 1986: 5).

Overlay: The signature, the artist, the brand

The artist Gavin Turk asked a number of "key" individuals (contemporary artists, musicians, photographers, designers) to submit their favorite item of clothing to Oki-ni, a concept store in Soho that, like Turk, addressed the question of rarity, value, branding, and authorship as determinants of fashion value.

The items were signed by Turk and photographed, catalogued, displayed in a high-profile "installation" at the flagship Oki-ni store on Savile Row, London, to which regular customers and celebrity "fans" of Gavin Turk and Oki-ni (or both) were invited. Oki-ni then ran an online competition for consumers who had to "match" the celebrity with their (anonymous) donated garment—the garments were displayed and described, but their owners were anonymized. The project not only generated new design ideas for future garments but, crucially, it questioned the notion of authorship, authenticity, and value in the production of fashion labels. Many of the donated garments were "vintage," one-offs, or handmade; many had been worn by the "celebrity" who donated them, and thus bore their bodily traces and held memories (individuals who donated items included, for example, Paul Smith, Sam Taylor Wood, Nick Knight); they now additionally bore the original signature of controversial Brit artist Gavin Turk and

Gavin Turk

OKI-NI
...another signature "real" or "forged"

10th December 2002

You are invited to take part in a dynamic analysis of the artistic process.

Renowned British artist Gavin Turk joins forces with oki-ni, the pioneering fashion project, to create a show questioning the process by which a label can bestow value upon clothing.

Much of Gavin Turk's work questions issues of ownership and authorization with respect to artistic creation. Why is the artist required to sign his work? What creates the value, the art or the signature? A lot of Gavin's work is based around his signature and this project explores the method by which a label (in effect a signature) is able to create value upon articles of clothing.

Gavin has rendered a "unique" version of his signature which oki-ni have used to create the label included here. We invite you to stitch this label into one of your own garments and loan the piece to oki-ni in preparation for showing at the oki-ni flagship store in Savile Row, London and also on-line at oki-ni.com.

You are part of a select group of people chosen to participate in this project.

Throughout the show at Savile Row, the names of the participants will be made available but they will not be linked to the individual garments. Resulting from the show a "collection" of pieces will be re-produced in extremely limited numbers. The reproduction will ensure that all the characteristics of the garment, as a result of usage by the owner, will be replicated exactly; another presence of signature.

To be part of the process, simply follow the instructions attached for the loaning of your personal garment of choice.

oki-ni, 25 savile row London w1s 3pr

t 020 7494 1716 f 020 7434 3212

Figure 6.1 Nicole Farhi × Gavin Turk × Oki-ni worn belt. © author's photograph.

were also inscribed with an Oki-ni label lauding "rarity is value. We don't make many." One example is the soft, black leather belt in Figure 6.1.

The belt was originally purchased from Nicole Farhi, and had been worn, cherished, and loved by the owner who sent it, as requested, to Oki-ni where it had a new "brand" label stitched into it bearing the artist's signature (Gavin Turk) plus Oki-ni's label. The question posed here is how do the effects of the label, the brand, a store, rarity, possession, ownership, and use influence value? Is the belt now more "valuable" to the owner as it carried an artist's signature, or less, as it has been "defaced," amended, and labeled? Has this layering of labels diluted the original brand value or enhanced it? Have the traces of wear and use on the garment been eroded, erased, or tainted by the addition of another commercial brand overlain on top of the original label? This hybrid commercial and artistic exploration raises a number of questions that are central in our quest to understand fashion's value. Quite where do authorship, value, creation, and ownership lie in such complex systems of co-production? Does the layering of additional labels (Gavin Turk and Oki-ni) make the original object more valuable and rare, or less? Does the fact that the donated objects were worn, worn-in, personal, render the item more or less valuable? Clothes are a means through which to examine how people use things to transact certain aspects of being-in-the world at a direct sensory level of experience. The very act of wearing clothes is in itself transformative. While the brand, label, signature, or author may have originally informed the initial purchase decision, cycles of use and wear transform clothes and their meaning. Garments are among the single most personal and the single most global objects we possess. They affirm their sense of genuine specificity and individuality despite this enormous homogenizing world.

Ghosts in the wardrobe

The weekly feature in the Guardian newspaper titled Pieces of Me in which a "famous" person is invited to reveal, photograph, and discuss their fifteen most significant possessions underscores the significance of social relations in understanding why things matter and where value might reside. Again not surprisingly, the selected objects are rarely described as meaningful because of their brand, cost, or label. Rather, these significant possessions are predominantly idiosyncratic and often peculiarly personal belongings that reveal the ways in which value resides less in price and more through object: subject connections that are intertwined with history and memory. The filmmaker and director Mike Lee, for example, discusses the importance of the notebooks he uses in which he lists and details individual actors, the evolution of their character, and the spaces and places in which they rehearsed and filmed. The significant point here is the way in which the books absorb and hold the sensory traces of Lee's body and location. He explains:

> I work individually with each actor to create the character, but they don't make notes: I do. Each has his or her own, numbered reporter's notebook according to when they start the rehearsals. The most famous things associated with me are my tiny pocket scripts, cut to fit my shirt pocket. They absorb sweat and weather and location-catering and fuck knows what. It's great not to be cluttered with crap. Like scripts. (Lee 2008)

As Sherry Turkle argues so persuasively, "we think with the objects we love. They help us to make up our minds, reaching out to us to form active partnerships" (2007: 308). Objects engage the heart as well as the mind and the "longevity of the relation assimilates them in some sense to the person and makes parting from them unthinkable" (Koptyoff 1986: 80). In another Pieces of Me feature the novelist Isabel Allende discusses the slippers that her prematurely deceased daughter Paula used to wear. She tells how "[O]nce a year we have a ceremony to remember Paula and we take them out" (Allende 2008). The unexpected and unanticipated death of Allende's daughter endows her slippers with untold significance. The tiny, dirty-white slippers hold the very essence of her daughter: her smell, skin, shape, and feel. Their form has evolved as an effect of this particular person's inhabitation, and they now act as a repository of accumulated sensory biography, caught between the warp and the weft, fused into the dirty white fur, layered, and accumulated. They store and reveal corporeal traces of presence and intimacy. The furry slippers and Paula, their wearer, are combined and entwined, inseparable in mind and memory. Paula inhabited her slippers, brought them to life, and they now carry untold symbolic resonance. The material and the immaterial, fabric and feeling, are woven together in and through the slippers. The slippers are almost unbearably evocative. They reveal how small and intensely personal objects have profound capacities to move us. Their affective charge is out of all proportion to their market worth and underscores the hugely consequential significance of materiality. A beautiful illustration of the power of absence can be found in Sarah Scaturro's article in which she reflects on who might have worn a garment she is preparing for the Cooper-Hewitt textile archive. Scaturro tells how she

> gently lay the ripped and faded child's dress on the sterile muslin-covered table. Its cavity, open to the waist, references the long-absent body of the girl who used to wear it. Glimpsing the interior I see the exposed mending stitches wrought over a century and a half ago. By who? The little girl's mother or aunt?… And what was it about this plain calico-print dress that caused it to be passed down…Why did it win that race of selectivity?… I believe that if I try hard enough, imagine long enough, then a small amount its previous life will transfer to me and I will truly know her. (2010: 21)

Like Scaturro's dress, the tattered babies' Christening gown in my wardrobe holds traces of its former life—worn, tattered, ripped, and decayed, the little dress has been treasured, nurtured, wrapped in tissue paper, and stored, passed through families and holding precious memories in its paper-thin cloth. As all of these examples reveal, clothes are a particularly potent biogeographical category of good echoed here by Stein as she recalls the memories trapped within her dress "When I opened up the box …, tears came into my eyes…I was wearing it when I had my first kiss with the guy to whom I would later become engaged and also when I first met his family. It never failed me. The dress never disappeared. I know exactly where it is in my closet" (Stein, S. in Heti et al. 2014: 60). As a number of commentators have argued so persuasively, clothes retain the history of our bodies within their fabric. "Bodies come and go; the clothes which have received those bodies survive" (Stallybrass 1993: 37). We wear clothes, clothes wear, they are and become us. Creases, stains, smells, and rips testify to the "way in which things become materially, in their consumption as much as their production" (Hauser 2004: 293). Used clothes simultaneously hit a whole number of sensory registers: touch, smell, sight. They also reveal the inextricable relation between clothing and memory. Clothes tell stories and store corporeal traces of presence and intimacy. They suggest an instinctive, imagined closeness and trigger strong and vivid memories (Granata 2010). They are repositories of accumulated biographies, their stories caught between the warp and the weft, fused into the thread, layered, accumulated. They are also enduring, potent, powerful, inarticulate, and at times unbearably evocative. And so it may be that objects exert their value and holding power because of the particular moment and circumstance in which they came into someone's life and through the intimate connections we make with our things (Turkle 2007: 8). This suggests that we need new conceptualizations that move beyond value as located at points of production, via the movement of things (Appadurai 1986), as a result of the politics of exchange (Appadurai 1986), or due to branding or design (Gregson et al. 2009). Rather, it is argued that value may have altogether more intimate roots that center on our personal relations with them. The key theoretical point here is that to understand the value of commodities we need to reflect on emergent systems that constitute the object and subject as grouped around the idea of human-possession encounters, the social lives of our things, and the affective power of material things. This requires no less than a disentangling of the assumed connections between creation, sale, and use, decoupling of production from consumption in the creation of value. It is valorization through presence and attachment—the coming together of desire.

Reflections

I always want a relationship that feels like a block of steel—but perhaps consider instead: love that feels like the thinnest man's undershirt, in many places ripping. (Heti et al. 2014: 179)

I conclude with two conceptual points that connect to the statement by Heti above. The first relates to significance, evocation, and space. The second argues that we need to foreground subject: object encounters and the intimate biogeographical relations we share with our possessions if we are to more fully understand clothing value. First, I have shown how the most mundane, ordinary, invisible, and seemingly uninteresting things can be as significant and revealing as the most dramatic. By casting illumination onto that which was previously unremarkable, I have revealed the powerful evocative agency of ordinary objects. Meaning lurks in surprising spaces, in the lowly and lost, the abandoned, and damaged. It is important to look at this stuff in the background "both as the resonance or fall-out of things in the foreground and, at some level, something that contributes to it. The foreground is made up of the information that we more regularly notice, although the background things who we chat with or what we sketch out probably takes up more of our everyday engagement" (Julier 2004). The important point is to acknowledge how much "we construct the complexity of our lives from minutiae; and how little, from inspecting the minutiae, can we deduce that complexity" (Bywater 2001: 53). Second, I argue that value emerges through practices of possession, loss, and memory as well as through production and purchase. In order to understand ourselves, we need to understand the story of how the self comes to be through a continual process of re-experiencing and redescribing the fragmented narratives encoded within objects. The objects and their stories reveal the weighty materiality of lifetimes of acquisition, use, display, and disposal. They reveal, too, poignant insights into the most personal reaches of people's subjectivities, vestigial traces of secrets, loves, losses, and desires. Our clothes may tell us more than we might imagine about ourselves, our connections to objects, and our social relations with others. They are fragments, shreds, and traces of lives that linger, endure, remain, and haunt in both material and immaterial forms. This is conceptually significant as it requires that we consider clothing as a key component in the making of subjectivity. This takes us theoretically further than the literatures on commodities and the politics of value (Appadurai 1986; Koptyoff 1986) by foregrounding possession, rather than exchange and movement, as a key determinant of value. The chapter has revealed how the biographical histories and geographies of things, and their connections to people and places really do matter (Miller 2009, 2010). Value and significance can be seen to reside in the most unlikely of places and may emerge through practices of loss and remembering as well as through more conventional processes such as production and purchase (Baudrillard 1997). Value lingers and endures. It can be both immaterial and stubbornly resistant. I suggest that the locus of value may reside less in the sphere of the market and more in the accumulated biogeography of objects. Things rarely hold value in themselves as objects but act as material memory joggers to an emotional state or moment that their owners want to recapture. The object that is received at the point of emotional transaction is the one the human will value. It is the closest thing to the memory of the moment. This may go some way to explaining why the materiality, autotopography, and biogeography of an object matter so much, and why an exact copy or replica never quite works: while a laptop or memory stick may store our photographs, documents, letters, or music, the memorizer knows that this digital storage is one step removed. A laptop full of letters will never be as significant as a handful of the original objects, with the traces and memories of reading, holding, receiving, touching, feeling. Our relations to our things are sensory, bodily, evocative, and profound. Things come to matter through our interactions with them, object and subject combined and entwined, inseparable in mind and memory. This reworked approach to value based on the intimate biogeography of possessions acknowledges the importance of the relational geographies of both present and absent things, the material and the immaterial, and the subject and object. The chapter has revealed the autotopographical nature of clothes and underscored the complex ways in which garments narrate personal histories and geographies. Clothes are intimate. We wear them and feel them and leave our bodily effects on and in them, trapped between the fibers. Our clothes become us. We inhabit them and they tell stories about us: where we bought them; when, where, and with whom we wore them; the places we went; the stains from the party, the rip from the fall as marks of value not distain. They touch us and reveal significance and memory-value. Clothing is an object in the space between self and surround, a second skin, porous, absorbent, soaked in memories and steeped in stories.

7

SOFT: WARE: WEAR: WHERE—VIRTUAL FASHION SPACES IN THE DIGITAL AGE

This chapter explores the impact of the digitally mediated communications technologies on the fashion sector, analyzing the impact of the internet on the spaces, times, business models, and consumption practices of fashion. It argues that material and virtual fashion worlds are perpetually intersecting social realities that coexist relationally, simultaneously, and in mutual connection. Specifically the chapter explores how conventional fashion spaces (cities, stores, magazines, designer firms, shows) might variously compete, coexist, or coalesce with digitally mediated spaces and how the relational networks between the two might unfold. How are fashion producers and consumers adapting to emergent worlds where touching or stepping through the screen becomes part of the daily routine of everyday life, and where windows are properties of both physical and virtual stores? How do fashion worlds function when they are carried with us on mobile devices, permanently in transit, always on, and what might be the impact of this on the existing geographies of fashion space? The chapter explores these shifting fashion landscapes in three particular ways in order to understand how fashion worlds are being transformed, enhanced, and reproduced in space and time. First, it is argued that emergent digital technologies are *remediating* and *refashioning* existing cultural forms of signification such as fashion magazines and photography. Second, the chapter explores the potential *disintermediatory* effects that the internet is having on fashion markets and consumption, questioning to what extent digital technologies are enabling the devolution of fashion authority from traditional power brokers such as magazine editors and designers toward a more diversified assemblage of participants, including fashion bloggers and consumers. Finally, the chapter explores the transformative effects that digital technology is having on fashion consumption. The internet has opened up new spaces of fashion consumption that are unprecedented in their levels of ubiquity, immersion, fluidity, and interactivity. Fashion spaces are increasingly portable, must follow us around, travel with us through time and space. The network effects made possible by the internet are enabling the creation of always-on, always connected consumer communities. Increasingly we are adrift *without* the internet, not with it. This is generating new ways of being in space where the absence of physical presence becomes second nature. Taken together, the collision between virtual and material fashion spaces requires a fundamental rethink about the role of fashion production, consumption, knowledge, and the laws of markets. In part the answers to these questions depend on how one conceptualizes the fashion sector. It is now widely acknowledged that fashion is rarely, if ever, simply a moment, or a point of purchase, or a reflection of supply and demand (Entwistle 2000, 2006a, 2010; Rantisi 2006, 2009, 2011; Scott 1996; Tokatli 2011, 2012a). Fashion has never been simply transactional, whether through a store, a catalogue, or a computer, and thus the impacts of the internet on the sector need to be evaluated in beyond-market terms. The most significant effects relate to shifts in the distribution and reproduction of fashion practices and knowledge rather than to quantifiable fluctuations in sales by volume, value, or distribution channel. Under this theorization the virtual, material, embodied, and performative dimensions of the fashion sector become more significant than its empirical size or weight as digital technologies enable new possibilities for producers *and* consumers to see, explore, perform, and practice fashion. The outcomes, while still uncertain and evolving, are unlikely to produce a complete liquefaction of more traditional forms of fashion retailing and consumption. Rather, emergent technologies are probing and perforating the boundaries between firms and consumers, production and consumption, object and image, the material and the virtual. The emergent geographies of electronically mediated consumption may challenge our conventional wisdoms about consumption, space, and practice. Further, such fashioned geographies are generating new ideas about mind, body, self, identity, and object. When biology and technology kiss, the results can be unpredictable, exciting, transformative. The internet is far more than a technology: it transforms the way we connect to the world and understand it. Together, the collision between virtual and material fashion spaces requires a fundamental retheorization about the agentive capacity of consumers and their abilities to disintermediate existing industry hierarchies and to create and reproduce fashion knowledge and markets. The emergent computer-consumer-commodity nexus is thus of fundamental importance in that it holds the potential to reshape our understandings of organizations, consumers, and the mechanisms through which fashion knowledge is generated and circulated. Taken together, it is argued that these shifts provide the basis for a new conceptual framework through which we can understand how fashion worlds are being transformed, enhanced, and reproduced in space and time—a new theory of fashion time, space, and knowledge. Traditionally, brand narratives were transmitted unidirectionally, from designer/producer to audience/consumer through carefully choreographed photography and film. The emergence of interactive and fast-paced interface mechanisms is changing both the pace and form of fashion dissemination. But because they have developed within and alongside existing cultural and economic forms and formats, embedding themselves within a preexisting order yet forging new pathways through existing systems of signification, the effects are relational and depositional rather than straightforwardly disruptive. When physical, material, and virtual spaces coexist, coalesce, and collide, old and new fashion practices merge, are twisted together, hybrid, and relational (Fuery 2009). The remediating effects of digital communications reveal both the enduring significance of conventional fashion media such as magazines and photography and their translation and transposition into more immediate, mobile, and associative digital formats, the two relational and convergent. Second, the chapter explores the potentially disintermediatory effects that the internet is having on markets and consumption and suggests that we may be living through a critical moment where consumer participation offers the very real promise of a more open, transparent, and democratic fashion system (Rocamora 2011). It seems certain that the internet has empowered fashion consumers, transformed them from recipients or interpreters of brand messages into active players, brand storytellers, or "authors of their own lives" (Holt 2002: 87) who have a much greater range and influence on fashion markets than they (or we) could previously have foreseen, and pulling them into the process of value creation itself. This requires a critical rethink about how the fashion system operates and a disentangling of the assumed connections between creation, sale, and use—a decoupling of production from consumption in the creation of value (Tokatli 2012b). New relations between brands and consumers are slicing through market laws and business models and, in the process, are redefining what we understand as creation, knowledge, space, and time. This offers a very powerful reframing of the economy that will generate new understandings of what constitutes the producer and the consumer grouped around the idea of the market as a forum, of economies as hybrid heterarchies, and of strategy as a process of continuous co-creation (Benkler 2006; von Hippel 2005). Finally, the chapter explores the transformative effects that digitally mediated technologies are having on *fashion consumption*. Fashion spaces can increasingly be portable, can follow us around, travel with us through time and space. In contrast to accounts that predict social disconnection and fear that new technologies will usher in a "weightless economy" of isolated agents whose chief encounters are with machines not people, this chapter argues precisely the opposite and suggests that the network effects made possible by the internet are enabling the creation of always-on, always-connected consumer communities. Increasingly it seems we are adrift *without* the internet, not with it: the isolation of our physical bodies does not indicate our state of connectedness but rather quite the opposite. The chapter begins with an empirical appraisal of the recent growth, scale, and reach of digital communications and commerce. This is set alongside early pronouncements during the dot-com boom-and-bust debacle that fashion simply wasn't suited to e-commerce given the very materiality of the commodity—people simply wouldn't buy clothes online, it was argued, and fashion was positioned as an undigitizable product, unlike, for example, money or music. The infamous case of the fashion e-commerce retailer Boo.com is used as an exemplar of such arguments. The next section offers a rather different take on what is, and was, possible in terms of the internet's effects on fashion, focusing on processes of remediation. Drawing on the cases of Burberry, SHOWstudio, and Boudicca, all acknowledged pioneers in operationalizing digital technologies in the fashion sector, the chapter argues for the powerful remediating effects of digital forms of communication and display, effects that reveal the sensory capacity, responsiveness, reach, scalability, and complexity of digitally mediated fashion sites. Third, the chapter questions to what extent digital technologies are enabling the disintermediation (or at least reconfiguration) of "trusted" fashion intermediaries and knowledge providers, resulting in a devolution of fashion authority away from traditional power brokers such as magazine editors and photographers toward a more diversified assemblage of participants, including bloggers and consumers (Rocamora 2011). Fourth, the chapter explores the ways in which emergent forms of fashion dissemination have the capacity to absorb the consumer with unprecedented multidimensionality, involving visuality, sociality, and interactivity at-a-distance. The chapter concludes with an evaluation of the significance of emergent forms of digitally mediated fashion creation, distribution, and representation for broader debates about production, consumption, knowledge, and markets.

Framing the recent history of internet fashion

The history of the effects of digitally mediated communication practices on fashion is both turbulent and little understood. Some fifteen years on from the media-hyped frenzy of the dot-com boom and the subsequent—and very precipitous—bust, there remains little critical analysis of the impact of new media technologies on the fashion sector. While e-business research has emerged as a key strand within the management strategy and marketing literature (see for example Armstrong and Hagel 1997; Kim et al. 2004; Liebowitz 2002; Porter 2001; Shapiro and Varian 1999; Tapscott and McQueen 1995), much of this work is remarkably insensitive to questions of geography and very little geographical scholarship has focused specifically on fashion and the internet. As with most innovations, the long-term and lasting implications of e-commerce were little understood at the outset of the boom and projections and impact analyses from a range of global consultancy organizations varied widely in their predictions (Deloitte and Touche 1999; Ernst and Young 1999). Following the dot-com boom and bust of the late 1990s, e-commerce activities have undoubtedly stabilized, become "normalized," and less erratic in their activities and impacts (Leyshon et al. 2005). Nonetheless, online business activity continues to grow apace. In crudely empirical terms it is undeniable that e-commerce has emerged as a significant economic force and it has been suggested that "everything we ever said about the internet is happening". Global e-commerce sales were predicted to grow by over 19 percent per year (Forrester Research 2011). The number of online shoppers globally increased by 40 percent in the two years 2006–2008, and the percentage of online consumers who made a purchase over the internet in 2009 reached 93 percent in South Korea, 89 percent in Japan, 75 percent in the UK, and 63 percent in the United States (Forrester Research 2011). There are geographic variations in the rates of e-commerce consumption activity, with the Asia-Pacific region, which has 40 percent of the world's online population (Forrester Research 2011), predicted to grow by an estimated 27.5 percent per year until 2015, overtaking Europe as the world leader in e-commerce sales by 2012 (Forrester 2011). While Asia is experiencing the fastest growth rates in internet consumption, the UK has the highest per capita online spending in the world, with 31 million consumers purchasing online in 2009 (Boston Consulting Group 2010). Online commerce in the UK is predicted to account for between 10 and 13 percent of GDP by 2015 (Boston Consulting Group 2010). In spite of difficult recessionary conditions and a marked slowdown in consumer spending on the UK high street since 2009, £4.3 billion worth of clothes were bought over the internet in 2010 (Mintel Market Research 2010), a 40 percent increase in sales over the previous year. High street fashion stores in the UK experienced a decline in sales of 14 percent during 2010 while online sales increased by 10 percent and online fashion retailing is argued to be the sector that outperformed all others in 2010 (IMRG 2011), figures that are echoed across Europe, the United States, and the Asia-Pacific region. Interest in the unfolding developments occurring in the sector continues as traditional online commerce activities converge with newer mobile (m-commerce), location-based services, social networking, and person-to-person communications (P2P), signaling a new phase of development. It is predicted that more consumers in the United States will access the internet via mobile devices than via their desktop or laptop computer by 2012 (Morgan Stanley 2010) and that mobile commerce in the United States will replicate the developments underway in Asia. In the UK, two-fifths of retailers aimed to launch a transactional mobile site during 2011 (New Media Age 2010), a significant strategic investment given that 51 percent of consumers engage in m-commerce and there are an estimated 23.3 million mobile phone users in the UK (IMRG 2011). Existing e-commerce business models are being adapted for mobiles and new applications developed exclusively for mobile devices. These are having significant effects on the landscape of fashion retailing and consumption: M and e-commerce are not simply adjuncts, additional distribution, or sales channels— they are transformative technologies that are founded on new forms of economic behavior and have the potential to radically alter the ways in which retailers and consumers interact and share knowledge and expertise.

What, then, does all this add up to, and more importantly, what might its broader theoretical implications be? Beyond the obvious empirical growth in e- and m-commerce, and in more substantive terms, I argue that the digital revolution of 1980s has had lasting, unforeseen, and very real material and cultural impacts on the fashion sector. In some senses it could be argued that the internet has now sunk into the business background and is no longer a crisply demarcated "new" sector. Technological changes often filter into our lives in subtle, barely noticeable ways and not in the abrupt or startling ways that are sometimes proclaimed (Negroponte 1995). But this very mundanity, the ways in which computer-mediated communication has "slouched toward the ordinary" (Herring 2004) could also be one source of its transformative power and potential. If we unfurl the recent history of internet fashion a fascinating narrative emerges. Early accounts of the fashion sector positioned it as one of the most dramatic victims of the dot-com bust, with Boo.com being hailed by CNN as the most spectacular dot-com catastrophe in history. Launched in 1999, the founders of Boo.com appeared on the front cover of Fortune magazine with an estimated valuation of $390 million, before their website had even launched. Boo.com spent $135 million of venture capital in 18 months before it was placed into receivership and subsequently liquidated in May 2000 (Malmsten et al. 2001). With such a spectacular burn rate the aftermath of the Boo.com collapse was calamitous: creditors were owed over £12 million and 400 staff were made redundant. Lying dormant in the graveyard of binary has-beens (Lanxon 2008), Boo.com stands as a stark and sorry reminder of the very real dangers of trying to sell clothes online, a tragic sectoral icon of what not to do. Part of the explanation for the early failures of the fashion industry to succeed online undoubtedly relates to structural rather than specifically sectoral factors, most notably the limited bandwidth speeds associated with dial-up modems, the limited stockholding and fulfillment capabilities of e-tailers at the turn of the millennium (Wrigley and Lowe 2002), and the unsustainable funding regimes based on venture capitalists speculation and heady overexcitement. Undoubtedly too, part of the problem facing the fashion sector in particular lay in the vision, design, functionality, and aesthetic capacity of its early websites. Those organizations that attempted to create transactional sites, either as pure players or hybrid "bricks and clicks" retailers (Burt and Sparks 2002; Koontz

2002; Marciniak and Bruce 2004), all too often transplanted the layout of their conventional stores onto the internet, with dismal results. The visual presence of the sites seemed secondary to the desire to have some sort of online presence, however rudimentary or dysfunctional that might be. It is hardly surprising, then, that early e-commerce fashion sites that were visually unappealing, technically incompetent, functionally frustrating, and lacking aesthetic pull or interactive capability failed to seduce. They were, at best, little more than additional distribution channels—computerized catalogues that neither enticed nor excited consumers. Compounded by media dot-bust theories that suggest that some sectors (notably fashion) simply aren't suited to the web online fashion, it seemed, faced an uphill struggle. However, as this chapter argues, a significant part of the problem for the initial failure of online fashion relates less to the market constraints of capitalization, bandwidth capacity, or website functionality and much more to the instrumental, transactional, and narrowly marketized view of the fashion sector that underpins this particular e-commerce narrative. For the new technical media that typified the dot-com boom were not external agents that came from nowhere to disrupt an unsuspecting culture, catching it unawares and rewriting the rules. They emerged from within existing cultural contexts and refashioned, or remediated, other media that were embedded in similar contexts (Boulter and Grusin 1999: 19). Technological changes are geographically and institutionally embedded and work within existing practices, processes, representations, and formats (Dodge and Kitchen 2005: 170). Internet fashion sites have an ability to coexist, mediate, link with, and augment a range of more familiar fashion spaces such as the store, fashion show, and street (Dodge and Kitchen 2005: 169). As such, digitally mediated technological assemblages are evolutionary rather than revolutionary and are enabling the generation of new relations and mediations between hitherto disparate and disconnected nodes and actors within fashion's global networks (Currah 2002; Kitchin 1998; Rantisi 2009; Scott 1996; Thrift 1996). It is to the analysis of the capacity of the internet to remediate prevailing lines of connection within networks of fashion production and consumption that the chapter now turns.

Remediation, convergence, and heterotopia

If we adopt a more expansive take on what and where the fashion industry is, and can be, a rather different version of events unfolds, one which reveals the remarkable capacity of the internet to act as a multilayered choreographic tool that shifts and shapes both old and new fashion spaces in unanticipated and innovative ways. Fashion spaces can be described as heterotopias that contradict, neutralize, invert, and reflect sets of relations (Quinn 2003: 55).

Fashion is signified in a whole array of different registers: a garment, a body, a shop, a catwalk, an idea, a photograph, a memory, a moving image on a screen or a street, as a blog, or an application on our phone. And the capacity of the internet to remediate conventional representations of fashion such as stores, runways, magazines, and photographs to reanimate images in time and space and to conjoin different ways of seeing and doing fashion offers some potent possibilities for how we understand fashion. It reveals how fashion is increasingly operating through a range of collectivities, hybrid representational networks that are both and at the same time physical and virtual, social and solitary, aesthetic and transactional. Virtual remediation is generating additive effects and riotous forms—creating bastard spaces if you will and raising some key questions about how we understand fashion knowledge, space, and the making of markets. The sensory capacity, responsiveness, reach, scalability, and complexity of digitally mediated fashion sites may be one of their key strengths. A range of examples will be drawn on here to show how digital technologies are revealing both continuities and ruptures in the spatial organization and reproduction of fashion. Fashion is being remediated as old and new forms of distribution and reproduction, merge and mingle so that the product, its marketing, reproduction, retailing, and web space are not separately imagined, designed, or commodified but, rather, are incorporated into a coalescent spatial landscape. Burberry is one of the clearest examples of an organization that understands how traditional branding, editorial placement, and retail display can intersect with and be enlivened by digital technologies (Tokatli 2012a). The organization currently allocates 60 percent of its marketing budget to digital media as part of its accelerating digitization strategy—more than triple the industry average and an indication of the challenges facing traditional print media (Drapers 2011). Their A/W10 advertising campaign, for example, used motion responsive imagery that allowed consumers to choose the view and perspective of the video campaign and its cast and products. It featured fourteen images and six interactive videos of the brand's collections and the onscreen imagery could be rotated, paused, and dragged by 180 degrees. At the opening of their Beijing flagship store in April 2011, digital technologies were an integral element of their real-life and multi-angle digital runway shows which combined the use of live models with animated footage, life-like holograms, music, and the ability to purchase items viewed in the show immediately prior to their arrival in-store (Whiteside 2011). This evolving business model reflects both the history and heritage of the brand but also connects customers through music, technology, emotion, and product—the co-creation of desire through remediation, the convergence of a range of extant formats such as the flagship store, the logo, and printed copy, and the development of new forms of fashion reproduction and dissemination including livestream and interactivity (Figure 7.1).

Figure 7.1 Burberry Flagship Store, Regent Street, London. © author's photograph.

Burberry offers consumers total access to their brand across any device, anywhere, anytime. Digitally mediated fashion is here not simply a new transactional opportunity but is an additional space for the production of desire, a storehouse of signs, images, connections, and significations for consumers, producers, and intermediaries to work through and with. It reveals the evolving relationships between fashion, image, science, and technology through which new vocabularies and visions come into being. If we build on this broader view of a remediated fashion system and rewind back to the depths of the dot.com bust in 2001, an altogether different "business" model was being born, based not simply on the sales or market capitalization capacity of transactional fashion websites but upon their capacity to remediate and recalibrate the existing relations between and across fashion's networks and to generate new orchestrations between a range of cultural forms and practices, including art, design, fashion, production, and consumption. For much of the twentieth century, the promotion, transmission, and dissemination of fashion occurred primarily through biannual fashion shows in key global fashion cities (New York, London, Paris, Milan) and via printed global media publications such as Vogue, Tatler, and Womens Wear Daily (Entwistle 2010). The dissemination of designer fashion was choreographed by a handful of highly influential fashion editors such as Suzy Menkes (*International Herald Tribune*) and Anna Wintour (*Vogue*) who acted as global style authorities, were closely aligned to networks of fashion designers, stylists, photographers, and journalists, and were able to control the selection, circulation, and dissemination of fashion via their curation of international media publications and the lucrative advertising revenues that accrued to global fashion magazines and their reputational and authorial capital. This alliance between a group of highly influential fashion intermediaries working out of global fashion capitals such as London and New York ensured that knowledge about emergent fashion trends, directions, and stories remained in the restricted and privileged hands of key actors who shaped which, how, and where fashion stories were distributed to the consuming public (Rantisi 2006). The twenty-first century has seen the emergence of new forms of fashion reproduction and representation that have broadened and deepened fashion's reach and range. In its earliest incarnation this devolution of fashion authority emerged in the form of a new breed of fashion publications from the early 1980s onward such as *Dazed & Confused*, *Visionnaire, i-D*, and *Purple*. Edited by (now) iconic creative directors including Terry Jones, Neville Brody, Dylan Jones, Nick Knight, and Peter Saville, the magazines were a consistent source of inspiration for street style, fashion, and the creative arts, and both documented and shaped emergent street fashions, acting as an early template for the style press. *i-D*, for example, began as a hand-stapled fanzine under conditions of "controlled chaos" and established a reputation for enrolling the consumer in the production of its content and as a training ground for emergent talent in the industry. The publications emphasized the role of smaller, independent designers, the subversive and critical possibilities raised by alternative versions of fashion, the issue-based role that fashion photography can assume and the connections and symbioses that are evident across a number of cultural activities such as fashion, film, music, and photography. More recently these publications have extended their content online, revealing the powerful market effects that emergent and pervasive media offered in terms of reconfiguring the relations between printed media, retailers, producers, and consumers. Jefferson Hack, the founder of *Dazed & Confused*, launched *Dazed Digital* in 2010 to deliver fashion, film, music, and online events live via the internet to a global audience and became the channel category leader the same year. Acknowledging the powerful potential that viewers offer in terms of disrupting conventional hierarchies and closed systems within the fashion industry, a new site, *Dazed Digital Reactivate*, was launched by Hack in 2010 with a view to opening up new possibilities for fashion reproduction and for a realignment of existing relations between producers and consumers. Hack saw the very real limitations of static printed media and the radical new possibilities opened up by digital forms of display and communication, arguing that "The old media model is a frozen moment in time; a monthly magazine, a seasonal trend— it's over… Digital culture is a constant stream. Either you adapt to it, or you are a dinosaur and you will die" (www.DazedDigital.com). Here we see how digital fashion spaces have perforated and scrambled the temporal and spatial conventions of fashion (biannual runway shows, monthly magazines), opening up ongoing moments of immediacy. The fashion photographer Nick Knight's website SHOWstudio.com was one of the earliest and still most imaginative and exciting pioneers of digital fashion. Argued by Suzy Menkes, to be "the crucible of techno developments in fashion" (Menkes 2009), SHOWstudio.com harnessed the potential of digital technologies to reinvent how fashion images are communicated, reproduced, and relayed, in turn transforming the ways in which we consume and experience fashion. Since its inception in 2001 the site has in many ways defined the ways in which fashion is presented on the internet and has combined film, fashion, photography, art, and music in innovative ways to deliver fashion live, as it happens to a global community of thousands of viewers, freed from anchorage to a particular time, space, event, or occurrence. From the outset SHOWstudio's content and direction was determined by its audience and participants rather than by advertisers, a business model that remediated the existing practices of fashion production, reproduction, and dissemination and demonstrated that the internet is in many ways the perfect medium for the active co-construction of fashion. Founded on the convergent capabilities of a range of media, including the runway, film, photography, and music, this virtual concept space revealed perhaps more than any other the astounding capacity of fashion to move across and between different media modalities and in different material and immaterial forms—breaking down the binary between the two, and between creator and consumer, here and there, now and then. Nick Knight discusses the transformative impact that digital technologies had on fashion and how he saw the potential many years before he launched SHOWstudio, arguing that "designers create clothes to be seen in movement, so it could be said that any still representation of a garment is a compromise of the designer's vision" (Knight 2009). In an industry famed for its opacity and secrecy, Knight sought to prise open this closed world and saw the radical and progressive potential of transparency, free reveal, and fashion democracy. The concept of "live" was a key foundation for SHOWstudio who treated the internet as a live broadcasting channel. The site is founded on the belief that showing the entire creative process—from conception to completion— is important for the artist, audience, and art itself (Shinkle 2008: 115). Nick Knight saw too the exciting possibilities that new media offered in terms of fashion display and performance, as a means to animate the fashion image that had for so long been reproduced as a frozen still, flat, two-dimensional, and locked into the immobile and static frame that is the magazine or editorial photograph. The possibilities opened up by digital fashion began for Nick Knight in 1986 when he was filming a fashion shoot for the designer Yohji Yamamoto: "I was photographing a very young Naomi (Campbell) and she was dancing to Prince in a bright red Yohji Yamamoto coat. I thought it was just so thrilling. It was a piece of contemporary theatre and it was seen by no more than around seven people" (Knight 2009). Commenting on popular media representations of fashion, Knight argued that the industry has been trivialized, rarefied, and stereotyped, its potential as both a cultural and a commercial form underplayed. Just over a decade on, it is clear that SHOWstudio.com had a significant impact on the ways and spaces in which fashion is projected and reproduced. With an online archive detailing over 250 projects and monthly hits in excess of 120,000 viewers the range and reach of SHOWstudio is significant, as is its transformative impact on broader questions about fashion creation, authorship, and collaboration. Two particular projects are explored here in an attempt to sketch out the powerful remediating impacts that the digitally mediated communication is having on fashion. In the first example, called Virtual Accessories[1], we see how SHOWstudio actively questions corporate branding, creativity, and the power of the logo. SHOWstudio collaborated with the digital artist Daniel Brown to explore what fashion would look like without its logo and to create a virtual space in which viewers can imagine and experience the magical alchemy of a brand. Brown selected signature garments from four iconic global brands (Balenciaga, Marc Jacobs, Missoni, and Prada) and transformed stills of the clothes into interactive, three-dimensional designs overlain with interpretive sounds and the key symbolic referents of each brand's advertising campaign for Spring/Summer 2002.[2] The result is a unique, personal, and viewer-led experience of fashion where there is no product and no logo, but a layered set of sensory signifiers that capture what a brand is and what it symbolizes to a consumer. "As you introduce the cursor into the dark screen that opens Interactive 1, rays of textured colour fan out into star shapes, revealing wave-like printed patterns that could only belong to Missoni" (Martin 2002). Interactive images on computer screens can be beautiful, critical, passionate, provocative, and immersive. They extend the range and reach of designers and brands to consumers while simultaneously enabling the viewer to take an active role in the how a design or logo is reproduced, how and why it speaks to its audience, and how its representation can be curated, customized, challenged in ways that the original designer may not have anticipated. The second example of the way in which SHOWstudio harnessed the revolutionary power of the web to reframe and remediate fashion was the live streaming in 2009 of Alexander McQueen's final show before his death. McQueen is widely acknowledged as one of the most spectacular and provocative designers of the contemporary era and his catwalk shows have been legendary spectacles in the fashion world (Knox 2010). His collaboration with Nick Knight on the live streaming on SHOWstudio of the Plato's Atlantis collection has been seen as a pivotal moment in fashion history when "the rules of the game changed all over again" (Simpson 2009). Described as "the most dramatic revolution in 21st-century fashion" (Menkes 2009), this was the first runway show to have been streamed live on the internet from Fashion Week and gave industry outsiders across the world real-time access to a catwalk that had previously been the exclusive preserve of fashion's elite. The online broadcast captured the live spectacle of a McQueen fashion show and relayed it in real-time around the world. McQueen clearly saw the participatory potential of live online broadcasting and, through his collaboration with SHOWstudio, fulfilled his desire to be seen and heard rather than edited and reported. In suitably hyperbolic terms McQueen argued that:

> Every year, buyers and the press come to see the spectacle of my show. But I want to generate something else, something for a wider audience—for people…who don't have a seat at the show.… It'll be like live theatre—at home. The audience at home is actually going to see more than the guests at the show.… This is the birth of a new dawn. There is no way back for me now. I am going to take you on journeys you've never dreamed were possible. (McQueen, in Simpson 2009)

This venture undoubtedly led the way for the new generation of live streaming from the catwalk: by Autumn/Winter 2010 every major designer at every international fashion week streamed their shows live online. A second highly innovative fashion organization is Boudicca, based in Bethnal Green in London. Much of their work deals with the effects of new technology on human interaction. Like Lucy Orta and Vexed they use fashion to make sociopolitical statements. They make a concerted effort to integrate digital technologies into their work to keep it alive and have created a rich body of short films and videos to accompany their collections and exhibitions. This visual media work reinforces their creative ideas and reference the long and complex lineage that many of their designs share (author's interview 2013). As Broach argued:

> The product is not enough for us. It's the emotional potential of the interaction between the garment and the person that matters. Digital technology is our road towards the garment and away from it. Design isn't just product, it also an environment.… The process of making clothes is like another form of expression altogether, like a film or book, it all adds up. They all become part of the design. (author's interview 2013)

Boudicca's website reveals how digital media can be both visual and auditory, immersive and powerful—the images, music, and rich historical details are provocative and moving, taking the viewer far beyond the screen in space and time.[3] As with clothes, so too with the creation of a perfume, or in the case of

Wode, an anti-perfume. The fragrance took five years to produce in collaboration with scent designer Sissel Tolaas (who also worked with SHOWstudio on their fragrance "Violence") and Escentric Molecules. The fragrance is a blend of rare oils such as black hemlock and raw opium derived from wode, the dark blue extract used by ancient Britons to paint themselves with tribal markings as they went into battle. The original fragrance was produced in a spray can, highly resonant of graffiti as contemporary war paint. When the perfume is sprayed a blue mist appears on the skin that slowly fades leaving just the scent behind. Constantly probing the boundaries between different media, the radical perfume was visualized in a film in which the blue paint suddenly appears on the model's neck, like blood or poison[4] The fragrance "does something never done before and is applied in a new way." It also wasn't for sale, as Brian Kirkby argues "it will not follow the conventional route of a fragrance. And anyway it would be a huge cliché for us to do a fragrance as we all know it's a well-trodden path. We see it more as art" (Carter 2012).

As the front image to this book from the Stanley Picker Exhibition *The Liquid Game* demonstrates so potently, Boudicca's fearlessly uncompromising working methods are both meticulously considered and emotionally charged. The duo's richly researched work takes direct reference from cultural and political history, science and technology, nature and landscape, exploring the tailored silhouette while simultaneously exploiting a multitude of new disciplines—including 3D printing, processing, coding, film, and chrono photography—in an effort to examine, redefine, deconstruct, and atomize fashion and identity. Boudicca's *Liquid Game* is a wonderfully provocative audio–visual installation that probes the boundaries between art, fashion, design, technology, and corporeality—it provokes a sensory and bodily response in the viewer and emphasizes the transformative effects of technology. As with all of Boudicca's work, the aim is to "cause collision and rupture in known landscapes in order to create upheaval," describing their practice as "a hunt for the invisible…a casting up of all possibilities, experiments, history, identity, design, landscape, sound, body, breath, narrative."[5]

Through their collaborations with a range of artists, architects, photographers, and musicians, Boudicca has constantly questioned and extended their practice in a constant process of exploration and critique. Boudicca is constantly reflecting and questioning conventional practice and method and, latterly, has used digital media in particular to push the boundaries of existing modes of representation and display. Together these examples of Burberry, SHOWstudio, Boudicca, and the British youth-fashion style press show how fashion media can be simultaneously transactional, performative, interactive, and critical; they can offer both sensory seduction and critical political commentary and work on a number of layers as complex political, creative, visual, commercial, and ideological spaces. SHOWstudio and Boudicca demonstrate how fashion can be experienced in digital as well as physical space, virtually as well as materially, pointing to an imaginative, expansive, and future-oriented sense of experience. Digitalization has revolutionized the way fashion is designed, produced, and consumed. The rise of computing in the late twentieth century entailed a geographical separation of material and digital practice; fashion design, production and reproduction techniques have been partnered with the internet and new communication environments online that allow many industries, including the fashion industry, to evolve in new ways (Braddock Clarke and Harris 2012). As Bradley Quinn (2002) has suggested, fashion and technology are a perfect match; both give each other a wider frame of reference and room to discover new horizons. Technology and its rapid progression allow fashion's ever-evolving aesthetics to explore new terrain and create unseen design possibilities. Fashion and its technological abilities could allow fashion to have intelligence of its own; technology can be wearable as well as fashionable (Quinn 2002). This union between the two evolving industries has not only meant a revolution in fashion design and production but has also created unimagined possibilities in the field of technology. The integration of computing and computer parts into wearable fashion looks sets to change the future of clothing and fashion production. The potential convergence between fashion and technology is readily apparent, as the examples in this chapter testify; this convergence has the potential to enable the materialization of ideas and inspirations that past production modes could not produce (Quinn 2012). Future fashion garments could dramatically change the experience of wearing clothing. Adding a function beyond the original purpose of dress by integrating high-tech appliances to the clothing could unravel new purposes for wearables: reactive fashion products could be used for communication, protecting the body or empowering sensory abilities (Zhang and Benedetto 2010). Here we see how "virtuality has a more complex set of meanings which includes the practice of imagining urban space, the use of technology to simulate real spaces and a complex set of transactions in time and space" (Latham et al. 2009: 12). Far from acting simply as an additional distribution channel, we see how the web can act as a means of propagating and structuring creativity, reconfiguring existing nodes of knowledge and influence, offering shortcuts to inspiration, and creating highly accessible sensory worlds, fluid environments that entice and captivate, scrambling space and time in all sorts of powerful ways.

Disintermediation, co-creative communities, and heterarchy

Linked to the above, the internet is enabling the disintermediation (or at least reconfiguration) of "trusted" fashion intermediaries and knowledge providers and is reworking the relationships between producers, the media, and consumers.

This potential impact of the internet on business practices was acknowledged over twenty years ago by a number of management scholars and strategists. According to Malone et al.'s (1987) electronic market hypothesis, the growth of retail-focused electronic markets would bring about a reduction in the costs of economic coordination, resulting in a decline in the importance of hierarchies in favor of market coordination (see too Drucker 1993; Evans and Wurster 2000; Tapscott and McQueen 1995). The internet was seen to have the potential to disrupt and reconfigure established industrial networks and to shift the balance of power from market incumbents to relatively new market entrants (French et al. 2004). The emergence of the internet, and the growth of software devices such as search engines and intelligent agents, which purposely scan internet databases for specific types of information, makes it possible for consumers to conduct more effective searches of fashion markets and trends than before, at higher speed and at lower cost. This has the potential to greatly extend market spaces beyond their existing geographical boundaries and to enable consumers to access fashion knowledge that was hitherto concealed by corporations who controlled supply and distribution chains. For emergent media forms are not simply about increasing speed and reducing cost but are about shifts in the distribution of intelligence (Negroponte 1995). These processes of disintermediation, re-spatialization, and re-temporalization form part of the basis for claims that digitally mediated technologies will empower consumers by undermining the hold of large organizations over the production and distribution of fashion and its knowledge, creating heterarchies of relation where producers and consumers are more closely aligned in terms of knowledge, power, and authority. Such disintermediated networks offer powerful opportunities for the reconfiguration of the competitive bases and contestability of markets (French et al. 2004). There are a number of means through which digital technologies have enrolled the consumer in the production and dissemination of fashion knowledge. Based on Web 2.0, 3.0 and 4.0 capabilities, a range of social media practices such as social networking sites and collaborative projects such as wikis have enhanced and enabled consumer involvement in fashion creation and reproduction (Kaplan and Haenlein 2010). Two particular, and rather different, examples are drawn on here: crowdsourcing and user-generated content via blogging. Crowdsourcing as a concept was first coined by Jeff Howe in 2006 in a *Wired Magazine* article describing the process whereby the talent of the many (the crowd) can be leveraged to generate knowledges, products, capacities, and capabilities that were formerly the preserve of a specialized few (Howe 2009). Crowdsourcing depends on the capacity of the internet to create distanciated networks or communities of consumer producers who together collaborate, share, remix, fine-tune, and redesign products and processes. Crowdsourcing is actively being developed as an organizational strategy that harnesses the creative potential of consumer-producer communities to drive innovation and creativity (Corcoran 2010). The point about crowdsourcing is that it is a business-led strategy, an attempt by organizations to use digital capabilities to enroll the collective capacities of consumers into the creation, collation, and representation of their brand stories. Burberry's "Art of the Trench" project, for example, shifts the creative input from stylists, professional photographers, and editors to consumers who are sharing authorship for the many ways in which the iconic trench coat can be worn, displayed, performed. Users are invited to upload photographs of them wearing their Burberry trenchcoat which then appear on the official Burberry website—a perfect illustration of how organizations are crowdsourcing innovation and using the creative energies of their consumers to steer their corporate branding and marketing campaigns. Quite whether this represents a flattening of fashion's long-established authorial hierarchies and the emergence of a new set of relations between brands and consumers, or is simply another means through which capital can exploit consumer labor power in order to extract additional value remains to be seen. An arguably more powerful set of developments are underway that depend less on the corporate outsourcing of intelligence through crowdsourcing and more on disintermediating effects of social media operating outside but alongside professional organizational routines and practices. In a number of ways it can be argued that digital developments have given voice, knowledge, and power to larger and more diverse consumer groups, many of whom lacked any sense of authority or persuasion under the conventional hierarchical fashion system with its high barriers to entry and exclusionary practices. With the rise of social media and user-generated content such as blogs, the balance of power between fashion producers/intermediaries and consumers in terms of who shapes brand perception, fashion knowledge appears to be shifting. This is particularly significant because the fashion industry has long faced the threat of instability over the creation and dissemination of its knowledge. In spite of attempts by large organizations to control and orchestrate access to commodity and market knowledge, fashion has always been a difficult industry to govern, calculate, predict, or order because it requires change, pace, and unpredictability. This lack of brand certitude offers opportunities for consumers to subvert and reinterpret brand and trend messages and project their own dreams, desires, wishes, and identities on fashion's surfaces and spaces. The instantaneous digital global relay of fashion concepts across unbounded geographic spaces further flattens established hierarchies of access to knowledge. Now more than ever, communal consumer conversations have the capacity and critical mass to effectively challenge the assumed power of the producer and consumers are relying less on the authority of conventional branding and advertising campaigns for their consumption knowledge (Howe 2009). The powerful network effects made possible by the internet has enabled consumers to reach out into fashion worlds faster, further, and deeper than ever before and to redefine how and where fashion knowledge is created and disseminated to the point where it has been argued that the technologies of production are now increasingly in the hands, and minds, of consumers (Potts et al. 2008: 20). Consumers are able to connect to one another via digitally mediated communications in real time, all the time; physically absent from one another yet digitally connected. This ability to connect with others without co-presence is a powerful method of harnessing member-generated value in fashion consumption. It reveals the ability to mobilize strangers and to weave co-present interactions, distanciated connections, and mediated communications in a seamless web (Licoppe 2004: 135). And it suggests that people everywhere can participate not only in self-expression and entertainment, but in new ways of producing knowledge that is scaled up from the street, library, or bedroom to population-wide distributed networks (Potts et al. 2000: 20; Surowiecki 2005). Although still derived from individual actions that may be deemed insignificant in isolation, the emergence of social and technological consumer-to-consumer and consumer-to-producer networks generate forms of innovation that may be of large scale significance in shaping behavior (Howe 2009; Ritzer and Jurgenson 2010; Shirky 2009, 2010; von Hippel 2007). This ability for consumers to short-circuit the formerly concealed suite of corporate sales and marketing tactics is enabling new levels of transparency where there is less scope for hype and spin over pricing structures, the authority of the brand, the meaning of value, and conditions of production and distribution. This delayering of "trusted" experts may significantly empower consumers and offers the possibility at least for new forms of consumer agency and self-determination, enabling them to venture beyond the bounds of organizational intentionality. Such new technological means of doing fashion are resulting in a new blurring between firms, consumers, and the creative process to produce what might be described as a hybrid "mash culture," an accelerating "connective mutation" of cycles of production, consumption, and reproduction as consumers break into formerly closed systems and processes (Beer and Burrows 2010). As technological architectures shift from centralized providers to more personalized forms of collective intelligence, the possibilities arise for more democratic forms of fashion knowledge, distribution, and reproduction. Enhanced feedback loops enable new forms of active co-construction between producers and consumers and allow new forms of intelligibility to emerge on the back of active negotiation (Thrift 2011: 10). The example of fashion blogging is used to illustrate this broader conceptual intervention and to point to its limits. Blogs are internet sites where individuals post their thoughts, ideas, and inspirations online in an unedited and spontaneous style. Blogs began at the turn of the millennium and have grown to become a significant force in the field of fashion, a new means through which individuals can sift and sort through vast amounts of fashion information that they filter and distil into personally curated internet posts. It is estimated that there were 2 million fashion and shopping-related blogs in 2010 (Technorati Inc 2010). Fashion blogs can be broadly divided into corporate and independent blogs (Rocamora 2011). The former represents an institutional or organizational "voice," either a magazine (www.vogue.co.uk/blog; http://www.wwd.com/fashion-blogs/fashion) or a fashion brand such as Louis Vuitton (http://www.nowness.com/). The latter are personally curated postings, usually including photographs, that offer commentaries on fashion trends and directions. The most influential fashion blogs include Scott Schuman's *thesartorialist.blogspot.com*, which receives over 13 million views per month (Amed 2011) and is argued by *Time Magazine* to be one of the most important influences on contemporary design, London-based Suzie Lau's *stylebubble.typepad.com*, and Tavi Gevinson's blog *thestylerookie. com* which is part mood-board, part historical montage, part the curious musings of a quirky teenager and, increasingly, part of the front-row fashion media. Now 20, Tavi began writing her blog when she was 12 and is now regularly seated on the front row at Fashion Week, joining the rank and file fashion "A list" models, editors, and journalists, a coveted position where proximity to the front signifies seniority or authority—a clear spatial manifestation of the politics of power at play in the fashion world. That Gevinson's blog receives almost as many monthly hits as *Teen Vogue* illustrates what a significant force in the field of fashion blogs have become. Other notable fashion blogs that continue to appear on league tables include *jakandjil.com*, *thecherryblossomgirl.com*, *refinery29. com*, and *gofugyourself* (Blogrank 2010).[6] It is these independent or personal fashion blogs that have the potential to reshape the power relations in the industry. With minimal barriers to entry, the practice of blogging has enabled industry outsiders who may have no professional affiliation nor any formal qualifications to establish a credible, authorial voice that can stand alongside established fashion intermediaries such as editors and stylists and thus break into formerly closed and exclusionary worlds with speed and reach, shattering established hierarchies and modes of knowledge circulation. Bloggers represent a new form of fashion intermediary, one that is curiously positioned between insider and outsider, expert and lay-person. The disintermediatory power of blogging lies in its capacity for speed and immediacy, characteristics that conventional printed media simply can't compete with (Walker Rettberg 2008). Blogging has undoubtedly increased the speed and pace of fashion. A blogger can, for example, watch a fashion show and begin blogging immediately, creating conversations about brands or trends that can be watched, commented upon, and distributed in real time. The space and time between reader and author is reduced, removed even, and dense relational feedback loops and conversations can be developed without the need for institutional mediation or editorial curation. As a result fashion bloggers have the capacity to reappropriate and translate the intention of editors, brands, and marketeers. In this sense bloggers have the potential to assail the elitist world of fashion through transmitting their personal interpretations of fashion to audiences far and wide in geographical reach. Acting as new fashion mediators, bloggers can offer a more critical and democratic take on fashion, potentially challenging the exclusive hierarchical control that editorial elites formerly enjoyed over the creation and distribution of fashion. This shift in the long-held power relations that underpin the fashion system is well explained by Peterson, who argues that "viewers, readers, interpreters and consumers (are) producing, constructing, deconstructing and retrofitting ideas and objects to suit their individual wants and needs … (this) necessarily dispenses from power those who produce content for and edit major fashion publications." (Pederson 2011: 3). In other respects, however, there are signs that the boundaries between professional and non-professional blogs are blurring, which is in turn raising questions about their position as new intermediaries within the fashion system. As brands have quickly realized, being mentioned by a respected blog that has the potential to go viral can have significant income-generating impacts for business. The temptation here, for both brand and blogger, is to develop a more collaborative and advertorial relationship in which the blogger receives gifts, samples, or revenue in return for featuring a brand or having their copy checked by the sponsoring organization or their PR firm. In an industry where reporters and critics depend so heavily on the financial interests of those who control it for access, it is little surprise that many independent bloggers turn to large advertising campaigns or corporate "sponsorship" in order to gain entry into this formerly closed world, not least in order to ensure their economic security. Scott Schuman, the blogger who writes for the Sartorialist, for example, understood the importance of strategically aligning himself with the mainstream fashion media from the outset and wrote for GQ and Style.com alongside the Sartorialist, in addition to shooting and writing campaigns for Burberry and Kiehls. The vast majority of Schuman's income is now derived from advertising revenue from his blog. As the number of bloggers that become incorporated into the professional world of fashion and derive income from their branding messages or via advertising revenue increases, there are early indications at least that blogging may be undergoing a process of professionalization. The acquisition by Conde Nast of NOWMANIFEST.com that hosts personal style blogs including BryanBoy and Anna Dello Russo suggests a new phase in the evolution of personal style blogs such as BryanBoy, who began as independent outsiders and are now owned by one of the largest media companies in the world. At the very least the border between editorial, personal, and advertising content is becoming increasingly difficult to define and the relationship between individual bloggers and commercial actors is becoming both more blurred and more opaque. It is possible to argue that these developments are part of a new technological and social democracy that allows for more public deliberation on products and more input into their design. Blogging has undoubtedly transformed the relationships between designers, editors, magazines, shows, and consumers, enabling the latter to actively and rapidly represent, interpret, and modify fashion consumption.

Fashion bloggers are becoming increasingly important in defining innovation and can be seen as a mechanism for redistributing fashion knowledge and democratizing fashion via open-source branding (Neff and Stark 2002; Prahalad and Ramaswamy 2004). Bloggers have "altered the language, delivery methods and hierarchically ordered designations of those who could be truthfully considered as producers versus those considered mere consumers" (Pederson 2011: 3). These emergent forms of fuzzy consumer power enable consumers to be active producers not simply in the consumption of things but in the creation of worlds limited only by the imagination. Craft consumers (Campbell 2005), producers (Bruns 2005), and prosumers (producer-consumers) (Beer and Burrows 2010; Ritzer and Jurgenson 2010) engage with the market as a means of creative self-expression and play an active role in the production of contemporary fashion as part of a broader and more significant shift toward participatory web cultures founded upon user participation and user-generated content (Beer and Burrows 2010: 6). In this way bloggers are challenging the conventional wisdom that the spheres of production and consumption are separate (Firat and Venkatesh 1995) and raise the possibility for innovative forms of participatory engagement. In turn it could be argued that this vision of a permanently heterarchic, emergent, and interactive economy may become a primary means through which the fashion system is reproduced—an architecture of participation if you will. Through the accelerated and heterogeneous forum of the internet we are seeing the emergence of new relations between markets, fashion, and everyday lives, relations that are producing new cartographies of fashion knowledge and new geographies of fashion consumption that provide significant insights into the role of consumer agency in the fashion system and are suggestive of an emergent fashion democracy.

Real time, all the time: Immediacy, hypermediacy, and mobility

Third, and connected to the above, the internet is raising important new possibilities in terms of mobility, temporality, and subjectivity. The internet has opened up new spaces of consumption that are unprecedented in their levels of ubiquity, immersion, fluidity, and interactivity (Currah 2002; Kenney and Curry 2001; Zook 2000). Emergent forms of pervasive media are available anytime, anywhere, and are immersive and interwoven into our everyday lives. The internet has the capacity to absorb the subject with unprecedented multidimensionality, involving visuality, sociality, interactivity at-a-distance: immersive environments that communicate with all of our senses all at the same time, all of the time: emotional performances. Increasingly it seems that the "human body and digital information need to be thought of in conjunction with one another, and indeed, one might say, quite literally as a conjunction: a labile, processual and contingent entity" (Boothroyd 2009: 334). Technology is as much an architect of our passions and preferences as it is about our solitudes (Turkle 2008: 29). Again we can look to any number of organizational examples that demonstrate new levels of producer-consumer fluidity, openness and mobility. New levels of media literacy and the technological competence of consumers demand that the future fashion industry be digitally integrated into people's lives wherever (and whenever) they are. Net-a-Porter is a good illustration of how the contemporary consumer moves in multiple ways and across a number of modes. Consumers with no time or inclination to go out shopping or who are not geographically proximate to design stores can still participate whenever and wherever they choose. The site offers so much more than "just shopping" and includes an online magazine, trend guides, notes, online boutiques that enable consumers to "shop the catwalk by phone," and a pop-up, augmented reality-interactive "shop" called *Window Shop* that enables customers to scan photographs of products on the wall using an image-recognition app on their phone or tablet and purchase them for next-day delivery. By any conventional reckoning this is proving to be a successful business model: 3 million women log on to Net-a-Porter each month, of whom 10,000 are new customers and the average order price is £500. Turnover has increased by 67 percent year on year for the ten years it has been running and currently stands at £120 million with a company valuation of £350 m. The new head office mirrors the company ethos, with screens throughout the slick interior so that everyone working there can see what is selling in real time (Retail Week 2011a). In an ironic twist of fate the HQ is located above London's Westfield Centre where it floats whitely over Europe's largest mall which increasingly looks like a monument to old-fashioned walk-in and browse shopping. Part of the success of Net-a-Porter undeniably relates to precision buying and editing of stock. But the founder, Natalie Massenet, attributes at least 5 percent of the company's sales to the 400 independent bloggers who drive traffic and increase sales, further evidence of how old and new forms of media representation are refashioning one another as content flows across multiple platforms and networks, bleeding into one another through the process of remediation. The company has also recently introduced a new tool that allows consumers to see exactly what other consumers are buying and from where. This marks a dramatic departure from the secrecy and opacity of corporate sales data in the conventional retail world and simultaneously fosters a sense of a community among consumers and offers enormously rich market intelligence for marketers and fashion buyers (Figure 7.2).

ASOS (As Seen on Screen) is another example of the growing power and presence of e- and m-commerce. Founded in 2000 the company offers 36,000 fashion products, employs 570 people, has 13 million unique visitors every month

Figure 7.2 Net-a-Porter meets DKNY, London, 2014. © author's photograph.

(de Teliga 2011) of which 700,000 visits are via mobile devices and wants to be "as ubiquitous as possible" (Hart 2010). Revenue grew by 35 percent in the fiscal year 2010 to reach £223 million and pre-tax profits increased by 44 percent to £20.3 million (Boston Consulting Group 2010). International sales increased by 142 percent to £140 million, accounting for 43 percent of ASOS' total (Retail Week

2011). As the UK's biggest online retailer, with separate sites in the United States, Germany, France, and Australia, this internet-only model of retailing appeals to customer's demands for 24 hour, 7 days per week hassle-free shopping, with free delivery and returns, and a dedicated marketplace where shoppers can browse hundreds of small independent boutiques, shop for ethically sourced garments in the Green Room, and sell their unwanted garments, a strategy that replicates online auction sites such as Ebay. ASOS rely on social media, including a Twitter customer-help line and multiple Tumblr, Facebook, and Pinterest accounts to build social consumer communities. ASOS co-founder draws on explicitly geographical metaphors to describe the concept: "Imagine putting a roof over Oxford Street...ASOS is Oxford Street, Net-a-Porter is Bond Street" (de Teliga 2011). ASOS has pioneered a number of technological innovations including "Catwalk view," first introduced in 2006 and now a defining feature associated with the website. Catwalk view attaches life to clothing that a mere photograph is unable to do. The feature advises the customer of the movement of the garment, allowing better assessment of fit, color, and fabric and helps visualize how the apparel would look on. Not only does this feature increase purchase intent but also it contributes to the hedonic experiential nature of online consumption.

Digitally mediated retailing is arguably bringing about transformative shifts in the spaces, times, and practices of fashion consumption. It has expanded the boundaries between how, when, and where we consume, and has reduced the search and transaction costs associated with fashion consumption and the acquisition of commodity knowledge by harnessing the mutually constitutive strategies of generating immediacy and vastly expanding fashion's range and reach. The internet has brought new fashion worlds into the homes, screens, and minds of consumers, creating imaginative possibilities and provoking us to reflect on who we are and who we would like to be. The screen or the surface becomes a gateway into new and multiple spaces and interface design, just as store design or shop window display did before it. These new ways of seeing, feeling, looking, and doing fashion are increasingly reliant on digitally enabled communication practices that are mediated via the interface and architecture of the screen (computer monitor, mobile phone, tablet, or television). The ubiquitous (and increasingly mobile) screen is a key means through which fashion consumption is shaped, transmitted, called forth. The fashion landscape is shifting so quickly that monitoring the monitor may represent an important means of keeping up to speed. New fashion worlds have literally been brought to life through the internet and an emergent online–offline choreography is offering huge potentiality for reconfiguring ways of practicing and performing fashion. Virtual spaces can be every bit as vibrant as physical ones and the internet has revealed a number of ways in which fashion can assume and inhabit unanticipated forms and formats. The historical binary divide between active, agentive, communicative humans, and passive, silent, fixed objects looks increasingly untenable as we move into an era saturated with the "technological unconscious" (Clough 2000; Thrift 2005). This is in turn redefining the relations between people and objects as "constituent elements of a mutually constitutive moving 'frame' which is not really a frame at all but more of a fabric that is constantly being spun over and over again" (Thrift 2011: 7).

Reflections

The chapter concludes with an evaluation of the significance of emergent forms of digitally mediated fashion creation, distribution, and representation for broader debates about production, consumption, and the relations between the two. As Elizabeth Wilson argued so well, "Fashion is as much a part of the dream world of capitalism as its economy" (Wilson 1985: 14).

Together, these reflections offer the possibility at least for a theory of fashion for the contemporary era. First, the developments discussed above demand that we recalibrate our understandings of fashion practice and process, space and place. Certainly the bipolar narratives that dominated early e-commerce literature (physical versus virtual, clicks versus bricks, material versus immaterial) seem singularly unhelpful in understanding the complex spatialities and temporalities at work when digital technologies and fashion collide (French et al. 2004). Rather, "people and things are located within complex networks of mobilities, interactions, and transactions that bind them together across scales…creating multiple, simultaneous but partial time-space configurations that are at once 'local' and 'beyond'" (Dodge and Kitchen 2005: 174). Electronic space interweaves and is intertwined with the spaces and places of our physical worlds; practices, processes, and products cannot be isolated from one another whether online or off-line; printed and digitally mediated formats are co-connected, relational, and reveal mutual influence. Old and new modes of doing fashion rebound on one another, are recursively connected—convergent even—and are challenging and disrupting conventional dualisms about here and there, now and then, surface and substance, object and subject. The precise impact of the internet on fashion's geographies and practices is complex and still evolving, and will continue to be in part shaped by the spatial configuration of existing value chains, power relations, and network structures by virtue of the remediation effects at work. In some respects the developments discussed above may be reinforcing existing geographies of global fashion and throwing fashion's world cities such as London, New York, Paris, and Milan into yet sharper relief. And yet in other important respects we may well be seeing the opening up of new fashion spaces and actors that previously didn't figure on fashion's map. There is certainly evidence that the digitally mediated developments discussed here may be reworking and decentering the geographies of fashion, displacing the authority of traditional experts. The disintermediation that has been made possible through new mechanisms of transmission such as personal blogs and livestream suggests a flattening of fashion's long-established hierarchies, a new kind of virality that is rhizome-like in its spread and reach. The relationship between the consumer and the fashion industry is fundamentally changing. The recasting of the relations between old and new forms of fashion representation is generating new ways of making markets, new worlds of possibility that require that we reformulate what is understood as innovation, knowledge, and expertise. The transformations outlined above suggest new affordances based not on time-worn hierarchies and sectoral power asymmetries but on new and more democratic modes of doing and seeing fashion that together are reconfiguring the power bases of the fashion system in what may be only the beginning of a broader enfolding of consumers into the networked process of innovation (Benkler 2006). Finally, the developments discussed here raise a number of more substantive questions about production, consumption, power, space, and the reproduction of markets. Quite how this will unfold and take shape remains uncertain and there are a number of possible readings about the longer-term implications of digitally mediated communications on the fashion sector. The depressing interpretation is that crowdsourcing, livestreaming, and active enrollment of consumers into the creation of brand messages is little more than capitalism's latest tactic to co-opt the consumer in the relentless pursuit of surplus value creation. Is this simply a new means of doing business whereby organizations actively put the consumer to work (Tapscott and Williams 1996), a ratcheting up of long-held forms of exploitation, but at the places of consumption rather than production? The professionalization of personal style blogs is one example of such occurrence. While this is a possibility I would like to think that the developments discussed here really do offer transformative possibilities for fashion and its participatory politics, possibilities founded upon new modes of knowledge generation and circulation and new recursive links between production and consumption which, together, might form the basis for a new, more transparent, dynamic, and participatory industry. In combination, the processes of remediation, convergence, disintermediation, and hyperarchy are transforming the fashion landscape. The tendencies at work here signal both disruption and disturbance to the conventional power relations that structure fashion. They suggest the emergence of new, hybrid geographies in which certain distance-transcending activities can be enacted while simultaneously being embedded in the performer's positionality in material space (Graham 2011: 10). And they reveal new sorts of temporality within fashion characterized by immediacy, virality, and more interactive forms of engagement. Together these developments point to exciting times ahead in the practice and theory of fashion and its geographies. Finally I have demonstrated how we are living through exciting moments of new understanding and possibility. These findings offer us something that breaks with conventional wisdom and implies that we need to find new languages and syntaxes to talk about fashion technologies in ways that don't follow the standard script. In theoretical terms we have great opportunities to rework our understandings of embodiment and subjectivity through the collapse of distinctions between body, commodity, and technology. Above all there can be no end to fashion's geographies for they are continually being re-enacted, replayed, relayed anew. We increasingly inhabit multiple spaces whose interplays and relationalities are throwing up fascinating questions about business models, market, and consumption. This strikes me as a great way to debate the shape and form that technology, fashion, and space will interweave and evolve in the future.

Notes

1 The examples drawn upon in the discussion can be explored further on the SHOWstudio website.

2 http://showstudio.com/projects/vac/vac_start.html

3 http://www.essays.boudiccacouture.com/Presentation01.html

4 http://www.wode.platform13.com/

5 http://www.stanleypickergallery.org/participation/projects-and-events/listen-online-poetry-inspired-by-boudicca-the-liquid-game

6 There are a number of publications that rank the influence of blogging sites according to a range of metrics, including RSS subscribers, unique monthly visitors, number of incoming links and the Alexa rank. See Blog Rank 2010; Net-a-Porter's The Blog Power List 2010; Top Sites Blog Fashion 2010; Signature9 Top 99 Fashion blogs 2011. While the precise ranking of the blogs varies according to the particular metrics used, a handful of key names, including those listed here, occur repeatedly across all league tables.

REFERENCES

Abbas, R. (2005) "Team spirit," in Moreno, S. (ed.), *Forefront: The Culture of Shop Window Design*. Amsterdam: I.B. Tauris, pp. 52–67.

Abrams, F. and Astill, J. (2001) "The story of a pair of jeans," *The Guardian*, May 29, 2001.

ACG. (2007) *The crime of the 21st century*, High Wycombe: The Anti Counterfeiting Group, available at: http://www.a-cg.org/guest/index.php, Last accessed September 30, 2016.

Agnew, J. (1998) *Geo-Politics: Re-visioning World Politics*. London: Routledge.

AIM. (2005) *Faking It: Why Counterfeiting Matters*, Briefing Paper April 2005, Brussels: Association des Industries de Marque (European Brands Association).

Allende, I. (2008) "Pieces of me," *The Guardian*, April 14, 2008.

Amed, I. (2011) "The business of blogging: The sartorialist," available at: www.thebusinessoffashion.com, October 3, 2011.

Amin, A. and Thrift, N. (2004) *Cultural Economy Reader*. Oxford: Blackwell.

Andrews, M. (1997) *The Acceptable Face of Feminism. The Women's Institute as a Social Movement*. London: Lawrence & Wishart.

Antonelli, P. (2007) "Bias-cut architecture," in Gabellini, M. (ed.), *Architecture of the Interior*. New York: Rizzoli, pp. 60–70.

Appadurai, A. (1986) *The Social Life of Things: Commodities in Cultural Perspective*. Cambridge: Cambridge University Press.

Appadurai, A. (1990) "Disjuncture and difference in the global cultural economy," *Theory Culture and Society*, 7, 295.

Armstrong A. and Hagel, J. (1997) *Net Gain: Expanding Markets through Virtual Communities*. Cambridge, MA: Harvard Business Press.

Arnold, R. (2001) *Fashion, Desire and Anxiety: Image and Morality in the 20th Century*. London: I.B. Tauris.

Arvidsson, A. (2006) *Brands: Meaning and Value in Media Culture*. London: Routledge.

Aspers, P. (2010) *Orderly Fashion: A Sociology of Markets*. Oxfordshire: Princeton University Press.

Assouly, A. (ed.) Proceedings of the 13th Annual Conference for the International Foundation of Fashion Technology Institutes (IFFTI) Fashion & Luxury.

Assouly, O. (2008) *Le Capitalisme Esthetique*. Paris: Cerf.

Atkinson, P. (2006) "Do it yourself: Democracy and design," *Journal of Design History*, 19 (1), 1–10.

Atsmon, Y., Dixit, V. and Wu, C. (2011) "Tapping China's luxury-goods market," *McKinsey Quarterly*, April 1–5.

Atwal, G. and Williams, A. (2007) "Experiencing luxury," *Admap*, March, pp. 30–2.

Atwal, G. and Williams, A. (2009) "Luxury brand marketing—the experience is everything!," *Journal of Brand Management*, 16 (5), 338–46.

Auster, P. (2006) *Travels in the Scriptorium*. London: Picador.

Aynsley, J., Breward, C. and Kwint, M. (1999) *Material Memories: Design and Evocation*. Oxford: Berg.

Bain, M. (2015) Luxury Goods Worldwide Study. December 2015, Altagamma.

Bain, M. (2016) "Zara is an unstoppable sales machine," *Business of Fashion*, 2016.

Bair, J. and Gereffi, G. (2003) "Upgrading, uneven development and jobs in the North American apparel industry," *Global Networks*, 3, 143–69.

Barnett, J. M. (2005) "Shopping for Gucci on Canal Street: Reflections on status consumption, intellectual property, and the incentive thesis," *Virginia Law Review*, 91, 1381–423.

Barreneche, R. A. (2008) *New Retail*. London: Phaidon Press.

Barthes, R. (1967) *The Fashion System*. Paris: Editions du Seuil.

Baudrillard, J. (1996) *The System of Objects*. London: Verso.

Baudrillard, J. (1997) *Fragments*. London: Verso.

Baudrillard, J. (2000) *Vital Illusion*. New York: Columbia University Press.

Baudrillard, J. (2009) *Why Hasn't Everything Already Disappeared?* Chicago: University of Chicago Press.

Bauman, Z. (2007) *Consuming Lives*. Cambridge: Polity.

BBC. (2008) 'Primark on the Rack' *Panorama*, available at: http://www.bbc.co.uk/programmes/b00cf06z, Last accessed September 30, 2016.

BBC4. (2009) *Savile Row*. London: BBC.

Beckert, J. (2011) "The transcending power of goods," Chapter 5 in Beckert, J. and Aspers, P. (eds), *The Worth of Goods*. Oxford: Oxford University Press, pp. 106–27.

Beckert, J. and Aspers, P. (2011) *The Worth of Goods: Valuation and Pricing in the Economy*. Oxford: Oxford University Press.

Beecroft, V. (2009) *Maison Martin Margiela*. New York: Rizzoli.

Beer, D. and Burrows, R. (2010) "Consumption, prosumption and participatory web cultures," *Journal of Consumer Culture*, 10 (3), 3–12.

Belk, R. (1988) "Possessions and the extended self," *Journal of Consumer Research*, 15 (2), 139–68.

Bell, Q. (1976) *On Human Finery*. London: Allison and Busby.

Benjamin, W. (1936) *The Arcades Project*. Harvard: Harvard University Press.

Benkler, Y. (2006) *The Wealth of Networks*. Yale: Yale University Press.

Bennett, J. (2004) "The force of things: Steps towards an ecology of matter," *Political Theory*, 32 (3), 347–72.

BFC. (2014) *Facts and Figures*. London: BFC.

Bhardwaj, V. and Fairhurst A. (2010) "Fast fashion: Response to changes in the fashion industry," *The International Review of Retail, Distribution and Consumer Research*, 20 (1), 165–73.

Bhattacharjee, A., Roy, A., Bhardwaj, K. and Ghosh, S. (2015) *Towards an Asia Floor Wage: A Global Initiative for Garment Workers in Asia*. Bangalore: Books for Change.

Bigolin, R. (2011) "Faux pas? Faking materials and languages of luxury," in Ebel, S. and Assouly, O. (eds), *Proceedings of the 13th Annual Conference for the International Foundation of Fashion Technology Institutes: Fashion and Luxury—Between Heritage and Innovation*, Paris, April 11–15, pp. 219–26.

Bingham, N. (2005) *The New Boutique*. London: Merrell.

Birch, A., Mott, G. and Schneider, D. (1999), *The Age of E-tail: Conquering the New World of Electronic Shopping*. Oxford: Capstone.

Bird, L. (2007) *Holidays on Display*. New York: Princeton Architectural Press.

Bissell, D. (2009) "Inconsequential materialities: The movements of lost effects," *Space and Culture*, 12, 95–115.

Black, A. and Burisch, N. (2010) "Craft hard, die free: Radical curatorial strategies for craftivism in unruly context," in Adamson, G. (ed.), *The Craft Reader*. Oxford and London, pp. 609–19.

Black, S. (2011) *Eco-Chic: The Fashion Paradox*. London: Black Dog Publishing.

Bloomberg. (2012) Hermes wins $100 million damages from counterfeit websites Bloombery.com/news/articles/2012-04-30, Last accessed September 26, 2016.

Bloutin Artinfo. (2011) www.blouinartinfo.com/photo-galleries/monumental-makeovers -prada, Last accessed September 26, 2016.

Boeglin, N. (2006) *Washing your jeans could cost the earth*. France: BioIntelligence Service.

Bohdanowicz, J. and Clamp, L. (1994) *Fashion Marketing*. London: Routledge.

Boothroyd, D. (2009) "Touch, time and technics: Levinas and the ethics of Haptic communications," *Theory, Culture and Society*, 26, 330–45.

Boston Consulting Group. (2010) *The Connected Kingdom: How the Internet Is Transforming the UK Economy*. Boston, MA: BCG.

Bosworth, D. (2006) "Counterfeiting and piracy: The state of the art," *Intellectual Property in the New Millennium Seminar*, Oxford Intellectual Property Research Centre, May 6, 2006, available at: http://www.oiprc.ox.ac.uk/EJWP0606.pdf, Last accessed September 30, 2016.

Boulter, J. and Grusin, R. (1999) *Remediation*. Cambridge: MIT Press.

Bourdieu, P. (1984) *Distinction*. London: Routledge.

Bowlby, R. (1997) "Supermarket futures," in Falk P. and Campbell C. (eds), *The Shopping Experience*. London: Sage, pp. 92–110.

Braddock Clarke, S. E. and Harris, J. (2012) *Digital Visions for Fashion and Textiles: Made in Code*. London: Thames and Hudson.

Bratich, J. and Brush. H. (2011) "Fabricating activism: Craft-work, popular culture, gender," *Utopian Studies*, 22 (2), 233–60.

Breward, C. (2003) *Fashion*. Oxford: Oxford University Press.

Breward, C. and Gilbert, D. (2006) *Fashion's World Cities*. Oxford: Berg.

Britten, F. (2008) Future proof your look *Sunday Times*, August 24, 2008, p. 16.

Brook, I. (2012) "Make, do, and mend: Solving placelessness through embodied environmental engagement," in Brady, E. and Phemister, P. (eds), *Human-Environment Relations: Transformative Values in Theory and Practice*. Dordrecht, Heidelberg, London and New York: Springer, pp. 109–20.

Brooks, A. (2013) "Stretching global production networks: The international second-hand clothing trade," *Geoforum*, 22, 10–22.

Brooks, A. (2015) *Clothing Poverty: The Hidden World of Fast Fashion and Second Hand Clothes*. London: Zed Books.

Brooks, L. (2009) "Amid the economic rubble, a revolution is being knitted," *The Guardian*.

Brooks Young, A. (1937) *Recurring Cycles of Fashion 1730–1937*. New York: Harper & Brothers Publishers.

Brown, A. (2009) "Are we being spun a yarn?" *The Sunday Times*, April 12, 2009.

Brown, B. (2001) "Thing theory," *Critical Inquiry*, 28 (1), 1–22.

Brown, B. (2004) *Things*. Chicago: Chicago University Press.

Brown, S. (2010) *Eco Fashion*. London: Laurence King.

Bruns, A. (2005) "Some explanatory notes on produsers and produsage. Institute for distributed creativity," available at: http://distributedcreativity.typepad.com/idc _texts/2005/11/some_explorator.html, Last accessed September 30, 2016.

Bruzzi, S. and Church, P. (2011) *Fashion Cultures: Theories, Explorations and Analysis*. Oxon: Routledge.

Buchanan, V. (2011) "VM and display award winners," *The Window Shopper*, [blog] 7.

Burkitt, L. and Chao, L. (2011) "Made in China: Fake stores," *The Wall Street Journal*, August.

Burt, S. and Sparks, L. (2002) "E-commerce and the retail process: A review," *Journal of Retailing and Consumer Services*, 10, 275–86.

Business of Fashion. (2015) "The race to control the luxury leather business," *Business of Fashion Intelligence*, November 17, 2015.

Butler, S. (2013) "Chinese demand for luxury goods boosts Kering," *The Guardian*, July 25.

Butler, S. and Rankin, J. (2014) "Primark profits surge 30% after 'magnificent year,'" *The Guardian*, November 14, 2014.

Buszek. (2011) *Extraordinary: Craft and Contemporary Art*. Durham: Duke University Press.

Bywater, M. (2001) "How I learnt the secret of life in GA," *The Independent*, February 25.

Callon, M. and Law, J. (2004) "Absence-presence, circulation and encountering in complex space," *Environment and Planning D: Society and Space*, 22, 3–11.

Campbell, C. (2005) "The craft consumer: Culture, craft and consumption in a postmodern society," *Journal of Consumer Culture*, 5 (1), 23–42.

Candy, F. (2003) The fabric of society: A proposal to investigate the emotional and sensory experience of wearing denim. Proceedings of Conference on Designing Pleasurable Objects and Interfaces Pittsburg, USA, June 23–26.

Caniato, F., Caridi, M., Crippa, L. and Moretto, A. (2012) "Environmental sustainability in fashion supply chains: An explanatory case based research," *International Journal of Production Economics*, 135 (2), 659–70. doi: 10.1016/j.ijpe.2011.06.001.

Capgemini. (2013) *World Wealth Report*. London: Capgemini.

Carcelle, Y. (2007) "Betts K Art Lessons," *Time*, October 11.

Carmichael, M. (2011) "What customers want from brands online," *AdAge Digital*, February 27.

Carr, C. and Gibson, C. (2015) "Geographies of making: Rethinking materials and skills for volatile futures," *Progress in Human Geography*, 40 (3), 297–315.

Carrell, S. (2012) "Harris tweed returns to global boutiques after island's renaissance," *The Guardian*, November 9, 2012.

Carter, L. (2005) "Connect the dots," *The New York Times Style Magazine*, New York.

Carter, L. (2012) "Boudicca Boudicca – Concept is King," *Hint Magazine*, May 1–3.

Castells, M. (2001) *The Internet Galaxy: Reflections on the Internet, Business and Society*. Oxford: Oxford University Press.

Castets. (2009) *Art, Fashion & Architecture Louis Vuitton*. New York: Rivoli.

Castle, H. (2000) "Fashion and architecture," *Architectural Design*, 70, 6.

Catry, B. (2003) "The great pretenders: The magic of luxury goods," *Business Strategy Review*, 14 (3), 10–17.

Cattaneo, O., Gereffi, G. and Staritz, C. (2010) *Global Value Chains in a Post-crisis World*. New York: World Bank.

Celant, G. (2003) Prada Aoyama Tokyo: Herzog and de Meuron Milano, Fondazione Prada.

Cervellon, M. C. and Coudriet, R. (2013) "Brand social power in luxury retail: Manifestations of brand dominance over clients in the store," *International Journal of Retail & Distribution Management*, 41 (11/12), 869–84.

Chadha, R. and Husband, P. (2006) *The Cult of the Luxury Brand: Inside Asia's Love Affair with Luxury*. London: Nicholas Brealey International.

Chalayan, H. (2002) "Designing, dwelling, thinking," in Quinn, B. (ed.) *The Fashion of Architecture* Oxford: Berg, pp. 119–32.

Chamberlain, G. (2016) "How can Lidl sell jeans for £5.99? Easy … pay people 23p an hour to make them," *The Guardian*, March 13, 2016.

Chapman, J. and Gant, N. (2007) *Designers, Visionaries and Other Stories*. London: Earthscan.

Chaudhry, P. E. (2006) "Changing levels of intellectual property rights protection for global firms: A synopsis of recent U.S. and EU trade enforcement strategies," *Business Horizons*, 49, 463–72.

Chevalier, M. and Mazzalovo, G. (2008) *Luxury Brand Management: A World of Privilege*. London: John Wiley.

China Customs Statistics. (2014)' (HK TDC Research), available at: http://china-trade -research.hktdc.com/business-news/article/Fast-Facts/China-CustomsStatistics/ff/ en/1/ , Last accessed September 30, 2016.

Cline, E. (2013) *Overdressed: The Shockingly High Cost of Cheap Fashion New York: Penguin*. London: Portfolio/Penguin.

Clough, P. (2000) *Auto-affection*. Minneapolis: Minnesota University Press.

Cohen, J. (2007) "Cyberspace as/and space," *Columbia Law Review*, 107, 210–56.

Collins, N. (2010). "Selfridges named world best department store," *The Telegraph*, June 14, 2010.

Collins, S. (2010) "Digital fair: Prosumption and the fair use defence," *Journal of Consumer Culture*, 10 (1), 37–55.

Comaroff, J. and Comaroff, J. (2006) *Law and Disorder in the Postcolony*. Chicago: University of Chicago Press.

Contactlab/Exane BNP Paribas. (2015) *Luxury Goods/Digital Frontier: The New World Luxury of 2020*. London: Exane BNP.

Coppard, A. (ed.) (2010) *Aware: Art, Fashion, Identity*. Italy: Damiana.

Corcoran, C. (2006) "The blogs that took over the tent," *Women's Wear Daily*, February 6, 2010.

Corcoran, C. (2010) "Rule of the masses: Reinventing fashion via crowdsourcing," *Women's Wear Daily*, July 26, 2010.

Cotton Incorporated. (2005) "Lifestyle Monitor," available at www.cottoninc.com/ LifestyleMonitor/LSMDenim2005/, Last accessed October 28, 2008.

Craciun, M. (2014) *Material Culture and Authenticity: Fake Branded Fashion in Europe*. London: Bloomsbury.

Crewe, L. (2003) Markets in motion. *Progress in Human Geography*, 27 (3), 352–62.

Crewe, L. (2008) "Ugly beautiful: Counting the cost of the global fashion industry," *Geography*, 93 (1), 25–33.

Crewe, L. (2010) "Wear: where. The convergent geographies of fashion and architecture," *Environment and Planning A*, 42, 2093–108.

Crewe, L. (2011) Life itemized: Lists, loss, unexpected significance and the impossibilities of erasure. *Environment and Planning A*, 29 (1), 27–46.

Crewe, L. (2013) "Tailoring and Tweed: Mapping the spaces of slow fashion," in Bruzzi, S. and Church Gibson, P. (eds), *Fashion Cultures*. London: Routledge, pp. 200–14.

Crewe, L. and Davenport, E. (1992) The puppet show: Buyer supplier relations in clothing retailing. *Transactions of the IBG*, 183–97.

Crewe, L. and Martin, A. (2016) "Looking at luxury: Consuming luxury fashion in global cities Chapter 16," in Hay, I. and Beaverstock, J. (eds), *Handbook on Wealth and the Super Rich*. Cheltenham: Edward Elgar, pp. 322–38.

Cuito, A. (2005) *Store Window Design*. New York: Te Neues Publishing.

Cumming, T. (2001) "The happiest day of my life," *The Guardian*, February 17, 2001.

Cumming, T. (2002) "Stuff and nonsense," *The Guardian*, February 13, 2002.

Currah, A. (2002) "Behind the web store: The organisational and spatial evolution of multichannel retailing in Toronto," *Environment and Planning A*, 34, 1411–41.

Currah, A. (2003) "The virtual geographies of retail display," *Journal of Consumer Culture*, 3 (1), 5–37.

Currid, E. (2007) *The Warhol Economy: How Fashion, Art and Music Drive New York City*. New Jersey: Princeton University Press, pp. 373–91.

Currid, E. (2012) "The social life of art worlds: Implications for culture, place and development," in Crane, R. and Weber, R. (eds), *Oxford Handbook of Urban Planning*. Oxford: Oxford University Press, pp. 373-91.

Curtis, E. and Watson, H. (2007) *Fashion Retail*. Chichester: Wiley.

Danziger, P. (2005) *Let Them Eat Cake: Marketing Luxury to the Masses*. Berkshire: Kaplan Business.

Davidson, A. (2016) "The luxury of Nature: The environmental consequences of super-rich lives, Chapter 17," in Hay, I. and Beaverstock, J. (eds), *Handbook on Wealth and the Super Rich*. Mumbai: Edward Elgar, pp. 339–62.

Davies King, W. (2008) *Collections of Nothing*. Chicago: Chicago University Press.

Davis, M. (1990) *City of Quartz*. London: Verso.

Davis, M. and Monk, D. (eds.) (2007) *Evil Paradises: Dreamworlds of Neoliberalism*. New York: The New Press.

Dean, C. (2003) *The Inspired Retail Space*. Beverley, MA: Rockport.

De Brito, M. P., Carbone, V. and Meunier Blanquart, C. (2008). "Toward a sustainable fashion retail supply chain in Europe: Organisation and performance," *International Journal of Production Economics*, 114 (2), 534–53. doi:10.1016/j.ijpe.2007.06.012.

Debo, K. (2008) *Maison Martin Margiela 20: The Exhibition Paperback*, September 1, 2008, Momu.

Debord, G. (1994 [1967]) *The Society of Spectacle*. New York: Zone Books.

De Certeau, M. (1998) *The Practice of Everyday Life*. Berkeley: University of California Press.

De Seyne, G. (2015) Executive VP, Hermes International.

De Teliga J. (2011) "E-tail giant rises" The Australian features section, August 17, p. 9.

Deloitte. (2015) *Global Powers of Luxury Goods 2015: Engaging the Future Luxury Consumer*. London: Deloitte.

Deloitte and Touche. (1999) *The E-Business Tidal Wave—Perspectives on Business in Cyberspace*. New York: Deloitte and Touche.

Dercon, C. (2009) "Fashion like the dark side of the moon: The Moon Ray," in *Maison Martin Margiela*. New York: Rizzoli, p. 137.

Design Council. (2007), Creative and cultural skills sector skills council and the design skills advisory panel, *High-Level Skills for Higher Value*.

DeSilvey, C. (2012) "Making sense of transience: An anticipatory history," *Cultural Geographies*, 19 (1), 30–53.

Destefani, F. (2006) "The soul outside," in Guerriero, A. (ed.), *Dressing Ourselves*. Milan: Edizioni Charta, pp. 16–17.

Dewey, J. (1939) *The Theory of Valuation*. Chicago: University of Chicago Press.

DiMaggio, P. (1987) "Classification in art," *American Sociological Review*, 52 (4), 440–55.

Dion, D. and Arnould, E. (2011) "Retail luxury strategy: Assembling Charisma through art and magic," *Journal of Retailing*, 87 (4), 502–20.

Dodge, M. and Kitchen, R. (2005) "Code and the transduction of space," *Annals of the Association of American Geographers* 95 (1), 162–80.

Doesinger, S. (2008) "Virtually home," in Doesinger, S. (ed.), *Space between People*. London: Prestel, pp. 12–23.

Doherty, C. and Moore, A. (2007), *The International Flagship Stores of Luxury Fashion Retailers*. Oxford: Butterworth Heinemann.

Dorment, R. (2001) *The Daily Telegraph*, February 14, 2001.

Douglas, M. (1984) *Purity and Danger: An Analysis of Concepts of Pollution and Taboo*. Harmondsworth: Penguin Books.

Drapers. (2011) "Burberry switches marketing spend into digital media," *Drapers*, September 1, 2011.

Drucker, P. (1993) *Post-capitalist Society*. London: Routledge.

Duggan, G. (2001) "The greatest show on earth: A look at contemporary fashion shows and their relationship to performance art," *Fashion Theory*, 5 (3), 1–33.

Eco, U. (1973) "Social life as a sign system," in Robey, D. (ed.), *Structuralism: The Wolfson College Lectures*. London: Cape.

Edelman. (2012) *Louis Vuitton Marc Jacobs*. New York: Rizzoli Publications.

Edesnor, T. (2002) "Haunting in the ruins: Matter and immateriality," *Space and Culture*, 11 (12), 42–51.

Edensor, T. (2005a) *Industrial Ruins: Space, Aesthetics and Materiality*. Oxford: Berg.

Edensor, T. (2005b) "The ghosts of industrial ruins: Ordering and disordering memory in excessive space," *Environment and Planning D: Society and Space*, 23 (6), 829–49.

Edensor, T. (2005c) "Waste matter—The debris of industrial ruins and the disordering of the material world: The materialities of industrial ruins," *Journal of Material Culture*, 10 (3), 311–32.

Edensor, T. et al. (2010) *Spaces of Vernacular Creativity: Rethinking the Cultural Economy*. London: Routledge.

Edwards, T. (2007) "Express yourself: The politics of dressing up," in Barnard, M. (ed.), *Fashion Theory: A Reader*. London: Routledge, 191–6.

Entwistle, J. (2000) *The Fashioned Body: Fashion and Dress in Modern Social Theory*. Oxford: Polity.

Entwistle, J. (2006a) "The cultural economy of fashion buying," *Current Sociology*, 54 (5), 704–24.

Entwistle, J. (2006b) "The field of fashion materialized: A study of London Fashion Week," *Sociology*, 40, 735–51.

Entwistle, J. (2009) *The Aesthetic Economy: Markets in Clothing and Fashion Modelling*. London: Bloomsbury.

Entwistle, J. and Rocamora, A. (2006) "The field of fashion realized: A case study of London Fashion Week," *Sociology*, 40 (4), 735–50.

Ernst and Young. (1999) *The Second Annual Ernest & Young Internet Shopping Study: The Digital Channel Gathers Steam*. New York and London: Ernst & Young LLP.

Ervin Kelley, K. (2005) "Architecture for sale(s): An unabashed apologia," in Saunders, W. (ed.), *Commodification and Spectacle in Architecture*. Minneapolis: Minnesota University Press, pp. 47–59.

Evans, C. (2003) *Fashion at the Edge: Spectacle, Modernity and Deathliness*. New Haven: Yale University Press.

Evans, P. and Wurster, T. (2000) *Blown to Bits: How the New Economics of Information Transforms Strategy*. Boston: Harvard Business School Press.

Everest, T. (2008) BBC2 British Style Genius, October. London: BBC.

Featherstone, M. (2009) "Ubiquitous media: An introduction," *Theory, Culture and Society*, 26, 1–22.

Featherstone, M. (2013) "The rich and the super-rich: Mobility, consumption and luxury lifestyle," in Mather, N. (ed.), *Consumer Culture, Modernity and Identity*. New Delhi: Sage, pp. 3–44.

Fernie, J., Moore, C., Lawrie, A. and Hallsworth, A. (1997). "The internationalization of the high fashion brand: The case of central London," *Journal of Product & Brand Management*, 6 (3), 151–62.

Fibre to Fashion. (2012). "Window display the new retail mantra," available at: www .fibre2fashion/industry-article/2578/windowdisplayp2

Fionda, A. M. and Moore, C. M. (2009) "The anatomy of the luxury fashion brand," *Journal of Brand Management*, 16 (5), 347–63.

Firat, A. and Venkatesh, A. (1995) "Liberatory postmodernism and the re-enchantment of consumption," *Journal of Consumer Research*, 22, 239–67.

Fisher, A. (2012) "Fashion world warms again to wool," *The Observer*, September 2, 2012.

Fletcher, K. (2008) *Sustainable Fashion and Textiles: Design Journeys*. London: Earthscan.

Fletcher, K. and Grose, L. (2012) *Fashion and Sustainability: Design for Change*. London: Laurence King.

Fletcher, N. (2014) "Primark could be worth £19 billion says analyst," *The Guardian*, March 10, 2014.

Forrester Research. (2011) *The State of Retailing Online Forrester Research*. London: FPNY, pp. 2, 3.

Foster, H. (1988) *Vision and Visuality*. Seattle: Bay Press.

Foster, H. (2002) *Design and Crime*. London: Verso.

Foster, J. B. and Magdoff, F. (2009), *The Great Financial Crisis: Causes and Consequences*. New York: New York University Press.

Foucault, M. (1966) *The Order of Things*. Paris: Editions Gallimard.

Fox, I. and Chilvers, S. (2010) "Slow fashion: Forever yours," *The Guardian*, Wednesday July 7, 2010.

Fox, S., Marcuse, T. and Clark, J. (2010) *Fashion Projects: On Fashion and Memory*. New York: Fashion Projects.

Frankel, S. (2001) *Visionaries, Interviews with Fashion Designers*. London: V&A Publications.

Frankel, S. (2003) "Not a colour for cowards," *The Independent Review*, December 18, 2003.

Freeman, H. (2007) "Primark's £8 jeans and £2 bikinis cause stampede," *The Guardian*, April 6, 2007.

French, S., Crewe, L., Leyshon, A., Webb, P. and Thrift, N. (2004) "Putting e-commerce in its place: Reflections on the impact of the Internet on the cultural industries," in Power, D. and Scott, A. (eds), *Cultural Industries and the Production of Culture*. London and New York: Routledge, pp. 54–71.

Freud, S. (1917) Mourning and Melancholia. *The Standard Edition of the Complete Psychological Works of Sigmund Freud*, Vol. XIV, pp. 237–58.

Fuery, K. (2009) *New Media: Culture and Image*. New York: Palgrave.

Gauntlett, D. (2011) *Making Is Connecting: The Social Meaning of Creativity, from DIY and Knitting to Youtube and Web 2.0*. London: Polity Press.

Geczy, A. and Karaminas, V. (2012) *Fashion and Art*. London: Bloomsbury.

Gell, A. (1998) *Art and Agency* Oxford: Clarendon Press.

Gieson, B. (2008) *Ethical Clothing*. Saarbrucken Germany: VDM Verlag.

Gilbert, D. (2006) "From Paris to Shanghai: The changing geographies of fashion's world cities," in Breward, C. and Gilbert, D. (eds), *Fashion's World Cities* Oxford: Berg, pp. 3–32.

Gill, A. (1998) "Deconstruction fashion," *Fashion Theory*, 2 (1), 25–50.

Gill, A. (2011) "Suits you Sir: A man of the cloth," *Sunday Times*, March 13, 2011, 13.

Gill, A. and Lopes, A. M. (2011) "On wearing: A critical framework for valuing design's already made," *Design and Culture*, 3 (3), 307–27.

Gill, S. (2008) *A Series of Disappointments*. London: Nobody's Books.

Girard, M. and Stark, D. (2002) "Distributing intelligence and organizing diversity in new-media projects," *Environment and Planning A*, 34 (11), 1927–49.

Glenn, J. and Hayes, C. (2007) *Taking Things Seriously*. New York: Princeton University Press.

Goffman, E. (1971) *The Presentation of Self in Everyday Life*. London: Pelican Books.

Golbin, P. (2012) *Louis Vuitton Marc Jacobs*. New York: Rizzoli International Publications.

Goodman, M. K., Goodman, D. and Redclift, M. (2010) *Consuming Space: Placing Consumption in Perspective*. Surrey: Ashgate Publishing Group.

Goss, J. (1993) "The magic of the mall: An analysis of form, function, and meaning in the contemporary retail built environment," *Annals of the Association of American Geographers*, 83 (1), 18–47.

Goss, J. (1999) Once upon a time in the commodity world: An unofficial guide to the mall of America. *Annals of the Association of American Geographers*, 89 (1), 45–75.

Grabher, G. (2002) "Cool projects, boring institutions: Temporary collaboration in social context," *Regional Studies*, 36 (3), 205–14.

Graham, M. (2011) "Time machines and virtual portals: The spatialities of the digital divide," *Progress in Development Studies*, 11, 211–27.

Graham, S. and Upton, M. (2009) "LVMH successfully sues eBay for unauthorised sales of genuine products," in *Blake Dawson—IT, Communications & Media Update*, February 9, 2009.

Granata, F. (2010) "Fashion and memory," in Fox, S., Marcuse, T. and Clark, J. (eds), *Fashion Projects: On Fashion and Memory*. Granata, NY: NYFA.

Grant, P. (2010) "Football fashions suited me perfectly," in Salmond, C. (ed.), *Edinburgh Evening News*, February 19, 2010, p. 22.

Grant, S. (1997) MMM Exhibition at Boijmans Van Beuningen Museum, Rotterdam.

Greer, B. (2014) *Craftivism: The art of craft and activism*. Vancouver: Arsenal Pulp Press.

Gregory, A. (2014) "Art and fashion: The mutual appreciation society," *Wall Street Journal*, March 28, 2014.

Gregson N. and Crewe L. (2003) *Second Hand Worlds*. Oxford: Berg.

Gregson, N., Metcalfe, A. and Crewe L. (2007) "Moving things along: The conduits and practices of divestment in consumption," *Transactions of the IBG*, 32 (2), 187–200.

Gregson, N., Metcalfe, A. and Crewe, L. (2009) Practices of object maintenance and repair. *Journal of Consumer Culture*, 9 (2), 248–72.

Groom, A. (1993) "Belgian chic: From riches to rags," *Financial Times*, November 27, 1993.

Grossman, G. M. and Shapiro, C. (1988) "Foreign counterfeiting of status goods," *The Quarterly Journal of Economics*, 103 (1), 79–100.

Grumbatch, D. (2009) "From Worth to Margiela," in Bonifassi, C. (ed.), *Maison Margiela*. Paris: Rizzoli, pp. 56–8.

Guiness, D. (2013) "Foreword," in Oakley Smith, M. and Kubler, A. (eds), *Art/Fashion in the 21st Century*. London: Thames and Hudson, pp. 8–10.

Guthman, J. and dDu Puis, M. (2006) "Embodying neoliberalism: Economy, culture and the politics of fat," *Environment and Planning D,* 24 (3).

Guyon, J. (2004) "The magic touch," *Fortune*, 150 (5), 229–36, November 17, 2012, EBSCO Host database.

Habraken, N. and Teicher, J. (1998) *The Structure of the Ordinary*. Cambridge, MA: MIT Press.

Hackney, F. (2013) "Quiet activism and the new amateur," *Design and Culture*, 5 (2), 169–94.

Hale, A. (2000) "What hope for ethical trade in the globalised garment industry?" *Antipode*, 32 (4), 349–56.

Hale, A. and Wills, J. ((2005) *Threads of Labour: Garment Industry Supply Chains from the Worker's Perspective*. Oxford: Blackwell.

Handler, R. (1986) "Authenticity," *Anthropology Today*, 2 (1), 2–4.

Hansennov, S. (2012) "How Zara grew into the world's largest fashion retailer," *New York Times Magazine*, November 9, 2012.

Hanson, M. (2006) *Bodies in Code: Interfaces with Digital Media*. London: Routledge.

Harkin, F. (2007) "The cotton wars," *Financial Times,* March 2, 2007.

Harnett, S. (2014) "Made in Italy' may not mean what you think it does," available at: www.marketplace.org

Harris Tweed Authority (website www.harristweed.org)

Hart, J. (2010) "ASOS hunts for mobile agency as customers look to shop on the go," *New Media Age*, April 29, 2010.

Harvey, D. (1989) *The Condition of Postmodernity*. Oxford: Blackwell.

Harvey N. (2011) "History of Harvey Nichols luxury department store," available at: http://www.harveynichols.com/history, Last accessed September 30, 2016.

Hauser, K. (2004) "The clothes in the dock; or How the FBI illuminated the pre-history of a pair of denim jeans," *Journal of Material Culture*, 9 (3), 293–313

Hawkins, G. (2000) "Living with rubbish," *International Journal of Cultural Studies*, 4 (1), 2–23.

Hawkins, H. (2012) "Geography and art. An expanding field: Site, the body and practice," *Progress in Human Geography*, 37, 52–71 (online first, April 18).

Hawkins, H. (2013) *For Creative Geographies: Geography, Visual Arts and the Making of Worlds*. London: Routledge.

Hay, I. (2013) *Geographies of the Super-Rich*. Cheltenham: Edward Elgar.

Herring, S. (2004) "Slouching towards the ordinary: Current trends in computer-mediated communication," *New Media and Society*, 6 (1), 26–36.

Herships, S. (2014) "Think of it as an exclusivity tax," *Marketplace*, December 5, 2014.

Hetherington, K. (2004) "Second-handedness: Consumption, disposal and absent presence," *Environment and Planning D: Society and Space*, 22 (1), 157–73.

Hethorn, J. and Vlasewicz, C. (2008) *Sustainable Fashion: Why Now? A Conversation Exploring Issues, Practices and Possibilities*. New York: Fairchild.

Heti, S., Julavits, H., Shapton, L. and 639 others. (2014) *Women in Clothes*. London: Penguin Books.

Hieatt, D. (2013) "The best of British," in Rickey, M. (ed.), *The Guardian Style*, pp. 12–13.

Hill, C. (2009) "Body," in Quinn, B. (ed.), *Textile Designers at the Cutting Edge*. London: Laurence King Publishing, pp. 68–73.

Hills, G. (2011) "Fashion: Dashing tweeds," in Platman, L. (ed.), *Harris Tweed: From Land to Street*. London: Francis Lincoln, p. 123.

Hilton, B., Choi, C. J. and Chen, S. (2004) "The ethics of counterfeiting in the fashion industry: Quality, credence and profit issues," *Journal of Business Ethics*, 55, 345–54.

Hlubinka, M. (2007) "The datebook," Chapter 76 in Turkle, S. (ed.), *Evocative Objects*. Cambridge: MIT Press, pp. 76–84.

Hodge, B., Mears, P. and Sidlauskas, S. (2006) *Skin and Bones: Parallel Practices in Fashion and Architecture*. London: Thames and Hudson.

Hodkinson, P. (2007) "Interactive online journals and individualization," *New Media & Society*, 9 (4), 625–50.

Holgate, M. (1999) *Harvey Nichols Magazine*, London: Holgate Harvey Nichols.

Hollander, A. (1975) *Seeing through Clothes*. Berkeley: University of California Press.

Holt, D. (2002) "Why do brands cause trouble? A dialectical theory of consumer culture and branding," *Journal of Consumer Research*, 29, 70–90.

Holt, D. (2004) *How Brands Become Icons: The Principles of Cultural Branding*. Harvard: Harvard Business School Press.

Hopkins, D. M., Kontnik, L. and Turnage, M. (2003) *Counterfeiting Exposed: Protecting Your Brand and Customers*. New Jersey: John Wiley and Sons.

Hoskins, T. (2014) *Stitched Up: The Anti-Capitalist Book of Fashion*. London: Pluto Books.

Howe, J. (2009) *Crowdsourcing: How the Power of the Crowd Is Driving the Future of Business*. London: Random House Publishing.

Howell, M. (2012) "The outsider: Margaret Howell is British fashion's queen of minimalism," *The Independent*, May 25, 2012.

Huey, S. and Draffan, S. (2009) *Bag*. London: Laurence King Publishers.

Hughes, A. and Reimer, S. (2004) *Geographies of Commodity Chains*. London: Routledge.

Hutter, M. and Throsby, D. (2011) *Beyond Price: Value in Culture, Economics and the Arts*. Cambridge: Cambridge University Press.

IMRG. (2011a) *E-Retail Sales Index*. London: IMRG.

IMRG. (2011b) *Mobile Ad-spend Figures*. London: IMRG.

International Correspondence School. (1912) *The Window Trimmer's Handbook*. Scranton: International Textbook Company.

Isabella, G. (2010) *High Price—Art between the Market and Celebrity Culture*. New York: Sternberg Press.

Jackson, T. (2004) "A contemporary analysis of global luxury brands," in Bruce, M., Moore, C. and Birtwistle, G. (eds), *International Retail Marketing: A Case Study Approach*. Oxford: Elsevier Butterworth Heinemann, pp. 155–69.

Jackson, T. (2008) "Virtual flagships," in Kent, T. and Brown, R. (eds), *Flagship Marketing*. London: Routledge, pp. 186–94.

Jansson, A. (2002) "The mediatization of consumption: Towards an analytical framework of image culture," *Journal of Consumer Studies* 2 (1), 5–31.

Jarrett, M. S. (2006) *Street: The Nylon Book of Global Style*. New York: Universe Publishing.

Jenkins, H. (2006) *Convergence: Where Old and New Media Collide*. Cambridge, MA: MIT Press.

Jing Daily. (2014) "China's love affair with luxury lives on," *Jing Daily the Business of Luxury in China*, April 26, 2014.

Jing Daily. (2015) "China's luxury e-commerce boom means 'ostrich' brands lose out," *Jing Daily the Business of Luxury in China*, August 4, 2015.

Jones, D. (2013) "Menswear has designs on our creative economy," *Evening Standard*, June 14.

Jones, V. and Martin, M. (2015) *International Trade: Rules of Origin*. Washington: Congressional Research and Service.

Journeyman. (2014) Inside Malaysia's gruesome snake skin trade. November 17, 2014, Journeyman Broadcasts.

Julier, G. (2004) "The stuff in the background," available at: www.designculture.info/shorts/stuff, Last accessed November 29, 2004.

Kaal, R. (2004) "The great equalizer," *Frame*, 38, 56–7.

Kapferer, J. (2012) "Abundant rarity: The key to luxury growth," *Business Horizons*, 55, 453–62.

Kapferer, J. N. and Bastien, V. (2009) *The Luxury Strategy*. London: Kogan Page.

Karaminas, V. (2012) "Image Chapter 15," in Geczy, A. and Karaminas, V. (eds), *Fashion and Art*. London: Bloomsbury, pp. 177–88.

Karpik, L. (2010) *Valuing the Unique*. Oxford: Oxford University Press.

Kelly, K. (1999) *New Rules for the New Economy: 10 Ways in Which the Network Economy Is Changing Everything*. London: Fourth Estate.

Kennedy, K. (2011) "What she wore: The dialectics of personal style blogging," MA Thesis, University of Kansas.

Kenney, M. and Curry, J. (2001) "Beyond transaction costs: E-commerce and the power of the internet dataspace," in Leinbach, T. and Brunn, S. (eds), *Worlds of E-Commerce: Economic, Geographical and Social Dimensions*. Chichester: John Wiley, pp. 45–66.

Kerfoot, S., Davies, B. and Ward, P. (2003) "Visual merchandising and the creation of discernible retail brands," *International Journal of Retail & Distribution Management*, 31 (3), 143–52.

Kiessling, G., Balekjian, C. and Oehmichen, A. (2009) "What credit crunch?. More luxury for new money: European rising stars & established markets," *Journal of Retail & Leisure Property*, 8 (1), 3–23.

Kim, E., Nam, D. and Stimpert, J. (2004) "The applicability of Porter's generic strategies in the digital age," *Journal of Management*, 30 (5), 569–589.

King, A. (1995) *Global Cities: Post-imperialism and the Internationalisation of London*. London: Routledge.

Kitchin, R. (1998) "Towards geographies of cyberspace," *Progress in Human Geography*, 22 (3), 385–406.

Klein, D. (1999) *No Logo*. London: Random House.

Knight, N. (2009) *Nick Knight*. New York: HarperCollins.

Knox, K. (2010) *Alexander McQueen: Genius of a Generation*. London: A&C Black Ltd.

Komter, A. (2001) "Heirlooms, nikes and bribes: Towards a sociology of things," *Sociology*, 35 (1), 50–75.

Koolhaas, R. (2000) "Branding—signs, symbols or something else?" *Fashion and Architecture*, 70 (6), 34–42.

Koolhaas, R., Prada, M. and Bertelli, P. (2001) *Projects for Prada Part 1*. Milan: Fondazione Prada Edizioni (unpaginated).

Koontz, M. L. (2002) Mixed reality merchandising: Bricks, clicks and mix. *Journal of Fashion Marketing and Management*, 381–95.

Koptyoff, I. (1986) "The cultural biography of things: Commoditization as process," Chapter 2, in Appadurai A. (ed.), *The Social Life of Things: Commodities in Cultural Perspective*. Cambridge: Cambridge University Press, pp. 64–94.

Kozinets, R. V., Sherry, J. F., DeBerry-Spence, B., Duhachek, A., Nuttavuthisit, K. and Storm, D. (2002) "Themed flagship brand stores in the new millennium," *Journal of Retailing*, 78, 17–29.

Krugman, P. and Venables, A. (1995) "Globalization and the inequality of nations," *Quarterly Journal of Economics*, 106 (3), 669–82.

LaFerla, R. (2010) "The New Icons of Fashion," *The New York Times*, November 11, 2010, available at: http://www.nytimes.com/2010/11/11/fashion/11INFLUENCE.html, Last accessed September 30, 2016.

LaFerla, R. (2014) "Zara, Where insiders look for an edge," *The New York Times*, June 4, 2014.

Landy, M. (2002) *On Breakdown*. London: Artangel, available at: www.artangel.org.uk/projects/2001/break_down/about_michael_landy

Lang, H. and Bienale, V. (1996). "I smell you on my clothes." Exhibition Florence.

Langston, C. (2014) "Who needs Hermes when you can have Homies? New exhibition proves counterfeit can be cool," *Mail Online*.

Lanxon, N. (2008) "The greatest defunct web sites and dotcom disasters," *CNET*, June 5, available at: http://crave.cnet.co.uk/gadgets/the-greatest-defunct-web-sites-and-dotcom-disasters-49296926, Last accessed September 30, 2016.

Large, J. (2009) "Consuming counterfeits: Exploring assumptions about fashion counterfeiting," *Papers from the British Criminology Conference*, 9, 3–20.

Lash, S. and Urry, J. (1994) *Economies of Signs and Space*. London: Sage.

Latham, A., McCormack, D., McNamara, K. and McNeill, D. (2009) *Key Concepts in Urban Geography*. London: Sage.

Lean, G. (2007) "Chic and cheerful but no so great for the environment," *Independent on Sunday*, January 28, 2007, p. 16.

Ledbury Research. (2007) *Counterfeiting Luxury: Exposing the Myths* (2nd edn), London. Davenport Lyons, available at: http://www.a-cg.org/guest/index.php, Last accessed September 30, 2016.

Ledbury Research and Walpole. (2013) *The UK Luxury Benchmark Report*. London: Ledbury Research.

Lee, M. (2008) "Pieces of Me," *The Guardian*, March 25, 2008.

Lehdonvirta, V. (2010) "Online spaces have material culture: Goodbye to digital post-materialism and hello to virtual consumption," *Media, Culture & Society*, 32 (5), 883–9.

Leibenstein, H. (1950) "Bandwagon, snob and Veblen effects in the theory of consumer demand," *The Quarterly Journal of Economics*, 64 (2), 183–207.

Leinbach, T. and Brunn, S. (2001) *Worlds of E-Commerce: Economic, Geographical and Social Dimensions*. Chichester: John Wiley.

Leyshon, A., French, S., Thrift, N., Crewe, L. and Webb, P. (2005) "Accounting for e-commerce: Abstractions, virtualism and the cultural circuit of capital," *Economy and Society*, 34 (3), 428–50.

Li, F., Papagiannidis, S. and Bourlakis, M. (2010) "Living in multiple spaces: Extending our socio-environment through virtual worlds," *Environment and Planning D: Society and Space*, 28, 425–46.

Li, G. and Kambele, Z. (2012) "Luxury fashion brand consumers in China: Perceived value, fashion lifestyle, and willingness to pay," *Journal of Business Research*, 65 (10), 1516–22.

Licoppe, C. (2004) "Connected presence: The emergence of a new repertoire for managed social relationships in a changing communication technoscape," *Environment and Planning D: Society and Space*, 22, 135–56.

Liebowitz, S. (2002) *Re-thinking the Network Economy: The True Forces that Drive the Digital Marketplace*. New York: AMACOM.

Lindholm, C. (2008) *Culture and Authenticity*. Oxford: Blackwell.

Lingwood, J. (2001) "Michael Landy in conversation with James Lingwood Artangel," available at: www.artangel.org.uk/break-down/michael-landy-in-conversation-with-james-lingwood, Last accessed September 26, 2016.

Lipovetsky, G. (1994) *The Empire of Fashion: Dressing Modern Democracy*. New Jersey: Princeton University Press.

Lipovetsky, G. and Manlow, V. (2010) "The artilisation of luxury stores," in Brand, J., Teunissen, J. and de Muijnck, C. (eds), *Fashion and Imagination: About Clothes and Art* Berlin: Brand and Teunisson, pp. 154–67.

Lipson, H. and Kurman, M. (2013) *Fabricated: The New World of 3D Printing—The Promise and Peril of a Machine that Can Make Almost Anything*. Indianapolis: John Wiley & Sons Inc.

Luker, S. (2011) "Traditional media lose ground to social media," *PRweek.com*, May 26, 2011.

Lury, C. (2004) *Brands: The Logos of the Global Economy*. London: Routledge.

Maison Martin Margiela. (2009) *Maison Martin Margiela*. New York: Rizzoli.

Malmsten, E. Portanger, E. and Drazin, C. (2001) *Boo Hoo: A dot.com Story from Concept to Catastrophe*. London: Random House Books.

Malone, T., Yate, J. and Benjamin, R. (1987) "Electronic markets and electronic hierarchies," *Communications of the ACM*, 30, 484–97.

Manco, J. (2010) "Researching the history of shops," available at: http://www .buildinghistory.org/buildings/shops.shtml, Last accessed September 30, 2016.

Manning, P. (2010) "The semiotics of the brand," *Annual Review of Anthropology*, 24, 95–641.

Manovich, L. (2009) "The practice of everyday (media) life: From mass consumption to mass cultural production," *Critical Enquiry*, 3535, 319–31.

Mansvelt, J. (2007) *Geographies of Consumption*. London: Sage.

Mansvelt, J. (2009) "Geographies of consumption: Engaging with absent presences," *Progress in Human Geography*, 33, 264–74.

Manuelli, S. (2006) *Design for Shopping*. London: Laurence and King.

Marciniak, R. and Bruce, M. (2004) "The scope of e-commerce in retail strategy," in Bruce, M. (ed.), *International Retail Marketing*. Oxford: Butterworth-Heinemann.

Martin, P. (2002) "Garment as King," available at: www.SHOWstudio.com, *Virtual Accessories*.

Matarazzo, M. (2012) "Country of origin effect: Research evolution, basic constructs and firm implications," in Bertoli, G. and Resciniti, R. (eds), *International Marketing and the Country of Origin Effect: The Global Impact of 'Made in Italy'*. Chelrenham: Edward Elgar Publishing Ltd, pp. 23–4.

McIntyre, R. (2000) "Are workers rights human and would it matter if they were? P. 1," *Human Rights and Welfare*, 6, 1–12.

McKinsey and Co. (2013) *Understanding China's Growing Love for Luxury*. London: McKinsey.

McLeod. (1994) "Undressing Architecture: Fashion, gender and modernity," in Fausch, D. (ed.), *Architecture: In Fashion*. New York: Princeton University Press.

McLuhan, M. (1994) *Understanding Media*. Cambridge, MA: MIT Press.

McNally, D. (2009) 'From financial crisis to world-slump: Accumulation, financialisation, and the global slowdown," *Historical Materialism*, 17 (2), 35–83.

McNeill, D. (2009) *The Global Architect*. London: Routledge.

Mehta, M. (2013) "Passion, not profit: The tribe of passionate investors," available at: Luxpresso.com, October 4, 2013.

Melville, H. (1851) *Moby-Dick*. New York: Harper & Bros.

Menkes, S. (2009) "Special report: Fashion week," *The New York Times*, October 7, 2009.

Merleau, Ponty. (1968) *The Visible and the Invisible.* Evanston, IL: Northwestern University Press.

Miller, D. (ed.) (1995) *Acknowledging Consumption: A Review of New Studies*. London: Routledge.

Miller, D. (2005) *Materiality*. London: Duke University Press.

Miller, D. (2009) *The Comfort of Things*. Oxford: Polity Press.

Miller, D. (2010) *Stuff*. Cambridge: Polity Press.

Miller, D., Jackson, P., Thrift, M. N., Holbrook, B. and Rowlands, M. (1998) *Shopping Place and Identity*. London: Routledge.

Minahan, S. and Cox, J. (2007) "Stitch 'n' bitch: Cyberfeminism, a third place and the new materiality," *Journal of Material Culture*, 12 (1), 5–21.

Minney, S. (2011) *Naked Fashion.* Oxford: New Internationalist.

Mintel. (2007) Jeans UK Mintel Market Research Report, April, London: Mintel.

Mintel Market Research. (2010) "The changing face of the web—a ten year review" *Mintel Market Research*, London.

Mirzoeff, N. (2006) "On visuality," *Journal of Visual Culture*, 5, 53–79.

Mitchell, W. (1995) *City of Bits: Space, Place and the Infobahn*. Cambridge, MA: MIT Press.

Miyake, I. (2006) "One life, one thread and one piece of cloth," *Kyoto Prize Commemorative Lecture*. Kyoto: Inamori Foundation.

Miyake, I. and Fujiwara, D. (2001) *A-POC Making*. Japan: Issey Miyake Inc.

Modigliani, R. (2007) "Louis Vuitton and the luxury market," *Art Criticism*, 22, 69–81.

Montagu, A. (1986) *Touching: The Human Significance of the Skin*. New York: Harper & Row, 3.

Montague, J. (2006) *Stray Shopping Carts of America*. New York: Harry Abrams Inc.

Moor, L. (2007) *The Rise of Brands*. Oxford: Berg.

Moore, C. M. and Birtwistle, G. (2004) "The Burberry business model: Creating an international luxury fashion brand," *International Journal of Retail & Distribution Management*, 32 (8), 412–22.

Moore, C. M. and Doherty, A.M. (2007) "The international flagship store of luxury fashion retailers," in Hines, T. and Bruce, M. (eds), *Fashion Marketing: Contemporary Issues*. Oxford: Butterworth-Heinemann, pp. 277–96.

Moore, C. M., Doherty, A. M. and Doyle, S. A. (2010) "Flagship stores as a market entry method: the perspective of luxury fashion retailing," *European Journal of Marketing*, 44 (1/2), 139–61.

Moore, C. M., Fernie, J. and Burt, S. (2000) "Brands without boundaries: The internationalisation of the designer retailer's brand," *European Journal of Marketing*, 34 (8), 919–37.

Moore, R. (2003) "From genericide to viral marketing: On brand," *Language and Communication*, 23 (3-4), 331–357.

Moreno, S. (2005) *Forefront: The Culture of Shopwindow Design*. Germany: Frame.

Mores, C. (2006) *From Fiorucci to Guerilla Stores: Shop Displays in Architecture, Marketing and Communications*. Marsillio: Venice.

Morgan Stanley. (2010) *Internet Trends*. New York: Morgan Stanley.

Mower, S. (2008) "Margiela, be mine," *Vogue*, September 2008, pp. 595–8.

Murdoch, J. (2006) *Post-structuralist Geography – A Guide to Relational Space*. London: Sage.

Murphy, R. (2009) "Luxury meets modern art," *WWD: Women's Wear Daily*, 188.

Neff, G. and Stark, D. (2002) "Permanently beta: Responsive organisation in an internet era," *Centre on Organizational Innovation Working Paper*, Columbia University.

Negroponte, N. (1995) *Being Digital*. New York: Vintage Books.

Nobbs, K., Moore, C. M. and Sheridan, M. (2012) "The flagship format within the luxury fashion market," *International Journal of Retail & Distribution Management*, 40 (12), 920–34.

Norris, L. (2012) "Trade and transformation of secondhand clothing: Introduction," *Textile*, 10 (2), 128–43.

Norton, K. (2006) "Savile Row never goes out of style," *Business Week*, October 31, 2006.

Oakley Smith, M. and Kubler, A. (2013) *Art/Fashion in the 21st Century*. London: Thames and Hudson October, available at: http://www.thewindowshopper.co.uk/tag/vm-display-awards/, Last accessed September 30, 2016.

Oakley, S. et al. (2013) *Art/Fashion in the 21st Century*. London: Thames & Hudson.

O'Doherty, B. (1999) *Inside the White Cube: The Ideology of Gallery Space*. California: University of California Press.

O'Dwyer, E. (2009) "Style without a use-by date," *Sydney Morning Herald*, May 14, 2009, p. 6.

OECD. (1998) *The Economic Impact of Counterfeiting*, Organisation for Economic Co-Operation and Development, available at: http://www.oecd.org/dataoecd/11/11/2090589.pdf, Last accessed September 30, 2016.

Ojeda, O. and McCown, J. (2004) *Colours: Architecture in Detail*. Beverliny, MA: Rockport Publishers.

Okonkwo, U. (2007) *Luxury Fashion Branding*. London: Palgrave.

Okonkwo, U. (2009a) *Luxury Online: Styles, Strategies, Systems*. London: Palgrave Macmillan

Okonkwo, U. (2009b) "Sustaining the luxury brand on the internet," *Journal of Brand Management*, 6 (5), 302–11.

O'Neill, A. (2001) "Imagining fashion," in Wilcox, C. (ed.), *Radical Fashion*. London: V&A Publications, pp. 39–45

Orrell, P. (2007) *Lucy & Jorge Orta Pattern Book*. London: Black Dog Publishing.

Osborne, V. (2009) "The logic of the mannequin: Shop windows and the realist novel," in Potvin, J. (ed.), *The Places and Spaces of Fashion 1800–2007*. London: Routledge, pp. 186–99.

Oswald, L. (1992) "The place and space of consumption in a material world," *Design Issues*, 12, 48–62.

Pallasmaa, J. (2005) *The Eyes of the Skin: Architecture and the Senses*. Chichester: John Wiley & Sons.

Palmer, A. and Clark, H. (2005) *Old Clothes, New Looks. Second Hand Fashion*. Oxford: Berg.

Papastergiadis, N. (2002) "Traces left in cities," *Architectural Design*, 72 (2), 45–51.

Park, C., Jaworski, B. and MacInnis, D. (1986) "Strategic brand concept- image management," *The Journal of Marketing*, 50 (4), 135–45.

Parker, R. (1989) *The Subversive Stitch: Embroidery and the Making of the Feminine*. London: The Women's Press.

Participants in the Economic Geography 2010 Workshop. (2011) "Editorial: Emerging themes in economic geography: Outcomes of the economic geography 2010 workshop," *Economic Geography*, 97 (2), 111–26.

Pashigian, B. (1988). "Demand uncertainty and sales: A study of fashion and markdown pricing," *The American Economic Review*, 78 (5), 936–53.

Pasols, P. (2005) *Louis Vuitton: The Birth of Modern Luxury*. New York: Abrams.

Passariello, C. (2006) "Louis Vuitton tries modern methods on factory lines," *Wall Street Journal*, October 9.

Passariello, C. and Dodes, R. (2007) "Art in fashion: Luxury boutiques dress up as galleries," *Wall Street Journal*, February 16, 2007, p. 8.

Pederson, J. (2011) "Metamodernism in fashion and style practice," available at: http://www.inter-disciplinary.net/wp-content/uploads/2011/08/pedersonfapaper.pdf, Last accessed September 30, 2016.

Pereira, M., Azevedo, S., Bernardo, V., Moreira Da Sila, F., Miguel, R. and Lucas, J. (2010) "The effect of visual merchandising on fashion stores in shopping centres," *Fifth International Textile, Clothing and Design Conference—Magic World of Textiles*.

PETA. (2015) "Exposed: Crocodiles and alligators factory-farmed for Hermes luxury goods," available at: www.peta.org/investigations/, Last accessed September 26, 2016.

Pevsner, N. (1976) *A History of Building Types*. Princeton: Princeton University Press.

Phau, I. and Teah, M. (2009) "Devil wears (counterfeit) Prada: A study of antecedents and outcomes of attitudes towards counterfeits of luxury brands," *Journal of Consumer Marketing*, 26 (1), 15–27.

Pietrykowski, B. (2004) "You are what you eat: The social economy of the slow food movement," *Review of Social Economy*, LX11 (3), 307–21.

Piketty, T. (2014) *Capital in the Twenty-First Century*. USA: Belknap Press.

Pine, B. and Gilmore, J. (1999) *The Experience Economy*. Boston: Harvard Business School Press.

Pithers, E. (2014) "First look inside the new Chanel Flagship," *The Telegraph*, June 10, 2014.

Pinto, R., Bourriaud, N. and Damianovic, M. (2003) *Lucy Orta*. London: Phaidon, p. 40.

Polan, B. and Tredre, R. (2009) *The Great Fashion Designers*. Oxford: Berg.

Platman, L. (2011) *Harris Tweed: From Land to Street Francis*. London: Lincoln Publishers.

Pollin, R. (2005) *Contours of Descent: US Economic Fractures and the Landscape of Global Austerity*. London and New York: Verso.

Pookulangara, S. and Shephard, A. (2013) "Slow fashion movement: Understanding consumer perceptions—An exploratory study," *Journal of Retailing and Consumer Services*, 20 (2), 200–6. doi:10.1016/j.jretconser.2012.12.002.

Portas, M. (1999) *Windows: The Art of Retail Display*. London: Thomas and Hudson Ltd.

Porter, M. (2001) "Strategy and the internet," *Harvard Business Review*, 3, 63–78.

Potts, J., Hartley, J., Banks, J., Burgess, J., Cobcroft, R., Cunningham, S. and Montgomery, L. (2008) "Consumer co-creation and situated creativity," *Industry Innovation*, 15 (5), 459–74.

Potvin, J. (2009) *The Places and Spaces of Fashion, 1800–2007*. London: Routledge.

Poulain, R. (1931) *Boutiques*. Paris: Vincent Freal et Cie.

Prahalad, C. and Ramaswamy, V. (2004) *The Future of Competition: Co-creating Unique Value with Customers*. Boston: Harvard Business School Press.

Pyke, A. (2015) *Origination: The Geographies of Brands and Branding*. Oxford: Wiley.

Quinn, B. (2002) *Techno Fashion*. Oxford: Berg.

Quinn, B. (2003) *The Fashion of Architecture*. Oxford: Berg.

Ramsey, N. and Wrathmell, S. (2009) "Spotlight on … Fugitive denim by Louise Snyder and Confessions of an eco-sinner by Fred Pearce," *Geography*, 94 (1), 58–60.

Rantisi, N. (2006) "How New York stole modern fashion," in Breward, C. and Gilbert, D. (eds), *Fashion's World Cities*. Oxford: Berg, pp. 109–22.

Rantisi, N. (2009) "Cultural intermediaries and the Geography of designs in the Montreal Fashion Industry," in Rusten, G. and Bryson, J. (eds), *Industrial Design and Competitiveness: Spatial and Organizational Dimensions*. Hampshire: Palgrave, pp. 93–116 (Harvard: Harvard University Press).

Rantisi, N. (2011) "The prospects and perils of creating a viable fashion industry," *Fashion Theory*, 15 (2), 259–66.

Rantisi, N. M. (2014) "Gendering fashion, fashioning fur: On the (re)production of a gendered labor market within a craft industry in transition," *Environment and Planning D: Society and Space*, 32 (2), 223–239.

Rantisi, N. Leslie, D. and Christopherson, S. (2006) "Placing the creative economy: Scale, politics and the material," *Environment and Planning A*, 38, 1789–1797.

Reimer, S. (2009) "Geographies of production II: Fashion, creativity and fragmented labour," *Progress in Human Geography*, 33 (1), 65–73.

Reinach, S. (2005) "China and Italy: Fast fashion versus pret a porter. Towards a new culture of fashion," *Fashion Theory*, 9 (1), 43–56.

Reinach, S. (2009) "Fashion and national identity: Interactions between Italians and Chinese in the global fashion industry," *Business and Economic History*, 7 (Conference presentation).

Retail Week. (2011a) "Net-a-Porter live", June 29.

Ritzer, G. and Jurgenson, N. (2010) "Production, consumption and presumption: The nature of capitalism in the age of the digital 'prosumer,'" *Journal of Consumer Culture*, 10, 13–36.

Rivoli, P. (2009) *The Travels of a T-Shirt in the Global Economy*. Oxford: Wiley.

Rocamora, A. (2011) "Personal fashion blogs: Screens and mirrors in digital self-portraits," *Fashion Theory*, 15 (4), 407–24.

Rocha, C. (2013) "Shapeways shifts fashion, PC magazine digital edition: News and trends," available at: http://uk.pcmag.com/feature/15512/shapeways-shifts-fashion, Last accessed September 30, 2016.

Roddick, A. (2000) *Business as Unusual*. London: Thorsons.

Roper, S., Caruana, R., Medway, D. and Murphy, P. (2013) "Constructing luxury brands: exploring the role of consumer discourse," *European Journal of Marketing*, 47 (3/4), 375–400.

Rose, G. and Tolia-Kelly, D. (2012) *Visuality/Materiality: Images, Objects, Practices*. London: Routledge.

Ruddick, G. (2014) "How Primark changed the high street landscape, for shoppers and rivals," *The Daily Telegraph*, April 25, 2014.

Ryan, Z. (2012) *Fashioning the Object: Boudicca*. Chicago: Yale.

Saillard, O. (2009) *Louis Vuitton: Art, Fashion and Architecture*. New York: Rizzoli.

Sandvoss, C. (2005) *Fans: The Mirror of Consumption*. Oxford: Polity.

Saunders, W. (ed.) (2005) *Commodification and Spectacle in Architecture*. Minneapolis: Minnesota University Press.

Saunders, W. (ed.) (2007) *The New Architectural Pragmatism*. Minneapolis: Minnesota University Press.

Scardi, G. (2010) "The sense of our time," in Coppard, A. (ed.), *Aware: Art, Fashion, Identity*. Italy: Damiani, pp. 13–23.

Scaturro, S. (2010) Experiments in fashion curation: An interview with Judith Clark in *Fashion Projects 3*: On Fashion and Memory.

Schleifer, S. (2007) *Spectacular Buildings*. Germany: Taschen Books.

Schofield, S. (2011) "A man of the cloth: A. A. Gill," *Sunday Times*, March 13, 2011.

Scott, A. (1996) "The craft, fashion, and cultural-products industries of Los Angeles: competitive dynamics and policy dilemmas in a multisectoral image-producing complex," *Annals of the AAG*, 86 (2), 306–23.

Scott, A. (2000) *The Cultural Economy of Cities*. London: Sage.

Selfridges. (2013) www.selfridges.com/gb/en/content/article/no-noise-selfridges, Last accessed September 26, 2016.

Selinger-Morris, S. (2012) "Great Panes: Design," *Sydney Morning Herald*, September 15, 2012, p. 34.

Sen, S., Block, L. and Chandran, S. (2002) "Window displays and consumer shopping decisions," *Journal of Retailing and Consumer Services*, 9 (5), 277–90.

Shapiro, C. and Varian, H. (1999) *Information Rules: A Strategic Guide to the Network Economy*. Harvard: Harvard Business School Press.

Sharman, A. and Robinson, D. (2014) "Burberry rises on Chinese sales," *Financial Times*, April 16, 2014.

Shell, L. (2009) *Cheap: The High Cost of Discount Culture*. Harmondsworth: Penguin.

Shields, R. (2003) *The Virtual*. London: Routledge.

Shields, R. (2004) "One damned page after another," *Cabinet Magazine*, 15, The Average New York, pp. 88–90.

Shinkle, E. (2008). *Fashion as Photograph*. London: I.B. Tauris.

Shirky, C. (2009) *Here Comes Everybody*. London: Penguin.

Shirky, C. (2010) *Cognitive Surplus: Creativity and Generosity in a Connected Age*. London: Allen Lane.

Short, J. R. (2013) "Economic wealth and political power in the second gilded age," in Hay, I. (ed.), *Geographies of the Super-Rich*. Cheltenham and Northampton, MA: Edward Elgar Publishing Limited, pp. 363–80.

Shukla, P. (2011) "Impact of interpersonal influences, brand origin and brand image on luxury purchase intentions: Measuring interfunctional interactions and a cross-national comparison," *Journal of World Business*, 46 (2), 242–52.

Shukla, P. (2012) "The influence of value perceptions on luxury purchase intentions in developed and emerging markets," *International Marketing Review*, 29 (6), 574–96.

Sidlauskas, S. (1982) *Intimate Architecture: Contemporary Clothing Design*. Cambridge, MA: The MIT Committee on Visual Arts.

Siegle, L. (2008) "Why it's time to end our love-affair with cheap fashion," *The Observer*, Sunday August 24, 2008.

Siegle, L. (2011) *To Die For—Is Fashion Wearing Out the World?* London: Fourth Estate.

Siegle, L. (2016) "Is it time to give up leather?" *The Guardian*, March 13, 2016.

Simmel, G. (1904) "Fashion," *International Quarterly*, 10, 9130–55.

Simmel, G. (1957) "Fashion," *American Journal of Sociology*, 62 (6), 541–58

Simms, A. and Potts, R. (2012) *The New Materialism: How Our Relationship with the Material World Can Change for the Better*. London: Bread Print & Roses, The Real Press and Schumacher College.

Simpson, C. (2009) SHOWstudio, Nick Knight and Alexander McQueen in www.ifashion.co.za, November 27, 2009.

Smith, A. (2001) "The death of British art," *The Guardian*, Thursday February 15, 2001.

Smithers, R. (2007) "Cut-price jeans and denim sales soaring," *The Guardian*, June 1

Snyder, R. L. (2008) *Fugitive Denim: A Moving Story of People and Pants in the Borderless World of Global Trade*. London: Norton and Co.

Soja, E. (1989) *Postmodern Geographies*. London: Verso.

Solca, L. (2015) "The Truth about handbags," *Business of Fashion*, April 2015.

Sorkin, M. (2005) "The second greatest generation. Chapter 10," in Saunders, S. (ed.), *Commodification and Spectacle in Architecture*. Minneapolis: Minnesota University Press, pp. 113–20.

Spence, E. (2016) "Performing wealth and status: Observing super-yachts and the super-rich in Monaco. Chapter 14," in Hay, I. and Beaverstock, J. (eds), *Handbook on Wealth and the Super Rich*. Mumbai: Edward Elgar, pp. 287–301.

Stallybrass, P. (1993) "Worn worlds: Clothes, mourning and the life of things," *The Yale Review*, 81 (2), 35–50.

Stark, D. (2009) *The Sense of Dissonance. Accounts of Worth in Economic Life*. Princeton and Oxford: Princeton University Press.

Stark, D. (2011) "What's valuable?," in Beckert, J. and Aspers, P. (eds), *The Worth of Goods*. Oxford: Oxford University Press, 340–51.

Steele, V. (2001) "Style in revolt, in Wilcox, C. (ed.), *Radical Fashion*. London: V&A Publications, pp. 46–55.

Steele, V. (2012) "Fashion" Chapter 1, in Geczy, A. and Karaminas, V. (eds), *Fashion and Art*. London: Bloomsbury, 13–28.

Sternberg, E. (1999), *The Economy of Icons: How Business Manufactures Meaning*. Westport: Praeger.

Sudjic, D. (1990) *Rei Kawakubo and Comme des Garcons*. New York: Rizzoli.

Sudjic, D. (2001) "Editorial," *Domus*, 838, 4.

Sull, D. and Turconi, S. (2008) "Fast fashion lessons," *Business Strategy Review*, 19 (2), 4–11. doi:10.1111/j.1467-8616.2008.00527.x.

Surowiecki, J. (2005) *The Wisdom of the Crowds: Why the Many Are Smarter than the Few*. Boston: Abacus.

Tamen, M. (2001) *Friends of Interpretable Objects*. Cambridge, MA: Harvard University Press.

Tapscott, D. and McQueen, R. (1995) *The Digital Economy*. New York: McGraw-Hill.

Tapscott, D. and Williams, A. (1996) *Wikinomics: How Mass Collaboration Changes Everything*. New York: Portfolio.

The Economist. (2015) Luxury Goods: Counterfeit.com, April 21, 2015, London.

Thompson, D. (2012) "Zara's big idea: What the world's top fashion retailer tells us about innovation," *The Atlantic*, November 2012.

Thrift, N. (1996) "New urban eras and old technological fears: Reconfiguring the goodwill of electronic things," *Urban Studies*, 33, 1463–93.

Thrift, N. (2004) Intensities of feeling: Towards a spatial politics of affect. *Geografiska Annaler*, 86 (1), 57–78.

Thrift, N. (2005) *Knowing Capitalism*. London: Sage.

Thrift, N. (2011) "Lifeworld Inc—and what to do about it," *Environment and Planning D: Society and Space*, 29, 5–26.

Timmerman, K. (2008) *Where Am I Wearing? A Global Tour to the Countries, Factories and People that Make Our Clothes*. New Jersey: Wiley.

Tokatli, N. (2008) "Global sourcing: Insights from the global clothing industry—the case of Zara," *Journal of Economic Geography*, 8, 21–38.

Tokatli, N. (2011) "Creative individuals, creative places: Marc Jacobs, New York and Paris," *International Journal of Urban and Regional Research*, 35 (6), 1256–71.

Tokatli, N. (2012a) "The changing role of place-image in the profit making strategies of the designer fashion industry," *Geography Compass*, 6 (1), 35–43.

Tokatli, N. (2012b) "Old firms, new tricks and the quest for profits: Burberry's journey from success to failure and back to success again," *Journal of Economic Geography*, 12, 55–77.

Tokatli, N. (2013) "'Doing a Gucci: The transformation of an Italian fashion firm into a global powerhouse in a 'Los Angeles-izing' world," *Journal of Economic Geography*, 13 (2), 239–55.

Tokatli, N. (2014) "Made in Italy? Who cares! Prada's new economic geography," *Geoforum*, 54, 1–9.

Tranberg Hansen, K. (2000) *Salaula: The World of Second Hand Clothing*. Chicago: Chicago University Press.

Tucker, J. (2003) *Retail Desire: Design, Display and Visual Merchandising*. London: Rotovision.

Tungate, M. (2008) *Fashion Brands: Branding Style from Armani to Zara*. London: Kogan Page.

Turkle, S. (1995) *Life on the Screen: Identity in the Age of the Internet*. London: Simon and Schuster.

Turkle, S. (2007) *Evocative Objects*. Cambridge: MIT Press.

Turkle, S. (2008) *The Inner History of Devices*. Cambridge, MA: MIT Press.

Turkle, S. (2011) *Alone Together*. New York: Basic Books.

Van Dijk, J. (2009) "Users like you? Theorizing agency in user-generated content," *Media, Culture and Society*, 31 (3), 41–58.

Vanstiphout, W. (2005) "Rockbottom: Villa by OMA," in Saunders, W. (ed.), *Commodification and Spectacle in Architecture* Minneapolis, Minnesota University, pp. 78–87.

Veblen, T. (1934) *The Theory of the Leisure Class*. New York: Macmillan.

Velthuis, O. (2011) "Damien's dangerous idea: Valuing contemporary art at auction," in Beckert, J. and Aspers, P. (eds), *The Worth of Goods*. Oxford: Oxford University Press, pp. 178–200.

von Hippel, E. (2005) *Democratising Innovation*. Cambridge, MA: MIT Press.

von Hippel, E. (2007) "Horizontal innovation networks by and for users," *Industrial and Corporate Change*, 16, 293–315.

Walford, L. (2002) *Break Down*. London: Artangel.

Walker Rettberg, J. (2008) *Blogging: Digital Media and Society*. Oxford: Polity.

Walsh, C. (1995) "Shop design and the display of goods in Eighteenth Century London," *Journal of Design History*, 8 (3), pp. 157–76.

War on Want. (2016), "Rana Plaza: Three years on, garment workers still exploited," *WOW News*, April 21.

Warde, R. (2008) *Art v. fashion* Lecture delivered at Cornell Fine Arts Museum, Cornell, USE 2008.

Watson, L. (1992) *The Nature of Things: The Secret Life of Inanimate Objects*. Springfield, MA: Destiny Press.

Webb, I. (2012) *Fashion & Art in Fashion and Art Collusion*. London: Britain Creates, pp. 1–11.

Wells, R. (2009) "McFashion junked in the flight to sustainability," *Sunday Age*, March 15, 2009, p. 7.

WGSN. (2005) "Ethical fashion: myth or future trend?" *WGSN News*, October 15.

Whife, A. (2002) "Modern Tailor 265–71," in Breward, C. and Gilbert, D. (eds), *Fashion's World Cities*. Oxford: Berg, p. 574.

Whiteside, A. (2011) "The future of the catwalk," *Luxury Comms*, *Magazine*, May 22, 2011.

Wigley, M. (2001) *White Walls, Designer Dresses: The Fashioning of Modern Architecture*. Cambridge, MA: MIT Press.

Wilcox, C. (2001) "I try not to fear radical things'. Introduction," in Wilcox, C. (ed.), *Radical Fashion*. London: V&A Publications, pp. 1–7.

Williams, P., Hubbard, P., Clark, D. and Berkeley, N. (2001) "Consumption, exclusion and emotion: The social geographies of shopping," *Social and Cultural Geography*, 2 (2), 203–20.

Williams, R. (1982) *Dreamworlds*. University of California Press.

Wilson, B. (2012) "Harris Tweed Returns to Global Boutiques after Island's renaissance," *The Guardian*, November 9, 2012.

Wilson, E. (1985) *Adorned in Dreams*. London: Virago, p. 11.

Withers, R. (2001) "Michael Landy: Break Down," *Artforum International*, May 2001.

Wood, Z. (2008) "Slow fashion is a must have … and not just for this season," *The Observer*, Sunday August 3, 2008.

Wright, M. (2001) "Madman at C&A," *The Evening Standard*, February 1, 2001.

Wrigley, N. and Lowe, M. (2002) *Reading Retail*. London: Arnold.

Wylie, A. (2009) "Tweed goes to Tokyo," *The Scotsman*, March 16, 2009, p. 14.

Yeomans, L. (2012) "Foreward," in Webb, I. (ed.), *Fashion and Art Collusion*. London: Britain Creates, pp. 9, 10.

Zelizer, V. (2011) *Economic Lives: How Culture Shapes the Economy*. Princeton: Princeton University Press.

Zhan, L. and He, Y. (2012) "Understanding luxury consumption in China: Consumer perceptions of best-known brands," *Journal of Business Research*, 65 (10), 1452–60.

Zhang, B. and Kim, J. H. (2013) "Luxury fashion consumption in China: Factors affecting attitude and purchase intent," *Journal of Retailing and Consumer Services*, 20 (1), 68–79.

Zhang, D. and Di Benedetto, A. C. (2010) "Radical fashion and radical fashion innovation," *Journal of Global Fashion Marketing*, 194–204, 1–4.

Zook, M. (2000) "The web of production: The economic geography of commercial internet content production in the United States," *Environment and Planning A*, 32, 411–26.

INDEX

Note: The letter 'n' along with the locator denotes the note number.